"*The Integration Imperative* offers a potent cocktail of robust theory, insightful case histories, and lateral thinking—any marketer will find something to chew on here."
Sholto Douglas-Home, Group Marketing Director, Hays Plc

"This book will be an instant classic. Thanks to Suzanne Lowe's insights, we finally have practical guidance on overcoming an essential challenge for professional service firms: how to bridge the divide between marketing and business development functions."
Michael W. McLaughlin, Author, *Winning the Professional Services Sale*

"Professional service firms leave so much money on the table because of the lack of integration between marketing and selling, and this book demonstrates the path to getting it right."
Don Spetner, Executive Vice President and Chief Integration Officer, Korn/Ferry International

"An amazing blend of insight and in-depth real world examples. All professional firm marketers and managers should read this book."
David Maister, Author and Consultant

"Suzanne Lowe's depth of knowledge and thoughtful presentation, particularly the case studies, provide hands-on, targeted, and relevant information that helped me to gain some important and actionable insights. This book should be mandated reading for professional service firm marketers and would also be meaningful for marketers in many other sectors."
Barbara Gydé, Executive Director, Marketing and Business Development, Columbia Business School Executive Education

"Suzanne Lowe is so qualified to tackle this age-old challenge. She has been studying the role of the CMO in professional service organizations and leading CMO roundtable discussions for nearly 10 years, always with the goal of finding ways to do things differently and to do things better."
Connie Bennett, Retired Senior Vice President Enterprise Customer Management, The McGraw-Hill Companies

"As Suzanne Lowe highlights, the PSF mindset is one of continuous mastery of your profession through talent development, skill development, and an awareness of best practices in your field."
Juli Ann Reynolds, President and CEO, Tom Peters Company

"Suzanne Lowe makes a compelling argument regarding the often disconnected marketing and sales activities that take place in professional service firms. More importantly, *The Integration Imperative* offers the insights needed to overcome internal barriers to integration and offers examples of how it can be done."
Paul R. Brown, Executive Vice President, Global Market Development, CDM

"In extremely clear, well-documented fashion, Suzanne Lowe's *The Integration Imperative* makes a significant contribution to the requisite body of knowledge for leaders of professional service firms across the board and around the world."
> **Robert Galford**, Managing Partner, Center for Leading Organizations, and Co-author, *The Trusted Advisor*, *The Trusted Leader*, and *Your Leadership Legacy*

"*The Integration Imperative* is structured for maximum usefulness. Each section is self-contained, and it is easy to pop in at any point and pick up content of value. The case studies are especially accessible and get at the thinking behind why these marketers did what they did—what motivated them."
> **Eileen Harrington**, Vice President of Marketing, Analysis Group

"Lowe's latest book addresses the most fundamental issue that professional firms will face in taking their services to market over the coming decade."
> **Ford Harding**, Author, *Rain Making: Attract New Clients No Matter What Your Field*, 2nd edition

"Lowe again provides professional service firms with a template for making ourselves more effective and more successful. As in each of her preceding books she provides not only a construct for success but case studies that demonstrate best practices as well."
> **Leon Schor**, Vice President Sales and Marketing, L.E.K. Consulting

"Suzanne Lowe's new book is a perfect follow-up to her first book, *Marketplace Masters*. Now firms can know not just how vital marketing and selling functions are, but how to make them work together so that success will follow in good times as well as bad. No one can ignore the concepts in this book, nor find them anywhere else. Bravo!"
> **Ken Lizotte**, Author, *The Expert's Edge: Become the Go-To Authority That People Turn to Every Time*

"Successful marketing and business development is a fundamental mindset that, at its best, is fully integrated into every business practice. When reflected throughout the organization in every thought, communication, service, and behavior, this marketing attitude provides a powerful influence on the ultimate experience of each client."
> **Jon Alan Baker**, FAIA, LEED AP, Partner, NTD Architecture

"Once again Suzanne Lowe cuts the Gordian Knot of business and marketing with practical solutions. And she backs them up with lots of case studies to prove that they can actually be done."
> **Larry Bodine**, Esq., Apollo Business Development

"It is wonderful to see Suzanne Lowe's professional knowledge and insights put into book format."
> **Scott Adelson**, Senior Managing Director, Houlihan Lokey

"Marketing arms business development with the right information so that firms can better focus their people to clearly demonstrate the value, insights, and results the firm can deliver. The integration of marketing and business development is imperative for a successful firm."

> **Marc Busny**, Managing Director and Chief Marketing Officer, CBIZ Tofias & Mayer Hoffman McCann P.C. — Tofias New England Division

"[Suzanne Lowe's] ability to integrate the sales and marketing functions to ensure firms grow as a result of their efforts at branding and marketing communications is the 'missing link' we have all been waiting for."

> **Sally Glick**, Principal, Chief Growth Strategist, Sobel & Co.

"Suzanne Lowe's book provides great insight to the yin and yang of marketing and business development at professional service firms; it is a must read for marketers, business developers, and firm leadership alike."

> **Karen B. Hoy**, Chief Marketing Officer, Richards, Layton & Finger, P.A.

"Suzanne Lowe's new book comes at a perfect time. It has never been more important to have all members of professional service firms add marketing and business development to their job descriptions. This book provides proven ideas and methods that work."

> **Ed Kasparek**, Senior Vice President, Director of Business Development, Thornton Tomasetti

"Suzanne Lowe has tremendous insights in framing theory and implementation for *The Integration Imperative*. Beyond her professional wisdom, she involved marketing and practitioners in contributing their formulas for success. Managers who read this book will recognize their own bouts with 'internalitis,' develop a superior course, and be ready to walk in the clients' shoes."

> **Isidora K. Lagos**, Principal, Head of Brand Marketing and Communications, William Blair & Company

"Marketing, sales, culture, and a firm's people are the foundation of success, but success comes only when all four are in harmony. Suzanne Lowe explains how to make it so."

> **Patrick Lamb**, Founding Member, Valorem Law Group

"Suzanne Lowe addresses — with authority and uncommon skill — the two thorniest problems in law firm marketing — the disconnect between marketing and practice development, and between marketers and lawyers."

> **Bruce W. Marcus**, Author

"*The Integration Imperative* is a fabulous book! Right on target. Every professional service firm leader should read it cover to cover."

> **Mike Schultz**, President, Wellesley Hills Group and Author, *Professional Services Marketing*

"Suzanne Lowe has always been a strategic thinker. In her latest book, she provides practical and applicable solutions to the craziness surrounding the business world today. Her laser-sharp insight explains both why and how successful companies (and government agencies) must break down stovepipes if they are to survive."

Debrah A. Whitaker, President/ CEO, The Balanced Scorecard for Government, Inc.

"Services are different. Consequently, the rules for marketing and selling products don't apply. In this book, Suzanne Lowe provides an invaluable guide for those chartered with business development for professional services."

Julie Schwartz, Senior Vice President, Thought Leadership and Research, ITSMA

"Lowe's latest book, *The Integration Imperative*, is a must read for any executive in a professional service firm that knows their marketing and business development should be producing better results. She provides practical recommendations and real world examples that can have an immediate impact on your business."

David Munn, President and CEO, ITSMA

"Great book! Lowe addresses the challenges and dynamics that are unique to professional service businesses. Should be required reading for all marketers, business developers, and services practitioners looking to grow their business."

Erica Stritch, General Manager, RainToday.com

"Now is the time for marketing and sales disciplines to realize that they are part of the same purpose: to win, retain, and grow customers. Suzanne Lowe's latest book shows a practical and progressive way to integrate these interdependent business disciplines. It's a welcome antidote to silos and division of labor."

Charles Doyle, Chief Marketing Officer, Jones Lang LaSalle

"Finally, a book that gets to the heart of the disconnect between marketers and sales professionals! Suzanne Lowe's thoughts will enable leaders to improve significantly the effectiveness of their go-to-market strategies and ultimately lead to happier clients and greater business growth."

Meredith Callanan, Vice President, Corporate Marketing and Communications, T. Rowe Price

The Integration Imperative

Erasing Marketing and Business
Development Silos— *Once and for All*—
in Professional Service Firms

Suzanne C. Lowe

Professional Services Books

Concord, Massachusetts

Library of Congress Control Number: 2009929626

Copyright © 2009 by Suzanne C. Lowe

Text design, typesetting, and project management: Books By Design, Inc.

Manufactured in the United States of America.

ISBN: 978-0-615-29214-4

Contents

Resources

Acknowledgments

Although I am the author of this book, it was shaped by the collective thinking of many people whose contributions to professional and business-to-business service marketing continue to lead the best practices of this dynamic field.

In 2006 I co-published with Larry Bodine the findings of a significant research project, "Increasing Marketing Effectiveness at Professional Firms." Larry's enthusiasm and generosity helped create a viable springboard for this book. Also, I am indebted to the many hundreds of research respondents whose input helped form or verify the concepts that appear in this book. The "Increasing Effectiveness" research was guided by professional service firm management and marketing leaders David Bruns, Jason Dinwoodie, Anne Elvgren, David Fondiller, George Friedel, Maxine Friedman, Sally Glick, Allison Held, Karen Hoy, Isidora Lagos, Wendy Miller, Russ Molinar, Cherie Olland, Teresa Poggenpohl, Don Spetner, Debbie Stojanovic, Marianne Swallie, and Anne Malloy Tucker.

In addition to Larry Bodine's blog and leadership of the LawMarketing portal, I'm grateful to several "Increasing Effectiveness" study collaborators for assisting in the questionnaire's distribution and promotion: Michael McLaughlin ("Management Consulting News"); Mike Schultz and his RainToday colleagues; and the wonderful staff at the Society for Marketing Professional Services and the Association for Accounting Marketing. And, as with my earlier research initiatives, my crackerjack statistician, George Zipf, helped set up the questionnaire and conducted substantive analysis of the data.

I tested my ideas about the book's potential themes with a number of professional service marketing in-house leaders, consultants, and management experts. I could not have written this book without their invaluable advice and generous sharing of viewpoints. They are Charles Agin, Jayne Bates, Mark Beese, Marc Busny, Sharon Clark, Karen Courtney, Becky Sue Epstein, David Fondiller, Mary Garrett, Sally Glick, Ford Harding, David Harkleroad, Tom Kiely, Kate Kirkpatrick, Tom Kuczmarski, Patrick Lamb, Ken Lizotte, Ben Machtiger, Bruce Marcus, Regina Maruca,

Bill Matassoni, Wendy Miller, Judi Nitsch, Terrie Perella, Michael Reilly, Tom Rodenhauser, Teri Schram, Bill Viehman, and Ron Worth.

In my search for professional firms whose integration case studies could best illustrate the book's structural frameworks and cultural models, I interviewed more than 100 people. Their referrals to potential case study sources helped me choose the most powerful examples to feature in the book. I also held discussions with numerous authorities in organizational behavior, human resources, industrial psychology, performance management, and compensation. In every case, even with people who had never talked to me before, these individuals endorsed my pursuit of the integration topic, and encouraged me to push ahead to complete the manuscript. My heartfelt thanks to them will be individually delivered.

I could not have produced the book's case studies without the enthusiastic involvement of a small team of people at each of the companies profiled. They are: Michael Franzino, Michael Distefano, Hilary Dyson, Ana Dutra, and Marnie Kittelson of Korn/Ferry International; Mark Beese, Larry Wolfe, Jennifer Kummer, Brittaney Schmidt, and Emily Hager of Holland & Hart; Janice Barnes, Bill Viehman, Eileen Jones, Manuel Cadrecha, and Phil Harrison of Perkins+Will; Scott Jensen, Chris Schmidt, Rick Anderson, Heather Keen, Marilyn Monserud, and Amy Esary of Moss Adams; Mary Garrett of IBM; Sylvia Wheeler, Bruce Beverly, and Denise Coleman of Haley & Aldrich; Tea Hoffmann, Jerry Stauffer, Kim Low, Laura Hine, and Susan Wagner of Baker Donelson; Dave Kipp and Craig Toder of Ross & Baruzzini; Nancy Grimmer, Sarah Stanley, Charles Doyle, Paul Uber, and Molly Kelly of Jones Lang LaSalle; Jessica Reiter, Russ Stepp, and Susan Newton of R.W. Beck; and Frans Cornelis and Ineke Brandenburg of Randstad.

There were also several people whose intellectual capital is featured in this book, and whose sharing of study reports, charts, and slide presentations helped make my own content even stronger. For their generosity I am indebted to Diane Schmalensee, David Stone, Bob Buday, Tom Kuczmarski, Cindy Commander, Meagan Wilson, Jane Stevenson, and Granville Loar.

I referenced a small number of firms whose work to increase their go-to-market effectiveness served as excellent examples of the book's "doing things differently" points. For letting me showcase their work, I am grateful to Susan Arneson and Carl Roehling of SmithGroup; Jeff Durocher of RHR International; Ed Kasparek of Thornton Tomasetti; Jay Wager of

Wolf, Greenfield & Sacks; Kate Kirkpatrick of Gensler; and Jim Lanzalotto, formerly of Yoh.

My journey to complete this book could not have been completed without a fine team of specialists in editing, book production, graphics, and publishing. Regina Maruca's early enthusiasm for my pursuit of this book motivated me more than I can express. With her writing and editorial experience, Marie Gendron helped me begin to articulate my ideas in a coherent way. With his graphic design acumen, Scott Williams helped me envision ways to visually represent the book's themes. I was fortunate to work with Nancy Benjamin and the Books By Design team; each team member applied her extensive experience to the book's packaging and production. Lois Wasoff added her top-notch publishing law perspectives. I am enormously appreciative to John Butman and Ken Lizotte, who unselfishly provided me their invaluable book-publishing consulting expertise. I offer my heartfelt thanks to professional services management guru David Maister, who reviewed my manuscript and gave me important advice regarding the book's structure.

My Expertise Marketing team lent professional passion to every step of the book's creation, especially Laura Glennon, Andrea Harris, and my crackerjack virtual assistant, Kyle Sheldon-Chandler.

Behind all of these many individuals stands my family, without whose sustained investment of personal time, energy—and love—I could not have written this book. Each of them gave me courage to forge ahead, and every moment reminded me of all that is good. They include: Elisabeth Townsend and Jeff Greene, for being my incomparable book buddies from start to finish; the other cherished members of my Squam Lake family; and my amazing siblings Julie and Jim. My incredible husband John and my precious children Kerry, Elaine, and J.B. each offered unconditional enthusiasm, patient listening when I talked about my subject and my publishing journey, and heartfelt encouragement when I flagged during challenging moments.

Introduction

In 2004, after five years of research on thousands of professional and business-to-business service firms (PSFs and B2Bs), I published my first book, *Marketplace Masters: How Professional Service Firms Compete to Win* (Praeger Publishers). It outlined 11 organizational competencies shown by my research to be the hallmarks of a competitively effective enterprise. In the book, I called for professional and business-to-business service firms to develop an organizational **infrastructure*** in which **marketplace**-focused skills, processes, and tools were deeply embedded into a company's way of doing business.

Since then, I've been pleased to discover—through the growing literature and direct evidence from scores of business associations—that many organizations have begun to create the **market**-focused infrastructure I outlined in *Marketplace Masters* (and about which I continue to write elsewhere).

In 2005 a new trend caught my attention. Business management observers and leaders across a diverse array of professional sectors had begun to call for their companies to become more effective at **marketing**. This call to action was manifested in a hard-to-miss abundance of articles, webinars, blog posts, and industry conferences. They were all packed with information on capturing the return on investment (ROI) in marketing and **selling**. And they touted flavor-of-the-month toolkits, metrics, measurement techniques, and multistep processes. Most were directed at product-oriented companies, but the **professional and business-to-business services** arena also appeared to be rapidly recognizing the need to learn about marketing measurement.

From my standpoint, it was hard not to notice that something significant was taking place in services marketing. From small, private professional partnerships to enormous, publicly owned B2B services companies, the majority was insistently searching for real answers to how to grow market share, increase revenues, and provide more value to clients. It was

---

*Note: Terms that appear in boldface in the text are defined in appendix A at the end of this book.

clear they didn't think they had the right answers. It was also clear they hadn't yet harnessed their organizations to crack this nut.

Sure enough, in late 2005 my firm's research advisory council called for a study of effectiveness. And so in early 2006 I co-published with Larry Bodine a study of nearly 400 firms. From the findings in "Increasing Marketing Effectiveness at Professional Firms," I published numerous articles and made speeches and presentations reporting on how professional and B2B service firms were working to improve their marketing and **business development** effectiveness, how they thought they were doing, the obstacles they faced, and the results they had achieved.

During my travels from speech to speech and client project to client project, I began to notice a second trend, which I thought probably stemmed from the first: individual marketing and business development leaders, from both small firms and large global enterprises, were taking it upon themselves to champion initiatives they believed passionately would directly benefit the marketplace future of their firms.

Certainly, it's easy to applaud the success of these entrepreneurial efforts. But, once again, I couldn't help but notice a familiar pattern, one that I had addressed in *Marketplace Masters*: PSFs and B2Bs appeared quite unable to harness their people to work collectively toward common goals. And yet the cacophony (metaphorically, of course) to find some kind of "effectiveness Holy Grail" grew louder and louder.

I began to conceptualize some theories—that the "effectiveness Holy Grail" was actually *inside* a firm—and I began to talk to a new set of business advisors about some of my structural and cultural ideas on how to grow market share, increase revenues, and provide more value to clients.

My discussions of these parallel **integration** challenges were shaped by the flood of blog posts, podcasts, and research reports I found on the Internet while researching this book between late December 2007 and early March 2008. I also trekked through a blizzard of published articles and research studies on the **disconnect** between marketing and business development. The authors of these comments and publications sounded similar themes: "the classic sales vs. marketing debate"[1] and "Marketing and Sales play by different sets of rules."[2]

Every one of these sources, while decrying the sorry state of marketing and sales integration in businesses everywhere, pointed to the obvious: these **functions** should work together. Here is a sampling of some of the voices that have spoken out on this issue:

- Gale Crosley, in her 2007 article on connecting marketing and business development in certified public accounting (CPA) firms, asked, "Will it be teamwork for your marketing director and business developer? Or will there be strife between them? . . . When they are not in harmony, the result can be time- and resource-wasting initiatives." She encouraged CPA firm leaders to "create a fruitful team," and she had this advice: "As your firm moves toward hiring a business developer, consult the marketing director and take his or her feelings and reactions into account."[3]

- Barbara Sullivan and Graham Ericksen, in their December 2007 Booz Allen Hamilton Leading Ideas Online article primarily targeting product companies, blamed marketers for a "fundamental disconnect between getting the message out and closing the deal." More specifically, "marketers . . . don't pay enough attention to the point where their efforts should hit home, the moment of purchase decision." The authors went on to rap marketers for "treating sales support as an afterthought at best." They "should incorporate it into their overall strategic planning."[4]

- Cindy Commander, Meagan Wilson, and Jane Stevenson, authors of "The Evolved CMO," a 2008 study of 132 chief and senior marketers by Forrester Research's Chief Marketing Officer (CMO) Group and Heidrick & Struggles, called for "CMOs . . . to proactively create alignment and insert themselves into the strategic process," and encouraged them to take "overt actions to adapt and evolve their focus and behaviors to generate and wield influence across a new set of imperatives."[5]

- Mike Schultz, in a January 2008 comment on his Services Insider blog, cited The Yankee Group's 2002 study of the handoff of leads between marketing and sales. He referenced its findings that 40 to 80 percent of leads are dropped or lost. The reasons included "poorly defined roles and processes," "disparate sales and marketing systems," "no visibility into marketing effectiveness," and "poor qualification."[6]

- Julie Schwartz, writing for the Information Technology Services Marketing Association (ITSMA), a marketing association for technology, communications, and **professional service** providers, revealed in its March 2007 "Services Marketing Competency Report Card" that "marketers with more strategic roles have a greater impact on the business. [The Report Card] also shows that services marketers do not always have the skills to step up into a more strategic role."[7]

These and other viewpoints and data in the chapters that follow all corroborate my point that too many businesses are implementing their marketing and selling programs in a troubling state of "disconnectivity." Worse yet, some very negative implications thread their way through some of these articles, reports, studies, and blog posts.

In calling attention to disconnected marketing and selling functions, a subset of pundits, academics, authors, and bloggers fall into an all too common trap: *blaming individuals* for their organization's failure, or *setting up these individuals* to try to fix their company's functional hurdles all by themselves. Some of these researchers and writers fail themselves to recognize that the functional **structures** and cultural norms within which many marketers and business developers work do not support them in their efforts to integrate effectively their companies' marketing and business development initiatives.

It's certainly a slippery slope. Once one begins observing and writing about weaknesses, problems, or challenges (and especially from a distant keyboard or spreadsheet), it's so easy to start laying blame or finding fault. Such actions often have an unfortunate consequence: the notion emerges that marketers and business developers, instead of a firm's **management executives**, should be largely responsible for developing their own functions. The outcome likely spawns even more functional disconnects. Talk about creating **silos**!

This blame game also occurs in the professional and business-to-business service firm arena. Certainly, in my own research and consulting work I've encountered many examples of finger-pointing, frustration, and cynicism. But these examples, I thought, painted an unfairly bleak picture of what's happening in most professional firms.

So I had to assure myself that PSFs and B2Bs had the capacity to change. I admit it—I almost found myself believing those naysayers who bemoaned the oppressive traditions and dysfunctional go-to-market methods. I simply did not believe that PSFs or B2Bs were the lost causes I'd heard so much about.

To prove it to myself and others, I decided to devote all 2007 issues of "The Marketplace Master," my monthly newsletter, to the theme of individuals "doing things differently." My aim was to highlight the ways in which they are demonstrating professional bravery by pushing their professional and business-to-business service firms to achieve new marketplace gains and competitive effectiveness. For the monthly series, I largely chose the very same competencies I presented in *Marketplace Masters*.

I was surprised at how easy it was to find these "doing things differently" subjects—men and women who were willing to buck their firms' traditions and, in the words of one, to "stand in front of the [management] bus," bravely insisting that their firms embrace new marketplace pursuits. None appeared afraid of taking the risk. It's as if they said to themselves, "I've *got* to lead this initiative, because I'm the only one who will." What's more, these people, and many other experienced marketing and business development professionals, were increasingly articulating their aspirations to become more strategically well positioned within their firms. Seasoned professional service marketers, by and large, are indeed taking on new—and more strategic—challenges.

Why the Time Is Right for This Book

This book describes plenty of evidence that professional service firms "get it" about the importance of becoming more effective at marketing and business development. A lot of activity is under way to better connect functions, processes, and people.

Most **executive managers** of professional firms don't sit around idly, trying to put an unfair burden on their marketers and business developers to single-handedly retool dysfunctional structures and outmoded cultural standards. PSF and B2B executive managers are smarter than that. They're already looking at their organization's overall go-to-market productivity. They're already welcoming the initiative and professional passion of their marketing and business development professionals. They're already wielding a critical hand in driving the evolution of their functions toward greater strategic significance. Most marketing, business development, and administrative professionals are forward thinkers who proactively seek positive change.

I believe we are witnessing clear shifts in the ways in which professional and business-to-business service firms go to market. They are seeking, developing, and applying new knowledge. Leaders are willing to take responsibility for—and spearhead—change in the ways in which their firms go to market, pursue growth, and bring added value to clients. Marketers desire more accountability and influence. Everyone's expectations are rising in the areas of service marketing and business development.

Sounds rosy, doesn't it? But the "harnessing problem" has yet to be addressed. Sure, some admirable organizations are on the cutting-edge of marketing and business development effectiveness. (I'll tell you about them in this book.) But the bulk of professional and business-to-business service firms are still too far behind the "harnessing" curve. They haven't yet figured out how to integrate marketing and business development throughout their organizations. And they have not embedded marketing and business development into *every* person's job. They labor under numerous functional disconnects and silos that are entirely fixable. (Can't see them? Believe me, every firm has them, and I'll describe them in this book.)

This lack of integration, these functional silos, are a financial problem for firms. If PSFs and B2Bs have not yet harnessed their structures and cultures (or created the right models and paradigms) in order to grow their market share, increase the "right" kind of revenues, or provide significant value for clients, they are at a significant competitive risk.

In the chapters that follow, and in the case studies in particular, I discuss some real-life businesses that are hurt by lack of marketing and business development integration. For example, at RHR International, the organizational development and talent management consulting firm, the vice president of market development was pained to learn that his firm's business development gatekeepers were wasting a great deal of effort and money by not forwarding the company's thought leadership materials to their prospects and clients.[8] At SmithGroup, the architecture, engineering, and planning firm, the CEO and corporate marketing director could find no direct correlation between the marketing dollars spent and marketing effectiveness. The partners were busy, but they were just not generating the kind of return on investment that the firm had targeted.[9] There is, however, a good news ending for both of these stories. In both instances, executive managers teamed up with the marketing and business development professionals and came up with noteworthy solutions that weaned their firms away from their ineffective marketplace practices.

I wrote this book because I believe marketing and business development functions are the most critical engines for the growth of a professional or business-to-business service firm. Period. Together, these functions propel a firm forward in every way—helping it adapt to the shifting needs of its clients and serving as the springboard for mutually beneficial relationships between experts and clients. Integrating each person's involvement in marketing and business development, using the structural models and cultural approaches described in this book, gives an organization exponential advantages on many fronts. It's a competitive *imperative*.

Integration can create a business environment that gratifies all its participants—both practitioners and all **nonrevenue-generating professionals**. They not only can point to their own contributions, but also can benefit from the mutually generated profits and revenues that result from their collective efforts. Integration creates professional and personal growth opportunities and returns everyone to the most basic thrill of working alongside other people: learning and personal connections.

What's more, the "effectiveness Holy Grail" is in firms' own backyards. Using the concepts I've researched, tested, and discussed extensively, professional and business-to-business service firms will be able to create an environment that effectively harnesses everyone's talents to serve clients and, ultimately, the larger marketplace.

Who Will Benefit from This Book?

It's up to the leaders of a PSF or B2B service firm to tackle the issue of marketing–business development integration head-on, with drive and purpose. I wrote this book for the executives and managers who, even if they are the nominal figureheads of a collegial gathering of partners, are nevertheless charged with helping their enterprises grow and make marketplace gains. These leaders include executives and managers who serve on executive committees or internal boards, managing partners or chief executives and their C-suite colleagues, practice or sector leaders, and geography or line-of-business heads.

This book, then, is targeted at anyone who has decision-making responsibilities—or who shares in making growth decisions—for the marketplace future of a PSF or B2B service organization.

As David Maister wrote to me in an e-mail regarding key points in his 2008 book *Strategy and the Fat Smoker*, it's management's job to create the passion in other professionals that leads to disciplined execution.[10] These folks have to manage the changes that will help their firms move into the future—to *see* the challenges of marketing and business development functional silos and fix them. In this book, I echo Maister in calling on these senior executives and managers to adopt a new sense of passion and purpose to ensure that marketing and business development are more integrated, structurally and culturally, throughout the enterprise.[11]

These leaders "get it"; they understand their enterprises are facing an Integration Imperative. They seek a clear grasp of the scope and shape of their marketing and business development "disconnectivity" challenges. They're ready to contemplate some possible structural and cultural solutions and to see examples of how other professional firms are crafting their own integration solutions.

But what these leaders haven't yet seen—because this book is the first to provide it—is the big picture of marketing and business development integration. Executive managers need a compelling road map of the steps they can take to become even more competitively effective. Specifically, at which areas should they look? Where can they start to make changes, either structurally or with cultural initiatives? The Integration Imperative provides the road map, and the cases make it clear that changes can indeed be made. The impetus is competitive advantage, client benefit, and an engaged and deeply satisfied workforce.

What This Book Is—and Is Not

This book makes the point that there is an integration problem and that this problem prevents competitive effectiveness, impedes financial success, and hinders optimal **client service**. In these pages, I encourage leaders to begin or to continue an integration process at their own firms.

But this is not a "how-to" manual. It contains no cookie-cutter prescriptions that one can simply lift out and apply to an organization. I offer some high-level concepts, as well as some detailed templates in the appendix, that suggest some structural frameworks and cultural paradigms that firms could adapt. I also describe some customizable cultural approaches that could significantly break down the numerous organizational silos that have crept into professional and business service marketing programs.

Executive managers know integration is no small task. To undertake the changes I suggest, professional organizations must look internally to develop their own unique answers to the challenges of integrating marketing and business development. A one-size-fits-all solution simply will not work. The concepts described here must be considered in the context of the multitude of alternatives firms face each day, including the notion that "we're doing fine enough as is; let's not change anything too much." Each firm must tailor the advice in this book to its own situation.

I do not advocate that PSFs or B2Bs embark on efforts that paralyze the enterprise. I do, however, suggest that the structural frameworks and cultural approaches described in this book can offer these firms a greater probability of delivering better **value propositions** to their clients than most can do presently. I'm also convinced that clients will prefer to do business with organizations that make use of the Integration Imperative structural models and cultural approaches.

What This Book Contains

This "à la carte" book features cutting-edge research findings, outlines a set of emerging best practices, and offers a series of templates that can be adapted by professional firm managers. It also presents 11 case studies that highlight the compelling—and customized—approaches already being used by real-life professional and business-to-business service firms. An example of one of the book's structural frameworks, *The Process Imperative*, is found in the accounting firm Moss Adams, which developed new marketing and business development integration tools that dramatically accelerated the speed at which practitioners connected marketing to selling and selling to client service. These frameworks and new cultural norms are driving strong revenue gains (even in a slow economy).

An example of another one of the book's structural frameworks, *The Skills Imperative*, is a case about how a small engineering and architectural planning, design, and consulting firm, Ross & Baruzzini, adapted a big-time performance management tool (*The Balanced Scorecard*) and combined it with a marvelous **informal initiative**, a "guardian angel" mentoring program. And then there's Haley & Aldrich, an environmental, engineering, and management consulting firm that created a pathway to a "seat at the table" for its nonrevenue-generating marketing leader. This structural framework, coupled with the firm's mindful stewardship of a shared-accountability culture, has contributed to the enterprise's continued prominence in its sector.

The book's third structural framework, *The Support Imperative*, is illustrated by two cases featuring new **formal initiatives**—that is, collaborations between administrative functions aimed at improving marketing and business development effectiveness. At R.W. Beck, a management and engineering consultancy, marketing and human resource functional leaders teamed up on new performance improvement and organization development initiatives to improve the firm's internal collaboration and shared accountability on marketing, selling, and client **service delivery**. And Randstad, one of the world's largest temporary and contract staffing organizations, instigated innovative global collaboration between its marketing and finance departments, vastly improving the productivity of the company's marketing expenditures.

Because common definitions are so important in remedying the silos and functional breakdowns that exist in PSFs and B2Bs, defining terms makes sense. So in this book every term that could potentially be misunderstood or misinterpreted is boldfaced at first mention and its definition (where appropriate, vetted through my informal advisors) appears in the glossary in the appendix to this book.

Two examples of such terms are **function** versus **role**. By *function*, I mean a set of expected tasks that have a clearly identified boundary. Marketing is a function, not a role. A *role* is a subset of that function—say, a marketing coordinator whose job is to implement a variety of steps in a process. Or a CMO whose role is advisor, not implementer. Another example: **integration** versus **alignment**. Alignment isn't enough; it still allows silos!

The issue of managing change looms large throughout these pages. Although I found it tempting to insert a multipage manifesto on cultural change management as it relates to professional firms, I knew such a manifesto would distract from my central points. (That said, PSF and B2B executives do need to formally gain perspectives and build their skills in managing cultural change initiatives for their enterprises.) But change management is not the purview of this book, and so I decided to leave deep change management discussions to change management experts.

How to Read This Book

Each person reads a book differently. Some benefit most by reading stories that feature real people encountering the challenges that are related to the book's topic. Others prefer to understand the "argument," including research and data, before moving ahead to consider a book's proposed solution.

It makes sense, then, to suggest that this book be read in an à la carte fashion. It is broken into three sections, or parts, each of which can be consumed separately or in the order preferred. At the beginning of each section is a summary of its contents, and I encourage readers to skip to the next section if desired. Part I provides an overview of the marketing and business development disconnects found in professional and business-to-business service firms. Readers who most appreciate seeing evidence of the "problem," backed up by facts and figures, will want to start there. Part II outlines a "solution." Readers who learn best by first contemplating new ideas may enjoy the three structural paradigms I propose that could effectively integrate marketing and business development throughout a professional or business-to-business service organization. This section also highlights the reasons why integration ultimately benefits a firm and its clients.

Some readers may prefer to go directly to the stories, or case studies, that highlight both the problems and firms' own solutions to the challenges of marketing and business development silos. Part III features 11 stories about how real PSFs and B2Bs have worked toward greater functional collaboration, shared accountabilities, and individual competencies in each of the book's three Integration Imperative areas. The resources offered in the appendix will appeal to readers who appreciate the implementation of a concept. It contains both a glossary of terms and detailed templates and charts of the imperatives. It should help readers gain further insight into marketing and business development integration concepts.

Let's get to it.

A Solvable Problem

Read this section . . .

- If you didn't know there is a marketing–business development integration problem in professional and business-to-business service firms, or
- If you need to make a credible case to your colleagues that there really *is* an integration problem, and what it looks like.

Otherwise, feel free to skip to Part II.

■ ■ ■

The siloed and disjointed marketing and selling functions of professional and business-to-business service firms (PSFs and B2Bs) seriously hamper them from competing effectively and serving their clients optimally. So far, though, the attempts most professional firms have made to improve their effectiveness in marketing and business development have not addressed two core problems.

First, the traditional structure of these functions simply no longer works as well as PSFs and B2Bs need in today's complex marketplace. Second, this structural problem is exacerbated by cultural barriers, including a lack of common definitions of "marketing" and "business development" and their potential scope, and by obsolete cultural norms on marketing and business development.

The four chapters of Part I provide an overview of the marketing and business development disconnects found in professional service firms. Chapter 1 explores evidence of the numerous structural integration challenges, and makes the case that professional service firms can overcome them by adapting a deliberate focus. Chapter 2 outlines the cultural factors that have contributed to this relative state of marketing and business development ineffectiveness, and concludes that the executive managers of professional firms can have a direct impact on overcoming these challenges.

Chapter 3 summarizes the initiatives professional firms have undertaken so far as they try to address their marketing and business development disconnects. These efforts to increase effectiveness, while providing solid evidence that professional firms are indeed capable of "doing things differently," have yet to address in a substantive fashion the deep scope of the structural and cultural barriers to real integration. Chapter 4 introduces three structural frameworks and three cultural paradigms that could effectively integrate marketing and business development throughout a professional organization.

Chapter 1

Structural Challenges to Marketing and Business Development Integration

Professional and business-to-business service firms are part of a well-established global economic engine that generates revenues of more than a trillion dollars. Despite this apparent robustness, they continue to face numerous challenges to becoming more productive in their marketplace initiatives, more competitively effective, and, ultimately, more valuable to their clients and targets.

This chapter outlines several structural integration challenges, and it makes the case that executive managers should reconfigure their firms' marketing and business development structures to achieve better integration.

■ ■ ■

Clients begin forming impressions of the possible effectiveness of their service providers when they first encounter a firm's marketing and business development processes. Clients may ask themselves (sometimes subconsciously), "Has this firm targeted me well?" "Are its marketing and sales processes well coordinated?" "How astute is this firm in learning about my needs, trying to retain my business, and developing future-oriented solutions that I haven't even considered myself?" "How well will this firm deliver its services to my company?"

For their part, marketers and business developers know all too well the importance of personal, functional, and company-wide effectiveness in the marketplace. It's clear that firms are expending tremendous effort on a host of initiatives to better themselves in marketing and business development.

But, collectively, PSFs and B2Bs are only just beginning to recognize the serious structural and cultural disconnects that hinder their effectiveness in marketing and selling their services. Currently, the majority of professional firms manage their marketing and business development functions from separate functional silos. Most have no overarching structural integration models or integration cultural principles for marketers and business developers to follow, and little to no documented expectations of formal collaborations, shared accountabilities, or documented co-leadership among functions. All too often, in many PSFs or B2B service companies collaboration between these functions is the result of individual or small-team efforts.

This chapter looks at the structures that define how most PSFs and B2Bs go to market—and the challenges those structures have created. Most of these enterprises, even the smallest, utilize some form of management-endorsed marketing and business development department, formalized teams, or individuals designated to lead marketing and business development. Holding titles like "marketing director" or "business development partner," these professionals (who might also be practitioners of the firm's services) typically employ a recognized set of processes, tools, or protocols to help their firm market and sell its services. Together, these groups of people, reporting relationships, processes, tools, tasks, and methods comprise the structure of a firm's marketing and business development.

One of the best ways to address such a deeply systemic problem is to break it down into observable pieces. We'll now review four structural marketing and business development integration barriers.

A Lack of Process Coordination in Going to Market

Senior marketers and business developers from larger professional firms have told me about the logistical challenges of managing the handoff between marketing and business development within their **matrixed organizational structures**. Regardless of whether marketing and business development is led by **revenue-generating practitioners** or nonbillable marketers and business developers, people in these larger organizations know only too well how their matrixed organizational structures in some cases prevent their firms from deploying an overarching and integrated functional marketing-to-business development program.

Sometimes this lack of coordination has a technological underpinning. For example, information that resides in a centralized database should, arguably, be retrievable to discourage a team in Singapore from pursuing an engagement that another team in Los Angeles is also pursuing. Sometimes, the problem is found in the internal communication channels within the firm—for example, whether or not there is a regularly scheduled telephone conference call during which far-flung marketing and business development teammates share information about their marketplace pursuits.

More often than not, though, this lack of coordination, while observable at this tactical level, exists because the entire function of marketing is not seamlessly integrated with the function of business development. If one thinks about the ways in which clients make their buying decisions, it becomes clear that the function of marketing is at times underutilized at certain points along the clients' decision-making continuum and then overutilized at other points. The same thing occurs in the implementation of business development.

The Bloom Group's 2007 study "Integrating Marketing and Business Development in Professional Services Firms" corroborated this scenario. Of its 224 PSF respondents from North America and Europe, nearly half reported that they did not have strong coordination or integration between their marketing and business development functions. Arguing that marketers and business developers "aren't always cheek-to-cheek," Bloom Group researchers found significant variability in activities, including **targeting** the same clients or services, working off the same client database, working off the same marketing **campaign**, or working off the same timeline of activities.[1] When the Bloom Group analyzed the self-reported differences between the study's "leaders" and "laggards," the perspectives on integration became even more interesting. It found that the "leaders" reported much stronger coordination and integration between marketing and business development.

Respondents also reported that "the greatest obstacles in coordinating marketing and business development activities [were] lack of common measures of effectiveness, incentives, demand-generating processes or CRM [client relationship management] systems."[2] I, too, found evidence of this lack of process coordination in research I co-authored in 2006 with Larry Bodine. In that study, "Increasing Marketing Effectiveness at Professional Firms," nearly 400 senior-level respondents from a dozen professional and B2B service sectors revealed the functional silos in the way they coordinate (or don't coordinate, I should say) the handoffs from one marketing-to-business development process step to another.[3]

The "Effectiveness" study featured several questions on the five general steps that most firms follow in their process, and they are shown in table 1.1.

Bodine and I were surprised at how little emphasis respondents placed on the first of these five steps: "defining and identifying our most strategically appropriate clients and targets." In ranking their goals from 2002 to 2005, respondents ranked this marketing goal lower than all but one of their most important marketing goals (see top row of table 1.1).

Strategic marketing goals	Average importance in the last three years	Firms that ranked this goal *lowest*	Firms that ranked this goal *highest*
Define and identify clients and targets	2.8	23.6%	19.1%
Acquire clients	3.2	9.5%	18.6%
Retain clients	3.4	10.6%	26.3%
Build revenue	2.9	16.2%	13.5%
Increase perceived value	1.7	40.1%	22.6%

Table 1.1 Rankings of Strategic Marketing Goals by Professional Firms, 2002–2005
Source: Suzanne Lowe and Larry Bodine, "Increasing Marketing Effectiveness at Professional Firms," research report, Expertise Marketing LLC and Larry Bodine Marketing Inc., February 2006.
Note: Rank of importance: 5 = high; 1 = low.

The "acquire clients" step (see second row of table 1.1) has traditionally been the most riveting endeavor of a professional enterprise. In my days of serving as the in-house marketing director of a variety of firms, it was the single biggest focus for growing the company. The hunt was enthralling. So was the "kill," as it was sometimes called. Today, the hunt to acquire clients has almost taken on a life of its own.

In the "Effectiveness" study, one of the respondents commented on how important — and well-known — this benchmark was within his firm: "We want to maintain at least an 80% hit rate."[4] A law firm respondent stated it even more starkly: "We have revenue targets for 2006, and for the 2007–2010 periods. Those targets are higher than this current year. We also establish targets for new clients, and for total new files — calculated annually, and broken down monthly in patterns to match previous years' statistics."[5]

That's a *lot* of focus on acquiring new clients. But most professional firms swallow hard when clients walk away at the end of the engagement, perfectly willing to choose another service provider. Today, when clients decline to engage a firm in return assignments (even when they could do so), professional enterprises, appropriately enough, figure out that they need to shift away from their ongoing heavy focus on acquiring clients.

The respondents in the "Effectiveness" study confirmed this shift with their ranking of "acquire clients" in relation to the other four marketing goals. Although acquiring clients was, by average importance, the second highest-ranked strategic marketing goal and last among the lowest-ranked goals, it was in the middle of the pack in terms of the most highly ranked goals. These rankings corroborate my perception that the "acquire clients" goal has lost a bit of its luster. Acquiring clients—any old client— is understandably less helpful than identifying those clients best suited for building a long-term relationship and growing the firm.

For these respondents, retaining clients has become the new cure-all. Especially because contact database technologies have made it easier to manage the details of client relationships, marketers and business developers have made great strides in successfully pursuing this strategic goal. One respondent in the "Effectiveness" study described how her firm approaches this goal: "We measure the relationship on a matrix; identify the incremental business provided; identify the increases in specific client service relationship areas (extranet, face-to-face meetings, expense tracking processes, etc.)."

PSFs and B2Bs have also begun to implement more formal client satisfaction and postengagement evaluation feedback (although some sectors are doing so more programmatically than others). One information technology (IT) firm respondent said it well: "We get real feedback from our clients. It's very helpful in both managing the relationship and creating new products and services."[6]

The "Effectiveness" research findings bear this out. As compared with the four other strategic marketing goals shown in table 1.1, the goal of "retaining strategically appropriate clients" (see third row of table) was first in terms of average importance over the years 2002–2005. On a rankings scale, it also enjoyed the number-one spot in relation to the other marketing goals of our nearly 400 respondents.

At first glance, professional firms' emphasis on retaining clients looks great. Clearly, the respondents in the "Effectiveness" study have gotten the message that keeping the firm's best clients is a competitively astute move. But without the next strategic goal—building a firm's book of revenues with its most strategically appropriate clients—the enterprise simply maintains its current market share. If a firm overemphasizes the goal of retaining clients, it cannot make any competitive gains.

Of the five strategic marketing goals considered in the "Effectiveness" research, the goal of building a firm's book of revenues with its most strategically appropriate clients (see fourth row of table 1.1) presented professional firms with their most perplexing challenge. They encounter four

major stumbling blocks. The first is the fact that many firms underempha-
size the importance of achieving this goal, especially when compared with
the goal of constantly acquiring new clients. The other three stumbling
blocks are (1) professional firms' time-honored practice of implementing
"build revenue" programs that are tactical and simplistic; (2) "build revenue" programs that too often are overly internal and not strongly related
to a strategic marketplace growth rationale; and (3) "build revenue" programs destined to be hamstrung if they're not connected to the firm's innovation (or at least customized solutions) engine — most are not.

As for "increasing a firm's perceived value" (see last row of table 1.1),
since the formative early days of professional and B2B service marketing
this goal has received the lion's share of resources allocated by executive
managers. Not surprisingly, the main focus of their attention is outward,
on the client decision maker.

But this marketing goal has evolved beyond just an external focus. Especially because many firms have effectively harnessed the use of intranets in
the last dozen years, marketers have successfully added "internal marketing" to their scope of responsibilities. Although internal marketing still falls
largely in the comfort zone of "communications," this evolved purview
strongly indicates that the traditional scope of marketing is shifting.

But there is still evidence of some disparity among professional firms'
perceptions of this strategic goal. For example, according to the last row
of table 1.1, "Increase perceived value," almost twice as many firms
ranked this goal "least important" as those who ranked it "most important." None of the four other strategic marketing goals has this wide a
rankings gap.

This "Effectiveness" study finding confirms that for a distinct subset of
professional organizations the main marketing goal is still largely "communications." But what about the *other* subset of professional service
organizations — those firms that do balance "communications" with other
important strategic goals? Could it be that marketplace traction can be
gained more easily if "increase perceived value" initiatives are aimed
increasingly at targeted audiences rather than the amorphous "everybody"? Certain professional service sectors appear to be grasping this idea.
For example, management consulting and law firms have begun to put
in place discreet alumni relations programs. Others are also beginning
to create marketing programs directed toward their referral sources (as
opposed to potential clients).

A State of Confusion and Uneven Accountabilities in Marketing and Business Development

Is marketing from Venus? Is sales from Mars? Fundamentally, these questions reflect a lack of understanding of the optimal structure of marketing and business development functions. In a PSF or B2B service firm, what *is* marketing? What *is* business development? Who's supposed to do what, and how should it be structured?

Let's look closer at the confusion that exists in many professional firms today, stemming mainly from a less than optimal structure for deploying marketing and business development.

Business development (selling) is a one-to-one activity. Practitioners' brains (well, their brain power) are the "products" clients are considering for eventual engagement. But marketing is a one-to-many activity, and is best deployed from a firm-wide, centralized purview.

Without an optimal structure for marketing and business development, the potential for confusion creeps in when one-to-one **fee-earning practitioners** want to get involved in the one-to-many aspects of marketing. (Eventually, this dysfunctional structure leads to cultural challenges, but I'll address those issues in the next chapter.)

Let's consider the example of a professional firm putting on a seminar for its prominent clients in one of the firm's many business units. The content for the seminar will be developed by the business unit leader, who possesses the **intellectual capital** clients will eventually buy—that is, marketing her intellectual capital is a one-to-one initiative. The firm's nonrevenue-generating marketing director is responsible for developing and implementing the marketing program for the seminar. The marketing director is an expert in crafting positioning and branding messages for professional firms. The firm's marketing strategy is a one-to-many initiative, and thus the marketing director expects to "own" the invitation copy.

The marketing director brings the seminar invitation copy to the practitioner. He wants to ensure that he's articulated the practitioner's intellectual capital accurately. Instead, the practitioner insists on rewriting the entire invitation copy, even changing the way the company itself is described. Believing that her most important goal is to please her clients (a laudable one-to-one goal), she sees nothing wrong with her actions. But in doing so, she steps out of her own purview and wanders into the marketer's one-to-many territory. In doing so, she delays the marketing director's planning and production schedule for the seminar, which leads to cost and time overruns that affect other practitioners' planned marketing programs, and eventually the entire firm's clients. She's also undermined the one-to-many strategic positioning message that had been carefully crafted by the marketing director (and which was previously approved by the firm's equity shareholders).

There are no bad guys here. Indeed, professional firms need practitioners who can and who want to write and speak well. By packaging their one-to-one intellectual capital, practitioners can work effectively with their firms' one-to-many marketing programs. But any misunderstanding of the optimal scope of the marketing and business development function causes "disconnectivity" and waste.

And then what happens? More silos and less than effective marketing and business development. You get the idea: revenue generators conduct their own client perception research, develop their own sub-brands, or hoard names in their own personalized databases. These initiatives are best managed by a centralized unit of one or several professional marketers or senior executives who have an overarching and well-integrated one-to-many purview.

While it's tempting for marketers and business developers to be frustrated and perhaps even upset at the boundary-confusion picture I've just painted, the reality is that most revenue-generating practitioners are good people who earnestly want to work effectively on marketing and business development, whether their firm utilizes nonrevenue-generating marketing and selling professionals or not.

But there's another reality at work here, and it's directly related to the issue of boundary confusion—that is, when a professional firm unevenly assigns the formal accountability for marketing and business development throughout the organization. Too many firms expect their people to collaborate on marketing and business development initiatives without an adequate organization structure that includes formally recognized interdependent accountabilities for each function's success. "Formal" connotes a structural component such as a documented process, tool, or protocol. One of the most obvious is a job description that spells out what people are supposed to do and, in some cases, how.

So, in marketing and business development, who is supposed to have accountability, and for what?

Authors of the Bloom Group's 2007 study asked 224 respondents how they described their firms' definitions of the roles, responsibilities, and accountabilities of the following: sales/business developers, corporate-level marketers, practice/service-level marketers, and practicing partners with sales responsibilities. According to the study report, "Half of these respondents felt their roles are 'very clear' or 'clear,' but the other half weren't confident."[7] The Bloom Group also applied a self-reported "leaders" and "laggards" analysis here, and it found that "leader" firms were "clear" or "very clear" on the roles, responsibilities, and accountabilities:

- Sales/business developers: 67 percent were clear or very clear versus 42 percent for the laggards.

- Corporate-level marketers: 58 percent were clear or very clear versus 30 percent for the laggards.

- Practice/service-level marketers: 64 percent were clear or very clear versus 36 percent for the laggards.

- Practicing partners with sales responsibilities: 67 percent were clear or very clear versus 31 percent for the laggards.[8]

My reaction to these findings was that these margins aren't very wide. Shouldn't expectations be clearer?

The Bloom Group's 2007 study findings went even further, though, to hint at the true state of unevenly assigned accountability in PSF and B2B marketing and business development. To its question "Who is in charge of managing the process of creating demand for your firm's services?" one-third of responding firms reported they did not have an individual accountable for managing **demand creation**. Figure 1.1 shows that another one-third of responding firms assigned accountabilities for managing demand creation to practice or service-line heads. From there, accountability lies with marketing heads or sales heads or "another individual."[9]

Big deal, you might say. It's just that some of these firms have not formally designated someone as demand creation manager. Right? But it is a big deal when no one is accountable.

These results also bring up another critical concern. In figure 1.1, the Bloom Group's question was structured in a choose-one-answer format; respondents were not allowed to indicate they sometimes split accountabilities among functions. In reality, though, many professional firms do indeed assign partial or multiple accountabilities among the functions depicted in figure 1.1.

To the uninitiated, splitting responsibility for demand creation (or other marketing and business development initiatives) may seem like a reasonable

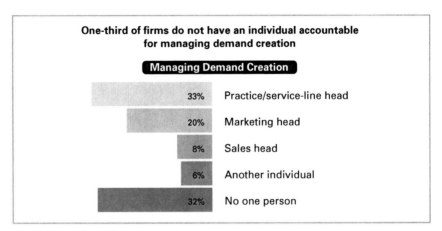

Figure 1.1 Managing Demand Creation

Source: Robert Buday, "Integrating Marketing and Business Development in Professional Services Firms: Findings from a 2007 Bloom Group Survey," research report, Bloom Group LLC, December 2007.

assignment of effort. But when professional firms split assignments for aspects of marketing and business development functions, they create built-in gaps or duplications in accountability. As the Bloom Group study's author Bob Buday and I agreed when we discussed its findings, even though the findings depicted in figure 1.1 don't specifically capture the issue of splitting responsibilities, this practice is exceedingly common in professional firms across all sectors.

Assignment splitting or duplication is a significant concern, especially if competitive effectiveness is on the line. Moreover, in these situations most marketing and business development function leaders aren't formally accountable *to each other* either. That, too, is an enormous problem—separate marketing head versus separate sales head, each working semi-independently, and so on.

And so the Bloom Group's 2007 study findings only show us the tip of the iceberg of uneven accountabilities. Moreover, as sometimes happens, professional firms make everything and everyone accountable to an overly narrow goal. Some firms, especially those with a strong tradition of private ownership, have traditionally assigned strategic marketing and higher-level selling to fee-earning practitioners or retiring **rainmakers**. This practice, although not intrinsically flawed, can sometimes glorify the seller-doer structural model to an unnecessarily unbalanced end.

Consider the highly successful rainmaker who becomes fixated on a tangential marketing or business development project. I recall the practice leader of a respected professional firm who wanted to produce a lush coffee table book chronicling his firm's long and celebrated history—it became his *cause célèbre*. For this project, he commandeered the attention and energy of many business developers and marketers whose time could have been better spent being accountable for more astute and strategic programs.

How does the formal accountability issue affect the way in which marketers and business developers work with their administrative counterparts in areas such as human resources, information technology, finance, and legal? In April 2008, in conducting research for this book, I ran an online "Administration Collaboration" survey. Respondents included senior business developers, marketers, and executive managers from PSFs and B2Bs.

The first question in the survey was whether, in the last three years, responding professional firms had deliberately structured new formal relationships, reporting lines, or shared accountabilities among marketing, business development, and other administrative functions. The respondents revealed that informality and a lack of structure are indeed their overarching paradigm. The majority reported that collaborating by "communicating" is popular. But only a few reported on the higher-impact forms of functional integration: recognized shared accountabilities, co-developed job descriptions, clearly delineated reporting relationships, and organizationally supported performance goals.

Some respondents protested the need for any kind of structural formality among marketing, business development, and other support functions: "We are small enough that we know what everyone is doing." Others downplayed the need for structure, saying that cultural ties exist in its place. For example: "We have a strong working relationship with our Finance Department personnel." "Everybody understands what's going on and the level of collaboration is fairly high." "We work closely with HR."

But there was strong evidence of increased effort—structurally—to formalize the working relationships between the firm's marketing, business development, and other administrative functions. These efforts fell into two categories:

- *Communication.* Some respondents were building collaboration and shared accountability through well-recognized communication vehicles. Several respondents referred to regularly scheduled meetings, often chaired by a leader in the C-suite.

- *New policies, assignments, and shared objectives.* Respondents used many words (italicized) that signaled their leaning toward formality:
  - "Legal, IT, Finance each have a *point person assigned* to Marketing."
  - "Marketing *handles* entry-level recruiting."
  - "Technology group has *designated* a 'Marketing Technology Specialist.'"

Some "Administration Collaboration" survey respondents reported they were formalizing the working relationship between just marketing and business development (and not other support areas). They considered this a positive step even without integrating these two functions with other enterprise-wide administration. But no respondents commented that their firms had taken the ultimate structural step of creating new reporting lines or recognized shared accountabilities among marketing, business development, and other administration functions.

Another study question asked PSFs and B2Bs if they formally compensate and reward administrative functions for collaborating and sharing accountabilities on marketing and business development. In this case, "formally" means executive managers *expect* their human resources, IT, legal, finance, and facilities management professionals (and beyond) to collaborate with their marketing and business development teammates, to share accountabilities, and to co-lead market-driven initiatives with them. "Formally" also means their performance evaluations will include assessments of how well they support achievement of the firm's marketing and business development goals.

More than two-thirds of respondents said "no." Of the one-third of responding firms that did compensate and reward their administrative and marketing and business development functions for formal collaboration, only a smattering thought their firms' efforts were "absolutely fantastic so far." Talk about a lukewarm endorsement!

The notion of structuring compensation inevitably raises the specter of performance measurement. Some of these professional firm respondents said they were ready to do the work that measuring performance requires, but they'd rather compensate and reward for *overall* teamwork on marketing and business development rather than go to the effort of unbundling the specific behaviors or accomplishments.

I'm not suggesting that professional service firms that don't add this level of formality are doomed to competitive failure. Indeed, friendly working relationships are vital to an organization's ability to succeed.

I am saying, however, that professional service firm executive managers could achieve more effectiveness in their marketplace pursuits if they are explicit about how they require everyone to contribute. In the research that I and others have conducted, we've seen that people need a common understanding of what's asked of them. Despite everyone's best intentions, "collaborate," for example, means different things to different people. Take the IT person who, when asked to collaborate on a new marketing initiative, may think, "Collaboration is a nice idea. But I'll only help those marketers when I can squeeze it in. It's really not my job."

By contrast, the IT person with a deep understanding of her managers' expectations for her contributions to marketing may say to herself in the same situation, "I'm clear that my function exists to help the firm compete as effectively as possible, and to serve the clients with as much value as it can. I'll not only shift my priorities to directly and promptly assist my marketing teammates, but I'll also co-lead this project, with suggestions for new and better ways for it to succeed."

There does appear to be an emerging awareness that structured functional integration among marketing, business development, and administration colleagues can offer substantive benefits for a firm. One "administration collaboration" respondent agreed: "[There are] still some thiefdoms to break down, but generally I think people are finding it far more rewarding to work together." (I enjoyed the mistaken, or perhaps deliberate, play on the word *fiefdom*.)

Arguably, professional firms are very good at structuring their formal expectations that revenue-generating practitioners will sell their and their colleagues' services. Indeed, the professional firm model would have never survived if this basic framework hadn't been etched in stone eons ago. But if a formal compensation and rewards structure has been built and is so workable among practitioners, why hasn't a similar structure been applied to their administrative functions related to marketing and business development?

It is only by formally integrating administrative functions with marketing and business development that the enterprise can truly gain marketplace traction. Many service businesses have already begun to encourage collaboration through communication. Once they begin seeing the positive results from informal collaboration among support functions, their enthusiasm will begin to pick up speed. They will shift gears into developing more explicit and more formally outlined shared accountabilities. And they will support these integrated functions with incentives, rewards, recognized shared accountabilities, or co-developed job descriptions.

Lopsided Marketing and Business Development Programs

You know it's an integration problem when you notice that a professional firm's marketing program is not effectively linked with its business development initiatives. The most obvious evidence of this "disconnectivity" is an unbalanced marketing program. For many PSFs and B2Bs, **marketing communications** (also known as marcom) is the 800-pound gorilla in the room, dominating all other marketing programs and creating disconnectivity at every step.

There are four ways to detect lopsided marketing programs. Each relates to the way a professional firm structures its marketing and business development functions. They are (1) a budgetary overemphasis on marketing communications; (2) an increase in calls, by PSFs or B2Bs themselves, for proof of a marketing communications program's return on investment; (3) position descriptions that overemphasize communications and designate these positions as "support" instead of pathways to strategic leadership; and (4) evidence of the commoditization of tactics-oriented marcom services.

First, let's look at the budgetary underpinnings of a lopsided marketing program. We see an overemphasis on marketing communications when a professional firm's marketing budget is heavily weighted toward biographical inserts in folders, brochures and taglines, new-hire press announcements, advertising or holiday cards—anything that features messages to influence prospective buyers. We see it when a professional firm's marketing budget allocates little or no resources toward what I've called "Looking Out" activities—that is, those endeavors that help a firm understand clients and their marketplace. We also see it when a firm's marketing budget allocates little or no resources to **thought leadership**, service portfolio management, or innovation—those endeavors I've called Embedding Innovation.[10]

Too many professional firms overweight the budgetary importance of marketing communications programs, even when there is evidence that their marketplace effectiveness could rise if they deployed Looking Out marketing program elements. My research, featured in *Marketplace Masters*, revealed that professional firms reported greater marketplace effectiveness when, for example, through formal client research they are able to understand more deeply their clients' own marketplace pain and unmet needs.[11]

And what about competitive intelligence, targeting and **segmentation, data mining**, and loyalty research? Too few professional service firms budget for these critical strategic elements in their marketing programs, leaving themselves competitively vulnerable, even as they work overtime to create undifferentiated and off-target marketing communications messages.

Finally, what about ensuring that the budgets for these marcom-heavy programs feature a more direct connection to business development? Budgets, as one of the structural tools professional firms use to help make marketplace gains, could serve as one of the means of breaking down marketing and business development silos. Yet many professional firm budgets don't link their marketing and business development budgets.

Nor do more than a very small percentage of firms include budgetary line items to fund measurement of their marketing-to-business development programs.

This point leads me to my second observation about detecting a general lack of balance in professional firms' marketing programs. Even though so few firms formally fund marketing and business development measurement, there are nevertheless growing calls for increased effectiveness of the marketing communications programs of PSFs and B2Bs. Indeed, in 2005 Larry Bodine and I both noticed the urgency with which our research advisors encouraged us to select "increasing effectiveness" as the focus of our 2006 co-authored research study.

In that "Effectiveness" study, we were struck by the enormous number of anecdotes from our 377 respondents, reporting their own and their firm managers' growing scrutiny of expenditures on marketing communications programs. Our respondents recounted their anxiety about having to defend their marketing and business development activities. These respondents essentially said, "How can we be certain that the investments we've made in communicating to our clients actually result in revenues for our firm?"

In due course, the "Effectiveness" study findings revealed the importance of—and success related to—measuring in a more integrated fashion. But the study wasn't the only one to shed light on the topic of effectiveness in professional and B2B service marketing. The investigators in the 2007 Bloom Group study asked respondents to rate the obstacles to coordinating the activities of marketing and business development in terms of difficulty. Their findings revealed that lack of common measures, incentives, and process are massive obstacles (see figure 1.2).[12]

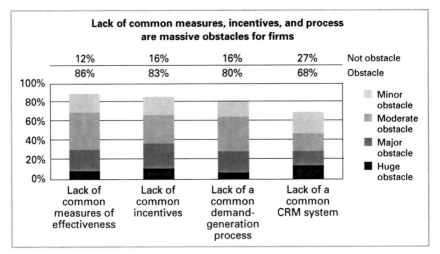

Figure 1.2 Marketing and Business Development Obstacles

Source: Robert Buday, "Integrating Marketing and Business Development in Professional Services Firms: Findings from a 2007 Bloom Group Survey," research report, Bloom Group LLC, December 2007.

Professional firms' executive managers, and, of course, their marketers and business developers, feel pressure to increase effectiveness precisely because they overrely on expensive, hard-to-measure, less than optimally researched and undifferentiated marketing communications tactics that are typically developed and distributed to less than well-targeted prospects and clients. But instead of perhaps creating better prioritization and integration for their marketing and business development programs, these managers and developers challenge the effectiveness of the unbalanced decisions they've already made. Instead of taking a step back and examining the disconnectivity in their overall marketing and business development programs, they chase tactical effectiveness. Without looking at the big picture about marketing and business development integration and its true potential, then, they toss the issue of measuring effectiveness onto the already hot disconnectivity fire.

This observation leads to my third point about detecting lopsided marketing and business development programs, and directly links back to organizational structures that could foster integration. The issue is that in many PSF and B2B service firms, marketing and business development position descriptions aren't structured to optimally integrate marketers and business developers, nor to recruit and retain marketers and business developers who have strategic or analytical capabilities.

This issue has many facets. In my consulting work, I have received a variety of senior marketing position descriptions from recruiters worldwide. These recruiters have asked me to make referrals or to pass the position descriptions along to worthy candidates in my network. But, in reviewing these position specifications, it became clear that many senior marketing positions were being set up to be siloed — that is, they were not structured for effective integration within the professional firm.

From 2006 through early 2008, I conducted a small, admittedly subjective study about the heavy marketing communications focus of chief marketing officer positions in globally prominent professional service firms. Every time an executive recruiter sent me one of these senior-level marketing position descriptions, I saved it in a folder on my desktop. What follows are summary descriptions of some of these positions, excerpted verbatim but cloaked for confidentiality purposes.

- In spring 2006, for a global executive search firm: "The Chief Marketing Officer will develop strategies, policies, and programs to define, support, enhance and communicate externally the identity of our firm. Working closely with firm leadership at the corporate, sector and regional levels, the Chief Marketing Officer will insure that the firm's 'brand identity,' as expressed in our well-defined values, cascades through all of the activities and programs conducted by the firm throughout its various markets. XXXX has developed a clear and distinctive vision regarding the firm's value- and principle-driven approach. Our positioning is 'XXXXXX.' Our marketing campaign, 'XXXX,' has been effectively launched with the publication of a XXXXX, the redesign of the firm's website and a clear strategy for raising the firm's visibility among key audiences, particularly XXX, XXX and XXX. The task now is to refine implementation of the strategy, working closely with the firm's sector and office leaders, and increase the momentum already established."

- In the second quarter of 2006, for a venerable management consulting firm: "The Head of U.S. Marketing will lead XXX's re-branding and marketing efforts in the United States. He/she will define and direct U.S. Marketing strategy and activities to support the achievement of aggressive growth objectives. The Director of Marketing will raise awareness of XXXX among key existing and prospective clients. He/she will create marketing and networking opportunities for [our practitioners], and will interface with the General Managers throughout the

United States to provide marketing support. This individual will build the Marketing function, hiring the staff, implementing Marketing structure and discipline, and establishing systematic Marketing practices that will add value throughout the United States. He/she will also interface with, and contribute to, the Global Marketing team."

- In mid-2007, for another global management consulting firm: "This newly created global Chief Marketing Officer position will lead the efforts to build awareness and equity in the XXXX brand to enable them to elevate, rival and ultimately overtake its main competitors, XXX, XXX and XXX. Major Responsibilities:

  - Lead and coach the marketing team to ensure the development of a highly performing function that achieves industry best practices and actively embraces the business values.

  - Evolve the XXXX brand positioning through a clear definition of brand values, visual identity and marketing communications to deliver differentiated brand value in an ever changing marketplace.

  - Lead the development and execution of annual marketing and communications plans including delivery of consistent messaging by all colleagues in areas such as public relations, practice and office marketing materials, website and intellectual capital projects.

  - Advise on 'packaging' intellectual capital into articles, reports etc. and distributing these to targeted clients.

  - Ensure the Firm's intellectual capital is leveraged into target media to develop relationships with journalists and thereby generate appropriate coverage."

It bothered me that these position responsibilities didn't explicitly include client perception or loyalty research. They didn't formally include analyzing competitive intelligence or economic trends. They didn't specifically seek skills in finance, statistics, or corporate strategy. They didn't require experience in managing for return on investment or tracking the life cycle of service lines. They didn't mention account or relationship management. They only highlighted communications responsibilities and not marketing strategy duties. They used code words that spoke to me about an overreliance on tactics—words such as "awareness," "messaging," "packaging," and "communications."

Could it be that these professional service firms—at the most basic structural level—are *creating* a lack of integration, right from the executive suite? And what happens if no one is assigned to lead client perception or loyalty research, account management, or other strategic marketing and business development initiatives? What happens if no one is leading competitive intelligence? And where will these functions connect with the firm's business development or other administrative functions?

What else did you notice about these three position descriptions? If you read them carefully, you probably caught what I did: the unmistakable spin of these roles toward "support" rather than "leadership." The support orientation of these supposedly senior-level marketing positions links back to the traditional foundation of marketing in the professions, when marketing and business development were viewed as peripheral, noncore activities.

There's evidence to corroborate my anecdotal observations. In their January 2008 study "The Evolved CMO," Forrester Research and Heidrick & Struggles co-authors Cindy Commander, Meagan Wilson, and Jane Stevenson shared their findings about the traditional responsibilities of the chief marketing officer role.

One of the study report's graphics (see figure 1.3) presented the areas in which their respondents indicated marketing had the highest levels of primary responsibility, including the three highest vote-getters: brand strategy and positioning, advertising and communications, and creative development. This study looked at 126 chief and senior marketers from both B2B and business-to-consumer (B2C) companies (across a variety of industries) with revenues of US$100 million and more. But its conclusions echo those in the professional service arena: lopsided marketing programs that too heavily emphasize communications.

When looking at figure 1.3, ask yourself: who in these firms is leading service or solutions development? Pricing? Sales training? Customer insights and analytics? The findings by Forrester Research and Heidrick & Struggles validate that B2B service firms manage these responsibilities elsewhere—not integrating them with the communications-focused responsibilities that hold sway. It's not a stretch to imagine the same of PSFs—it's likely that the various marketing and business development functions of these enterprises are not coordinated as well as they could be.[13]

A fourth and final observation about detecting the lopsidedness of PSF and B2B marketing programs relates to the commoditization of some areas of business-to-business service marketing. Specifically, there is evidence

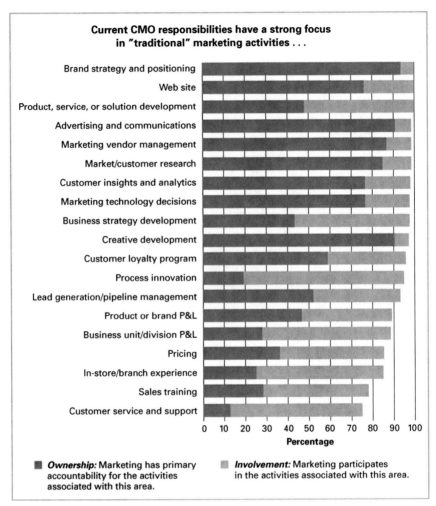

Figure 1.3 Marketing's Traditional Responsibilities

Source: Cindy Commander, Meagan Wilson, and Jane Stevenson, "The Evolved CMO," research report sponsored by Forrester Research and Heidrick & Struggles, 2008.

Note: Respondent base: 126 chief and senior marketers.

that firms are beginning to handle some of the more tactical aspects of communications externally, with senior marketers or CMOs supervising marketing services offered by outside vendors.

It's happening in legal services. Larry Bodine observed in an August 2006 blog post "Offshoring Marketing: How Law Firm CMOs Can Prioritize Their Efforts":

Clever CMOs [should] . . . join their firm's other efforts and offshore certain parts of their own jobs such as: advertising, desktop publishing, Web site design and coding, graphics creation and photo retouching, brochure creation, writing, invitations to events, . . . and PowerPoint templates and charts. That's because none of that is strategic work. In fact, it's the lowest-level, fungible work that top marketers have been trying to push down to other personnel for years. My suggestion is to take it a step further: Send it overseas.[14]

Law firms aren't the only professional enterprises to outsource or offshore tactical marketing and business development services. It's happening across sectors. The larger point, of course, relates once again to the perceived purpose of these functions. The earlier incarnations of the functions, as we've seen, were more support- and tactics-oriented. Now, senior marketers and business developers are seeking to delegate "execution-oriented" initiatives (and probably more so in the future). They view **offshoring** and **outsourcing** as options that will help them clear their plates in order to focus on making more deeply strategic contributions to their firms. Great idea. This kind of thinking represents astute resource allocation and cost-benefit judgment.

But if these senior marketers delegate some of these arguably tactical initiatives away, without a parallel initiative to ensure more optimal integration of the entire marketing and business development approach, they risk creating an unbalanced marketing–business development program. They risk exacerbating the functional silos that may have already crept in. And they risk creating an organizational vacuum and filling it with more disconnected activities (such as measuring tactical marcom initiatives), while not attending to the bigger issue of marketing and business development integration.

Professional firm executive managers should see outsourcing and offshoring decisions in a more strategic light, not just as opportunities to save money or reduce their firms' internal headcount. They should examine the bigger picture about *why* some service marketing tasks are becoming commoditized, and make careful enterprise-focused decisions about how to proceed. If they don't, they risk contributing to out-of-balance marketing and business development programs at own their firms.

Indeed, they should see marketing services commoditization, offshoring, and outsourcing as organizational opportunities to rebalance and integrate the marketing and business development functions. For example, in parallel with offshoring moves they could reconfigure the job descriptions of their marketers and business developers to expect different contributions to creating and leading implementation of the firm's growth strategies. They could examine whether their marketing-to-selling processes are functioning smoothly, and restructure them if not. They could explore ways to construct more formal collaborations internally among practitioners, marketers, and business developers, and administrative functions.

Underemphasized and Siloed Marketing and Business Development Skills

A professional service firm is essentially a collection of entrepreneurs who thrive on friendly internal competition and advancement. Practitioners jockey with each other to receive the next promotion or share of the firm's annual bonus. The big prize is owning a piece of its equity. For the firm's executive managers (who've already jumped through the hoops their predecessors set up), creating and touting the attainment of career advancement benchmarks is a very big deal; it is how the organization identifies its future leaders and outlines expectations for them to generate revenue.

You can imagine how riveting this culture can be to those who live within it. But there's a downside to all this fun. Practitioners can become overly attentive to the internal advancement game. The same cultures that foster such exhilarating jousting also distract people from growing their external acumen to keep pace with their clients or the marketplace. Practitioners become more interested in what their colleagues think than what the firm's clients think. Danger signs appear if advancement is not well tied to the marketplace, for example, or a firm's definition of a professional's thought leadership is somehow not tied to the client's perspective.

I've just described a concern about the silos of *practitioner* career advancement. What about marketers and business developers? Shouldn't executive managers be giving the same attention to the integrated skills growth and career advancement of their marketing and business development professionals that they give to the skills growth of their practitioners? Doesn't a lack of attention to the career advancement of their marketing and business development people lead to expensive position turnovers? Doesn't a lack of guidance for marketers and business developers on gaining strategic skills contribute to organizational silos and disconnectivity? Wouldn't it benefit the entire enterprise if executive managers could work with marketers and business developers to consider everyone's marketing and business development skills growth from a structural integration perspective?

Of course, the answer is yes. But most professional service firms have not built structures or formal pathways for training and skills growth for marketers and business developers. Most executive managers, perhaps still viewing the functions of marketing and business development as noncore, have yet to contemplate comprehensively the career pathways for these professionals.

To learn more about the ways in which professional and B2B service firms are seeing the scope of their marketing and business development functions evolve, I recently conducted a survey of 57 senior-level members of these firms. I published the results in March 2008.[15]

Let's review the good news from this "Evolving Scope" study. A majority of respondents provided details on their firms' efforts to increase the strategic impact of marketing and business development functions. Some specifically mentioned structural change work on "upgrading skills." Some described new developments in their roles, redefining the scope of the marketing function and making new or different allocations of staff in order to achieve new strategic goals. Notably, many firms were restructuring the entire function by bringing in entirely new staff members, or starting with a clean slate for the purview of marketing and business development for the entire firm.

I also asked respondents how their firms were going about increasing the skills and effectiveness of their marketing and business development professionals. They reported that their firms are implementing a variety of internal restructuring programs. The two programs with the highest number of votes ("changing marketing and business development job descriptions" and "creating a pathway to a 'seat at the table' for marketers and business developers") confirmed the structural approaches professional firms are taking to increase the effectiveness of marketing and business development.

That, then, is the good news from this small study: PSFs and B2Bs seem to be undertaking the work needed to boost the effectiveness and organizational pertinence of their professional service marketing and business development functions.

But the study also revealed that a clear subset of professional firm marketers and business developers feel "stuck" regarding the scope of their functions. Respondents in these firms spoke with a distinct tone of frustration and marginalization (the cultural ramifications of the marginalization issue are discussed in chapter 2).

The *structural* aspects of underemphasized skill development present at least two reasons for concern. The first reason relates to the overreliance of professional and B2B service firms on "soft" initiatives to grow marketing and business development skills, and their underreliance on structural skill growth pathways toward a clear vision of marketing and business development "success."

The majority of "Evolving Scope" survey respondents said their organizations were working proactively to make marketing and business development functions more strategic. And yet when asked for examples, a surprisingly large number of respondents could not identify *any* specific skills growth initiatives that their enterprises had endorsed or started.

Perhaps, I thought, my definition of "proactively working" differs from that of my respondents. I had hoped to track well-defined programmatic initiatives (*structure*, of course). Instead, these professional enterprises appeared to be adopting more culturally diffuse processes to make their marketing and business development functions broader, deeper, and more strategic. Respondents were using less formality than what I had thought I'd see.

Recognizing that my sample was only one subset of evidence, I then sought other examples of how professional service firms are developing structural solutions to grow the skills of their marketers and business developers. Perhaps skills growth is better achieved when "success" is formally articulated.

I found three research studies that may help executive managers envision the scope of skills their marketers and business developers should have eventually. However, each study stopped short of outlining exactly what competencies marketers and business developers should have, and when, in their careers.

In 2008 Diane Schmalensee and her colleague Dawn Lesh conducted a qualitative study on how to make marketing groups "indispensable" to their organizations. They discovered an enormous disconnect between the way a service company's practitioners defined "marketing success" and the way marketers did. In this study, practitioners said they felt "success" was achieved when they could "ask marketing for support or insights on complex, strategic issues—not just tactical ones," "view marketing as a partner," and "value marketing's instincts and judgments."

Marketers didn't have the same definitions of success. For them, successful marketing "introduces the voice of the customer," "influences better decisions," and "is a proactive force for success." One study respondent said, "I want to be seen as the first touch point when people need information and not as a group sitting off in a separate silo."[16]

In 2007, Booz Allen Hamilton (now Booz & Co.) published a book titled *CMO Thought Leaders: The Rise of the Strategic Marketer*. The firm followed this book with a *strategy + business* reprint that outlined the skills of a company's senior-most marketers. Although their work did not specifically target the service arena, the authors said marketers should possess the following capabilities:

- Curiosity to seek new ways to connect with customers
- Able to envision the future of a global brand
- Always listening to new voices and insights
- Can sniff out strategic direction
- Broad shoulders for carrying big ideas
- Fortitude to make marketing accountable
- Can work hand-in-glove with innovators
- Can think on his (her) feet
- Determined to be where his (her) customers are[17]

In these two studies, many leading thinkers provided well-corroborated perspectives on how to identify a true marketing leader. Each study correctly pointed out the importance of practitioners' defining their notion of marketing "success." Each did a good job of discussing appropriate business capabilities.

And yet, as I found in my own research, their guidelines were "soft" and open to broad interpretation (and misinterpretation). I couldn't help but wonder: exactly what skills should a marketer possess to give practitioners insights on complex, strategic issues? Exactly what makes marketing a "partner" (and pray tell, how does one get there)? Exactly how does a marketer "sniff out strategic direction"? How indeed does a marketer learn how to "work hand-in-glove with innovators"?

This observation leads me to my second reason to be concerned about the structural aspects of underemphasized and siloed skill development:

the fact that, collectively, professional firm executive managers have not demonstrated leadership toward the skills growth of their marketers and business developers. The vast majority of the advancement processes of professional firms are overly focused on practitioners, with the result that career and skill advancement pathways are not well outlined for nonpractitioners (the firm's administrative, marketing, or business development professionals).

It is perhaps understandable why the executive managers of PSFs and B2Bs don't appear to be as invested as they should be in helping their marketers and business developers grow their skills. Practitioners typically think of such skills in tactical terms: "We need to put on client events, so let's hire a marketing events person." "We need a good holiday card list, so let's hire a marketing database person." "We need to get our name mentioned in the press, so let's hire a media relations person." For practitioners, helping marketers and business developers to progress in their careers is a real challenge because marketers and business developers don't fit into the recognized growth pathways already in place for the revenue-generating side of the house.

To confirm this point, I contacted several professional firms across sectors to ask for examples of career advancement pathways for practitioners. Fortunately, I had no trouble gaining access to several examples for revenue-generating accountants, lawyers, and architects, among others. Their organizational growth pathways are well known and internally publicized.

But for marketers or business developers, it was a different story. In my conversations, I heard many cynical comments about the revolving door that most marketers face when they try to advance their careers. A former senior marketer at a world-class management consulting firm told me, "I doubt there are any real career paths at the major firms. Lots of outsiders— mostly journalists—still being brought in, and failing." A senior marketer from a different company told me his firm has no organizationally sanctioned growth pathway for members of his marketing team (and no plans to develop one either). The last time he promoted one of his team members, he said, was simply to acknowledge the individual's two years of fine work.

When a profession is young, as is professional service marketing and business development, and still forming a body of knowledge, hiring authorities have a hard time finding skilled and experienced people to direct and implement their programs. My esteemed friend Bruce Marcus, editor of "The Marcus Letter," summed it up well in an e-mail he sent to me on May 5, 2008:

Product people understood the role of marketing somewhere in the 1800s or earlier. The lawyers and accountants, with no such long tradition of marketing, still don't get it (with exceptions, of course). . . . I am easily stunned by people who get hired as marketers and don't know how to write a marketing plan, or are little more than party planners entirely directed by lawyers or accountants. I recently got an email from a marketing director who wanted to know what he could ethically say in advertising. As a "professional" marketing director, shouldn't he have known that? I recently saw an article by a marketing director about how to write an ad, citing the famous 5 Ws, which not only have nothing to do with advertising, but come from a now obsolete rule for writing press releases.

Marcus is right. Even though its history is brief, the field of professional service marketing and business development began as one largely populated by communication professionals. Early on, public relations executives, writers, and former journalists dominated the marketing ranks of professional service firms. This legacy remains. Many of today's marketing team members and leaders don't have a working knowledge of market research and analysis techniques. Do they understand corporate strategy? Behavioral psychology? Economics? Forecasting? Emerging markets? Service portfolio management?

Even beyond the principles of marketing, many marketing and business development professionals aren't as well versed as they should be in the principles of running and managing a service business. They aren't as immersed as they should be in the nuances of the industry in which they work.

Let's look at the issue of available sources for gaining skills. Because of the highly fragmented education and training landscape confronting service marketers and business developers, they face an unfairly daunting challenge in gaining the competencies they need to be better integrated and more strategically effective for their firms.

Consumer products marketing, which is a recognized discipline, is taught at the undergraduate and graduate levels in higher education institutions worldwide. But if one tries to get a degree or learn anything substantive on the recognized methodologies of service marketing, the sources practically dry up.

Of *U.S. News & World Report*'s top-ranked graduate business schools in 2008, only a few evidently offered a class or two on service marketing and management:

- MIT's Sloan School of Management: Business to Business Marketing[18]
- Northwestern University's Kellogg Graduate School of Management: Services Marketing and Management and New Products and Services[19]
- Columbia University's Graduate School of Business: a track in consulting, with a specific class in Services Marketing[20]
- University of Chicago's Graduate School of Business: Marketing of Services and New Products and Services[21]

Executive education sessions that cater to PSF and B2B firm leaders are available, but they're hard to find and sometimes expensive. Harvard Business School's one-week intensive mini-course called Leadership of the Professional Service Firm is a respectable example, although it's not targeted at marketing specifically.[22] Sales performance and training company Miller Heiman enjoys a respectable reputation in business-to-business sales training, but it does not appear to focus on marketing strategy and how it connects to sales.[23]

For knowledge-hungry service marketing and business development professionals, not to mention their firms' executive managers, these educational offerings are slim pickings indeed. And they are only available piecemeal. Generally, academia has not retooled its curricula to the enormous service sector, and has been slow to respond to the credentialing needs of the service marketing and business development population. There are, however, some sector-specific professional associations in the United States and Europe stepping in to fill this need (see figure 1.4).

The bottom line: for service marketers and business developers, there are not enough authoritative sources to gain knowledge, learn best practices or standards, or gain credentialing. The sources that do exist are hard to find, too sector-specific, too general, or still so new that they have not yet gained much traction in professional service marketing circles.

How is someone supposed to gain those skills? Do we expect marketers and business developers to simply explode into being, fully formed, as strategic leaders? They can't, unless they have more structural support from their executive managers.

Certification may not be the answer. Obtaining a service marketing MBA may not be the answer either. But inevitably, a lack of attention to skill

United States

In 1999 the *Society for Marketing Professional Services* (SMPS) launched its Certified Professional Services Marketer (CPSM) program for marketers and business developers in architecture, engineering, and the construction management industries. The CPSM currently tests for required knowledge areas and skill sets in the following domains of practice: marketing research; strategic, business, and marketing planning; client and business development; qualifications/proposals; promotional activity; and marketing and business performance.[24]

The *Legal Marketing Association* (LMA) offers a variation on this idea, but not with as much formality as SMPS, and not for certification. Its Quick Start program gives new legal marketers with five or fewer years of experience in law firms an opportunity to master the body of knowledge.[25]

As for credentialing for accounting marketers, executive director Granville Loar of the *Association for Accounting Marketing* (AAM) told me in a May 5, 2008, e-mail message that AAM had thought about developing a credentialing program but did not presently offer any kind of certification.

Europe

In the UK, the Chartered Institute of Marketing (CIM), which claims to be the leading international professional marketing body with some 50,000 members worldwide, ties membership to the achievement of certification. The institute began awarding its Chartered Marketer certification in 1998, and offers varying levels of certification (Introductory Certificate in Marketing, Professional Certificate in Marketing, Professional Diploma in Marketing, and Professional Postgraduate Diploma in Marketing).[26] Recently CIM began to offer a course that serves as a professional service alternative to its Professional Diploma in Marketing. It was developed through a partnership between the nonprofit Professional Services Marketing Group (PSMG) and the Cambridge Marketing Colleges. Although this credentialing program is professional service–specific, only about 100 students had taken the course as of 2008. This new credential is

(continued)

Figure 1.4 Sector-specific Professional Associations in the United States and Europe

---

Figure 1.4 (continued)

struggling, however, for recognition. On PSMG's Web site, Nigel Clark, a member of PSMG's executive committee, explained the challenge:

> In my eight years in professional services marketing I have contributed to many discussions and read even more articles about whether marketing really is "professional." This debate often rages amongst all marketers but is particularly pertinent to our sector, because we work in an environment defined by professional status. Whether you work with lawyers, accountants, surveyors, consultants . . . their professional qualification is their most treasured possession. It is their license to operate.
>
> Somewhat surprisingly, qualifications have not been fully embraced by marketers in our sector. Given that we work with people who hold them in such high esteem, we have been slow to address the issue.[27]

In some European countries, country-specific marketing associations have developed their own certification programs (some claiming to be more rigorous than the CIM certification programs). These include the 3,000-member Netherlands Institute of Marketing, which offers exams toward the achievement of the rigorous Registered Marketer status (awarded to only about 10 people each year).[28]

---

growth for marketers produces numerous negative consequences and contributes to organizational barriers. Strategically, it leaves professional firms vulnerable to the vagaries of the marketplace. If they are staffed with marketers who have underdeveloped expertise and who are relegated to more tactical than strategic initiatives, professional firms sacrifice the very agility, vision, and savvy they most need in difficult economic times. They also sacrifice agility, vision, and savvy in good economic times when they miss out on growth opportunities that could have been pursued by deeply experienced and highly skilled marketing and business development professionals. This lack of attention to marketers' skill growth presents tactical challenges as well because of the high cost of replacing marketers who leave, forcing underresourced and possibly underskilled teammates to function in their stead.

I'd like to see executive managers working more proactively with their marketers and business developers to create a respected training and professional development path. They also should work more closely with a body of service marketers and business developers to map out appropriate career advancement paths, just as executive managers have done for their firms' practitioners.

Time to Get Your Structural House in Order

"The main obstacle we have encountered is ourselves." Although this comment from the "Effectiveness" study could be interpreted as a bitter swipe from a frustrated individual, it accurately reflects the evidence I've presented in this chapter: the functional, and yet very solvable, causes of silos in professional firms' go-to-market practices are many.

But it doesn't have to be this way.

Think for a moment about what could happen if professional firms better coordinated their stepwise go-to-market processes. Or structured a better balance between their marketing program elements. Or reconfigured everyone's accountabilities so that practitioners, marketers, business developers, and other administrative functions could be better integrated. Or built a well-defined skills growth pathway for marketers and business developers.

Professional firm executive managers must ask themselves two hard questions: Are we competing for marketplace gains as effectively as we could? Are we substantively growing market share, increasing the "right" kind of revenues, or providing significant value for our clients? If the answers are anything less than a resounding "Yes!" these firms are vulnerable, especially in economic downturns.

It's imperative these managers begin today to reconfigure their firms' marketing and business development structures to achieve better integration.

In chapter 2, I outline a set of cultural challenges that also impede optimal marketing and business development integration. I'll make the case that the executive managers of professional firms should address these challenges in a more programmatic way than ever before in order to direct their organizations toward better cultural integration of marketing and business development.

Chapter 2

Cultural Challenges to Marketing and Business Development Integration

As the executive managers of professional firms address their organizations' structural barriers to marketing and business development integration, they will inevitably face the cultural side of the integration challenge: the internal standards and norms that underpin the operations of all professional and business-to-business firms, public or private. Tradition, history, and "the way we do things" are considered by many to be nearly immovable obstacles.

This chapter outlines these cultural integration barriers and makes the case that in order to most effectively erase marketing and business development functional disconnects, managers must take proactive steps to change their firms' traditional cultural patterns.

■ ■ ■

The professional and business-to-business service arena generates trillions of dollars of revenues globally, despite the fact that the businesses in this sector face some very intense and uncontrollable marketplace circumstances, including economic recessions, globalization of markets, and technological change. In the last chapter, I outlined a list of structural integration problems that impede the optimal integration of the marketing and business development of PSFs and B2Bs. These structural obstacles, I pointed out, are entirely within the control of executive managers to overcome.

But what about asking someone to change his or her *mind*? What about those cultural barriers that are so systemic, so "hardwired" that we barely know how to address them? What's their effect on a professional firm's marketing and business development integration, and what can executive managers do about them?

Let's take a look at six in particular.

Cultures of Distrust

In chapter 1, I discussed how less than optimal structures for marketing and business development can lead to unevenly assigned accountabilities and confusion. But cultural factors can affect the issue of accountability as well, and it's critical that the executive managers of professional firms examine and understand them. In real ways, these factors create a debilitating environment of distrust.

One distrust factor is that of avoiding accountability (and getting away with it). Because marketing and business development are so vital to the success of a professional enterprise, the most egregious examples of avoiding accountability involve these functions. I've seen people avoiding marketing and business development accountability whether or not their organizational frameworks for marketing or selling responsibility are well demarcated. Some firms *very quietly* allow their people to avoid marketing and selling. In these cases, others in the organization may not notice right away, but they do eventually.

The situation can become especially toxic when avoiding accountability becomes openly visible and nothing is done about it. I witnessed an example of this several years ago, during my keynote presentation to the senior leadership group of an enormous privately held professional service firm. My assignment was to set the stage for this firm's newly conceived growth initiative. All the company's bigwigs were gathered, and I delivered a rousing call to action. Then during the question-and-answer period, the head of one of the company's large lines of business raised his hand. He said, "Suzanne, you told us today about the importance of developing stronger relationships with clients. But I'm not as good at dealing with the clients as our business development executives. I'd rather leave it up to them, and not deal with the clients at all." As he concluded his remarks, you could hear a pin drop.

We should applaud his truthfulness, I suppose. His remark, though, spoke volumes about the level of marketing and business development disconnectivity within this firm. Indeed, he probably was *not* as good a "people person" as his senior colleagues might have liked. Likely, his technical expertise had propelled him into a position of prominence within the organization. Nevertheless, clearly he did not want to accept accountability for the relationship-building platform on which his firm planned its next stage of growth. And, from what happened next, he was going to be allowed *to continue* avoiding the accountability that was being expected of everyone else. His remark was addressed by one of his C-level counterparts, who replied blandly, "Well, it's something we will all have to work on."

My hope is that this C-level leader was privately shocked by his colleague's admission and took him aside after the session to discuss the importance of improving his people skills. But my experience has shown that few leaders are willing to face up to this huge obstacle—and the effect it can have on their firm's bottom line.

I do know this: from that moment on, the firm's efforts to encourage its leaders to endorse its new organizational growth initiative fell flat. And who could blame the others for their lack of enthusiasm? When people are allowed to avoid accountability, whether publicly or behind the scenes, it creates a culture of distrust. Distrust feeds cultural disconnectivity. And cultural disconnectivity builds barriers to effective marketing and business development.

There is evidence that other professional firms, having sprung from a collegial partnership culture, have trouble not only sharing marketing and business development accountabilities among professionals, but also assigning accountabilities to anyone at all. In our "Effectiveness" study, Larry Bodine and I asked respondents to describe the single biggest obstacle to achieving marketplace effectiveness. One respondent summed up the answers of many others: an "unwillingness to hold people accountable when it comes to sales and marketing activities."

And here is another example of professional or business-to-business practitioners avoiding accountability, and even assigning it elsewhere, inappropriately. The marketing team of a small U.S.-based accounting firm was asked by the firm's partners to organize a seminar at which CPAs would present their business insights to a group of invited clients. The marketing team directed the preparation for the event efficiently. As the day of the event approached, they reported a healthy number of preregistered participants. On the day of the seminar, however, the weather took a turn for the worse, and attendance was abysmal. Unbelievably, later the CMO who related this story and his team received a negative performance evaluation from the company's partners about their effectiveness for the event.

Bad feelings abounded: from the partners, who expected too much from the marketers for this one-time seminar, and from the marketing team members, who were unable to impress upon the accountants that a good marketing program relies on multiple tactical elements rather than one-shot client interactions. This CMO later related to me how much he wanted his firm to revise its performance evaluation structure for him and his team, so that unfair assignment of blame could be avoided in the future (I heartily agreed). He was wary of being asked again to put on a client seminar. With this demonstration of distrust—from both sides—it's not surprising that there was a palpable level of disconnectivity about the immensely vital function of marketing and business development.

I wish I were making up these examples. Imagine how these two firms could better achieve their growth goals if their revenue-generating and marketing and business development functions worked more collaboratively, and with more shared accountability, instead of one shunning or punishing the other. Imagine what marketing and business development achievements they could attain without such cultures of distrust.

Another distrust factor is when shared accountability for marketing and business development is denied to those who seek it. In particular, this problem occurs when revenue-generating practitioners don't trust their firms' nonrevenue-generating marketers and business developers enough to collaborate with them. In the "Effectiveness" study, respondents commented on this issue: "The partners still think of their firm as being a shop that is run by three individuals. They are not used to entrusting others to seek out new contacts and work. In a sense they resist marketing at all because . . . then they wouldn't be able to take the credit for finding the work. It's an ego thing right now."[1]

I've seen firsthand this distrust in my consulting work. Over the years, many professional firms have called me in to provide strategic marketing advice or lead important consulting projects for their executive management committees. In one of these cases, despite my recommendations that marketers and business developers be included in the work, they were *expressly excluded* from our conversations (not even allowed to listen in), and were only peripherally involved in our projects. When I pressed executive managers to explain their exclusionary behavior, they told me their marketing and business development functions were structured to be support-focused, and that they, the executive managers, were the leaders of marketing and business development.

There was no refuting the cultural distrust created by these practices of exclusion. In these projects, I was put in the position of amateur psychologist when confronted with the suspicious feelings of the marketers and business developers, many of whom asked me why they weren't trusted.

Even though the actions of these executive managers were based on well-defined structures and previously successful historical and traditional frameworks, their decisions to bar their marketers and business developers from sharing accountability released powerful doses of toxicity into their cultures.

Distrust directly feeds into marketers' and business developers' feelings of being marginalized.

Feeling Marginalized

The second cultural barrier to effective marketing and business development integration is manifested in marketers' and business developers' feelings of being marginalized. One of the most obvious reasons for marginalization is a structural arrangement — that is, when privately owned firms do not offer their nonrevenue-generating marketing and business development professionals a pathway to equity ownership.

As a case in point, a few years ago I received an e-mail from a client, the global head of business development at a large, widely respected management consulting firm. He told me that his latest and most senior-level direct-report had, after only 18 months with the firm, departed for another opportunity. He attached the firm's description of the position, and he asked me to keep my eyes and ears open for potential replacements. When I reviewed the job description, I was dismayed to see that the role — still pegged for a very senior marketer — was a nonequity position, with no potential to achieve shareholder status.

I shot him an immediate reply: why is this role, with its expected global prominence and potential for significant revenue generation, not included in the firm's partner track? I wondered whether it would be possible to find a senior-level professional marketer or business developer who would accept such a limited role. His almost sheepish reply revealed his embarrassment — he had been unable to convince the firm's equity owners of the merits of sharing ownership with someone whom they perceived to be a nonpeer, simply a business development operator.

Marginalization is based in historical precedent, and yet it is still supported by today's current economic conditions. The roots of today's organizational love-hate relationship toward business development (selling) and marketing in most professional firms are documentable.

I confirmed this love-hate relationship through the "Want to Market and Sell?" survey I conducted in February 2008. I was trying to find out whether professional firms were intentionally retooling their hiring guidelines to hire practitioners who *wanted* to market and sell (and had the instincts and skills to do so). As in my other online surveys, the respondents were senior marketing and business development professionals, and others in ownership or executive management positions for their professional firms across a variety of sectors. To introduce the survey, I reminded respondents that an increasing number of PSFs are employing carrot-and-stick programs to encourage their practitioners to market and sell. I then asked, "Would you like your PSF to make formal efforts to hire practitioners who *want* to market and sell?"

A huge majority of responding firms thought it was a great idea to hire practitioners who truly wanted to market and sell. But only a bare majority reported that their firms had actually made formal efforts to do so in the past year. These and many other PSFs fear that an embrace of overt selling would be off-putting to clients. "[Our firm would] never do this . . . ever!" Intentionally seeking to hire practitioners who want to market and sell appears to represent a frightening cultural hurdle. (And perhaps a structural hurdle, too, unless certain accountabilities are structurally redefined, as I discuss in Part II.)

When I asked their opinion on how well the effort was going to hire marketing and sales-savvy pros, only a very small group of respondents said, "Things are going absolutely great!" The vast majority were lukewarm or negative. Some of their comments revealed that their firms had been preoccupied with a need to focus only on hiring practitioner talent. Understandably, this distraction diluted their focus on hiring for marketing and business development skills or instincts.

But their comments also shed light on another critically important factor that contributes to the feelings of cultural marginalization articulated by marketers and business developers, both from this study and outside it: It can be a challenge to find the right set of marketing and business development capabilities, especially if the firm has yet to define them for itself. A firm's recruiters need standards, cutting-edge understanding of the optimal outlines of the function, and clear guidelines for the function's accountabilities in order to objectively evaluate marketing and business development skills. But because most professional firms and sectors use widely varying definitions of marketing and business development and generally lack understanding of the value these functions could deliver to their enterprises, it is no wonder that respondents rated their firms' efforts so harshly.

In my early years of marketing consulting across professions, I used to think that there would always be some people who feel marginalized, no matter the real circumstances. But since I began looking at the marginalization issue from a cultural point of view, I've come to believe that both sides—practitioners and nonrevenue-generating marketers and business developers—marginalize each other. This marginalization problem is more organizationally systemic than I had believed. And it further verifies a cultural norm that I outlined in my book *Marketplace Masters*. In the section entitled "A Historical Reticence to Compete" I wrote:

> Another root cause of the missteps so many professional service firms have taken in recent years is their historical reluctance to engage in "competition." In all too many professional service firms, asking the question "how will we compete" borders on the heretical. A brief history of professional services, offered in a fascinating 1998 article by U.K. academics Susan Hart and Gillian Hogg, offers an explanation for this claim. Hart and Hogg describe how the original professions of law, church and the military provided young aristocrats with a socially acceptable way of making a living. These were high status individuals; the term "professional" was synonymous with upper class. In time, a newer set of occupational professions developed such as medicine, pharmacy, and accountancy. In response, according to Hart and Hogg, the original professions fought to defend their status by encouraging principles that have come to define all other professions. These principles include a disdain for competition, self-promotion, advertising and bald profiteering; a belief in the principle of payment for work—rather than working for pay; and a belief in the superiority of the motive of service.
>
> Today's professionals still uphold these principles, a fact repeatedly made clear throughout my years of research about how firms address and overcome their marketing challenges. For example, in our 2001 study of more than 500 professional service firms, "using new approaches to compete against rivals" was one of the *least frequently used* of seven common methods to get closer to their clients. Some of the study respondents' comments revealed this discomfort in stark terms: an accounting firm respondent reported that ". . . focusing on external competition has never

been a key part of our marketing strategy." An engineering firm participant said it was "not profitable" to gather intelligence on competitors. Both remarks are simply astonishing; what's more, they could have originated within any number of other professional sectors. Regardless of the basis of their reasoning, these firms are inadvertently setting themselves up to be beaten by their more market-driven rivals. The professional service sector as a whole is maturing, and in order to survive and prosper, professional service firms must learn to compete. Ignoring the realities of the marketplace rarely, if ever, makes them go away.[2]

The respondents in the "Want to Market and Sell?" survey corroborated their firms' ambivalence about their marketing and business development functions. They spoke favorably about the notion of hiring practitioners who want to sell, or who have skills in the expertise-oriented aspects of marketing such as writing and speaking. But far fewer are actually following through on their endorsement of the idea. With these sentiments, it's no wonder that professional and business-to-business service marketers and business developers feel marginalized by revenue generators.

And it doesn't help when some prominent business publications fan the flames of fear and marginalization. In the June 2007 edition of *Fast Company* magazine, Ellen McGirt wrote a scathing article, "The Most Dangerous Job in Business." In it, she labeled the chief marketing officer as "the riskiest job in the American C-suite." She quoted a prominent source who said, "We're seeing CMOs getting ambushed." Another source observed, "CMOs are tempting targets. Because marketing is such a public function, and everyone has an opinion on what works."[3]

With a mindset like this, it's no wonder the position of marketing and business development, especially in professional and business-to-business service firms, has become a revolving door. (More on the high turnover of marketing and business development positions appears later in this chapter.)

But even journalists like McGirt keep returning to a salient point: "So what's it going to take to get the CMO off the endangered-species list? Perhaps a clearer definition of the position and what's expected—which is a job for the CEO."[4] I'd add to her point: executive managers will have to recognize that marginalization flows through their cultural norms and that they will have to address the issue aggressively if they hope to improve their firms' marketing and business development effectiveness.

Short-term Thinking

Professional and business-to-business service firms struggle with a third cultural impediment to effective marketing and business development: the tendency to engage in short-term thinking.

Recessions, globalization, rapid technological change, and other large marketplace shifts are riveting challenges for PSFs and B2Bs, and yet most engage in short-term thinking. The executive managers of most professional firms, for all they do so well, have not yet envisioned the critical cultural shifts that will be required in order to compete more effectively in the long term.

Marketing and business development professionals know all too well how their organizations respond to economic good times and downturns. When revenues are good, their organizations are typically more likely to launch new programs. When revenues are threatened, marketers know they will be asked to defend their budgets. Not surprisingly, the psychological aspects of an economic downturn force any businessperson to take a critical look at expenditures, and doing so is not necessarily a bad idea. Indeed, it's this kind of beneficial "defend my turf" mentality that drives marketers and business developers to seek ways to increase the effectiveness of their functions.

From a larger perspective, though, it's apparent that as a bloc, PSF and B2B service executive managers are challenged, culturally, to guide their firms to better address the inevitable ups and downs of economic cycles. How well equipped are these managers to insist on reinvestment and preparation for the next downturn, or when the economy is up and revenues are flowing?

One need only look at professional service firms' poor track record of funding innovation (or, as innovation is sometimes called in products businesses, R&D). How many professional service firms do you know that have a formally funded innovation program, or even a formally funded service delivery improvement program? My own research findings on PSF-funded innovation initiatives reveals what little regard PSFs hold for renewing their capabilities, or building on them to meet clients' future needs.[5]

Besides me, other business management observers also make this point. In his December 2007 article in the *Harvard Business Review*, Gary Hamel described how short-term thinking is manifested. He wrote that

It's surprising that so few companies have made innovation everyone's job. For the most part, innovation is still relegated to organizational ghettos — it is still the responsibility of dedicated units like new product development and R&D, where creative types are kept safely out of the way of those who have to "run the business." Today innovation is the buzzword du jour, but there's still a yawning chasm between rhetoric and reality. If you doubt this, seek out a few entry-level employees and ask them the following questions:

1. How have you been equipped to be a business innovator? What training have you received? What tools have you been supplied with?
2. Do you have access to an innovation coach or mentor? Is there an innovation expert in your unit who will help you develop your breakout idea?
3. How easy is it for you to get access to experimental funding? How long would it take you to get a few thousand dollars in seed money? How many levels of bureaucracy would you have to go through?
4. Is innovation a formal part of your job description? Does your compensation depend in part on your innovation performance?
5. Do your company's management processes — budgeting, planning, staffing, etc. — support your work as an innovator or hinder it?

Don't be surprised if these questions provoke little more than furrowed brows and quizzical looks.[6]

Although Hamel writes primarily about products-oriented enterprises, this same question could be posed to service firms. Arguably, they are even less prepared, culturally, to focus on preparations for the future than are their products company counterparts.

Author David Maister tackles this issue head-on in his book *Strategy and the Fat Smoker: Doing What's Obvious But Not Easy*. Maister addresses the uncomfortable truth that professional service firms too often choose the easy way out, even when they know the results may be uncertain or even detrimental to the firm's future:

The primary reason we do not work at behaviors which we know we need to improve is that the rewards (and pleasure) are in the future; the disruption, discomfort and discipline needed to get there are immediate.

To reach our goals, we must first change our lifestyle and our daily habits *now*. Then we must summon the courage to *keep up* the new habits and not yield to all the old familiar temptations. Then and only then we get the benefits *later*.[7]

As with other systemic cultural barriers to marketing and business development integration, PSF or B2B practitioners, and especially their firms' executive managers, have a clear choice: deliberately work to overcome the cultural barrier, or ignore it, and inevitably fall victim to the marketplace consequences.

Here, it's incumbent on professional firm executive managers to envision the cultural shifts their firms must make to weather the inevitable vagaries of the marketplace and to become prepared for the future. Because economic downturns are inevitable, these leaders have to erase the marketing and business development silos existing within their enterprises. They must proactively pursue integration and expanded go-to-market effectiveness. Their firms' very survival depends on it.

The "Immaturity" of Marketing and Business Development Functions

The negative ramifications of short-term thinking are exacerbated by a fourth cultural challenge that impedes the effective integration of marketing and business development: the relative immaturity of marketing and business development functions within professional firms, coupled with the fact that PSF and B2B executive managers, collectively, have not done more to encourage development of the field.

Compared with the long-held traditions and acknowledged best practices of the industries themselves, marketing and business development are newcomers. Even as of late 2008, it was not uncommon to hear about someone who had just joined a professional firm as its first ever marketing coordinator, manager, director, or even chief marketing officer. As relatively new professions on the business stage, service marketing, and especially professional and B2B service marketing, have yet to build a defined and widely acknowledged set of best practices. What may be acknowledged as a business development "best practice" in the construction management sector may not be so in management consulting or accounting.

What may be an acceptable marketing method in law may not be so in IT services.

With no instructions to follow about the role and purview of marketing or business development, or their overarching best practices, PSFs and B2Bs have had to build them from scratch, without a clear idea of these functions' optimal capabilities. It's a mosaic built by thousands of earnest but nearsighted artisans.

Consider a few examples from the many conversations I've had with senior marketing leaders and industry observers. Each makes sense on its own, and yet when looked at from a distant perspective, each only adds to a bewildering array of characterizations of the roles and their functions.

- From a management consulting firm CMO: "My definition of sales is 'one to one' and my definition of marketing is 'one-to-many.' If you have 'sellers' making decisions on messaging, positioning, events that we should participate in, writing by-lines, [or] talking to the press, they not only will send a very confusing message to the buyers (since everyone will have their own opinion and there won't be the consistency needed) but also cost the firm more money due to redundancy and bad decisions. In addition, if they are marketing they are not selling. A big problem is when consultants think that they have marketing chops and therefore make bad decisions on how to spend firm money on 'one to many' opportunities — how many advertorials have consultants agreed to sign up for before marketing became more controlled in most PSF firms. Marketing is easier then [sic] selling for most people's egos since with marketing the rejection comes later not immediately when the client says no. You want sellers out of the office calling on their clients. I am all for having the practitioners/sellers be supportive of marketing, participate when asked in conferences/events etc. and work closely with marketing to ensure that the handoff between marketing and sales is seamless and the targeting, messaging, positioning and deliverables are what is needed to make the sale. The skill sets between sales and marketing have some commonality but are vastly different as well."

- From law and accounting firm marketing consultant and author Bruce Marcus, in his May 5, 2008, e-mail: "Business development is — and as far as I'm concerned always has been — subsumed under marketing. That it is subsumed is true, whether you call [it] research or selling or training, or list management [or] business development, or something else, they're all practices under the marketing umbrella. Nor can it be done effectively except with other marketing activities as a background. Ultimately, the objective is to grow and sustain the practice, which can't be done effectively with promotion alone. Practice development skills play upon the promotional activities. It can be argued that 'business development' requires a different set of skills, but then each of the skills in a marketing program is distinctive. It is generally assumed that the good marketer has either a full or a smattering of each of the skills—public relations, writing, planning, etc.—and part of the problem with marketers is that few of us have all the skills to the same degree. There is also the problem that the lawyers (and accountants as well) don't truly understand the nature and value of those skills, which makes it tougher. . . . Party planners, for example, are hired as marketers and sophisticated marketers are hired to be party planners as well as to develop business."

• From the Bloom Group's 2007 study: "Business development is usually not a separate function, but there usually is a marketing function. In most cases, marketing and biz dev do not report to each other."[8]

If the opinions and remarks of just these marketing professionals and observers are enough to make my own head spin, imagine the many different interpretations they might elicit from PSF or B2B executive managers themselves, who have little or no grounding in marketing or business development. They know they need marketing and business development leadership, implementation, or just support, but inevitably they have to rely on their newest hire to shape their perceptions about the function and the capabilities to undertake it.

Meanwhile, fragmentation becomes hardwired. Except for the most enthusiastic marketing and business development champions, most PSF and B2B executives find that their eyes glaze over at these confusing discussions. I can just hear them say (and I have), "I don't want to know the background. Just tell me how to set this up." Their lack of comprehension is real, and it becomes culturally embedded. And the immaturity of the service marketing profession—fed by its lack of coalescence around best practices and standards—only exacerbates this confusion and cultural disconnects.

How does another maturity factor—the length of time marketing and business development have been utilized by the professions, and the formation of professional service marketing as a "field"—influence a professional firm's cultural perceptions of these functions?

Legally, United States law firms were unable to embrace marketing or selling until 1974. Other professions, especially those in which regulations require technical credentials and licensing, overtly deployed business development long before that. Engineering and construction management are good examples.

On separate timetables, then, each sector formulated its own set of norms for professional service marketing and business development. However, social networking and professional society memberships for practitioners in these fields lagged the formation and maturity of the professions they served. For example, in the United States:

- The American Bar Association was formed in 1878,[9] whereas the Legal Marketing Association (LMA) was not formed until nearly 100 years later, in 1985.[10] The Legal Sales and Service Organization was established in 2003.[11]

- The American Institute of Certified Public Accountants (AICPA) was formed in 1887.[12] But the Association for Accounting Marketing (AAM) was not formed until some 100 years later, in 1988.[13]

- The American Institute for Architects (AIA) was formed 1857,[14] followed nearly 120 years later, in 1973, by the Society for Marketing Professional Services.[15]

- The Association of Management Consulting Firms was founded in 1929[16] and the Association of Executive Search Firms in 1959,[17] and yet even as of 2008 there were no professional associations for marketers in either of these two sectors.

This situation is echoed in Europe as well. Several well-established sector-specific professional associations, and some very young overarching professional marketer groups, among them the Professional Marketers Forum, were established only as recently as 1996.[18] The nonprofit Professional Services Marketing Group has been holding its annual conferences since only the mid-1990s.[19]

Despite their late emergence in relation to each of their sectors, the "immature" fields of professional service marketing and business development are growing strongly:

- From 1997 to 2007, the membership of the Society for Marketing Professional Services grew nearly 60 percent, and its annual conference attendance grew nearly 40 percent.[20]

- From 2004 to 2007, the membership of the Legal Marketing Association grew more than 65 percent.[21]

- From 1997 to 2007, the Association for Accounting Marketing membership grew nearly 45 percent, and its annual conference attendance grew more than 40 percent.[22]

- From 1997 to 2007, the Information Technology Services Marketing Association catalogued the number of service marketers with whom it works within each of its corporate members. ITSMA's contact database grew from 5,000 to 25,000 people during this period, and about 9,000 of those contacts worked for member companies.[23]

The explosion of membership growth in these organizations reflects just how important they are to their members, who can turn to few other sources to help them share their emerging best practices and shape the cultural norms of their firms and their fields. Unfortunately, these sectors, regardless of their people-as-product commonalities (they are all based on an individual's intellectual capital, professional credentials, and experience), have remained largely separate from each other.

Thus the presence of these associations has yet to reduce the sense of isolation and cultural fragmentation that inevitably influences the perceptions of marketing and business development held by their sectors and their firms.

Since the late 1990s especially, the Web has also exploded with information on marketing and business development. Active and well-respected blogs, online newsletters, membership-oriented networking sites, and knowledge portals are helping to shape what might eventually become a body of knowledge about the field. Still, though, only a minority of these Internet sources are dedicated to service marketing and business development.

The cultures of professional firms certainly have not helped remedy the disconnects surrounding their marketers and business developers. Partners (or revenue generators in publicly owned professional service companies), focused on serving clients and bringing in revenue, have provided little opportunity for their marketers and business developers to coalesce around a set of established industry practices. But they certainly did so in their own professions. At some point early in their professions, accountants decided to build a set of standards for their industry. Lawyers did the same, and so did engineers, architects, and others. No functional or cultural disconnects there!

I think it's clear: service marketers and business developers are playing catch-up. The silos in professional service marketing and business development are real, with documentable historical underpinnings and cultural foundations. The result for this youthful, rapidly emerging field is a patchwork quilt of definitions, organizational structures, reporting relationships, and lack of any kind of agreed-upon industry standard.

It's no one's fault, then, that functional disconnects exist, or that their effects seep into professional firms' cultures. But "our youthful profession" won't serve as a good excuse to not push for more effectiveness and for integration. And it will be up to the executive managers of professional and business-to-business firms—within and across sectors—to help erase the silos that history and tradition still uphold.

Unrealistic Expectations, Demand for Talent, and High Turnover

The immaturity of marketing and business development feeds directly into a fifth cultural barrier to optimal integration: the revolving door of marketing and business development talent, which creates exaggerated and unrealistic demand for better talent, followed by further rounds of dashed expectations and more turnover. The elements of this complex cycle—and the cycle itself—create enormous cultural obstacles to marketing and business development effectiveness in professional firms.

Highly skilled professional service marketers and business developers are few and far between. Simultaneously, there is growing evidence that the demand of PSFs and B2Bs for experienced marketers and business developers is rising.

Let's look at the soaring demand for skilled service marketing and business development professionals. An increasing number of PSF and B2B executive managers, typically having risen to their own positions from the inside because of their deep competencies in their field, find their firms pressured by a progressively competitive environment. They know they need marketing and business development (or what they think it is), and more than ever are endorsing the idea of bringing on board (or upgrading) skilled marketing and business development leaders.

In some competitive sectors, this demand is characterized as desperate. In her December 2007 "Desperately Seeking CMOs" article in the *American Lawyer*, writer Amy Kotz wrote:

> Fifty-seven Am Law 100 firms now have CMOs, compared to 40 in 2005. . . . But the supply of marketing professionals with legal experience hasn't kept up, say consultants and headhunters. . . . The upshot: high turnover and even higher pay packages. The average tenure of a law firm CMO is three years. . . .
>
> Finding a new CMO can be just the beginning of the problem. As partners and CMOs report, both sides frequently harbor unrealistic expectations that are only fueled by the outsize pay packages. . . . "The biggest challenge is earning the respect and credibility of the lawyers for yourself and your profession," says Debbie Mandelker, chief marketing officer at Arnold & Porter, who joined from Merrill Lynch & Co., Inc.
>
> Few lawyers have training in the theory and practice of marketing, and many are still skeptical of its value. "You have to demonstrate your business acumen, give them reason to listen to you," says Roberta Montafia, a legal consultant and the former global director of marketing at Baker & McKenzie. "Lawyers are trained to find fault in everything."[24]

Law firm management consultant Biff Maddock concurred, in his "Maddock on Marketing" blog post "Chief Marketing Officers: Bigger Job, Bigger Expectations," from January 18, 2008: "law firms need to . . . clarify their expectations of their lawyers, their business development program and their CMO. In many firms, lawyers and even management are unaware of the firm's marketing program and the role they are expected to play."

These unrealistic expectations about marketing and business development are not confined to law (as a sector) or the United States (as a geographic region). Consider the findings cited in a February 2006 Australian Research Council study of the views of marketing of Australian professional service firms. In the press release entitled "Marketing Still a Dirty

Word to Many Professional Service Firms," study authors Janet McColl-Kennedy, Jill Sweeney, and Geoff Soutar cited several quotes that reveal the cultural perceptions held by professional practitioners:

> One respondent talked about "marketing princesses" who are "very good at handing out name badges at events," [McColl-Kennedy] said. The same person reported that their firm was "too scared" to get involved in marketing research and strategy. Another talked about the partnership structure often adopted by professional service firms and the consequent view among partners that money spent on marketing comes "straight off their bottom line."[25]

The trend toward high turnover contributes to the revolving door: short tenure for marketing positions.

Remember *Fast Company*'s "be very afraid" article regarding the issue of CMO tenure? It featured quotation after quotation about the treacherous cultural landscapes marketers must navigate.[26] But, beyond hyperbolic anecdotes, there are real data to support the marketing revolving door theme. Global executive search firm Spencer Stuart conducts a yearly study of CMO tenure. In the press release for its June 2007 report, the firm wrote, "The average tenure for chief marketing officers at 100 leading consumer branded companies . . . is now slightly more than two years." While cautioning observers to keep this tenure figure in perspective because of widely varying definitions of roles and expectations for them, Greg Welch, the leader of the Spencer Stuart Marketing Officer Practice, remarked that "there are twice as many vacancies in the top marketing role as there were last year."[27]

Professional services data about the short-tenure, high turnover of marketers echo the Spencer Stuart findings. In its "2006 Accounting Marketing/Sales Responsibility and Compensation Survey," the Association for Accounting Marketing reported:

> The accounting marketing profession is still in its infancy, as compared with other industries. Fifty-six percent of respondents have worked in marketing for more than 10 years in various industries, while 19% have worked in accounting marketing for more than 10 years. Additionally, 66% are either their first person to ever serve in their role within their firm or followed the first person in that job function. . . . The young age

of marketers in the profession, relative to the average age of managing partners, firms themselves and the CPA profession, creates a number of challenges/opportunities.[28]

Some law firm marketers think the low-tenure, high turnover situation is worse than that. According to Laura Schreier of Hartford Business.com, "Audra Callanan, president of the New England chapter of the Legal Marketing Association, put the tenure track at between one and two years. . . . Callanan bemoans the revolving-door scenario, and she and other marketers point to fundamental culture differences as a key source of friction."[29]

Data about this distressing turnover and tenure situation may be found for other professional sectors such as architecture, management consulting, IT services, or investment banking, but law and accounting are among the two most mature professional service sectors. If turnover and tenure challenges exist for these sectors, you can imagine similar problems are occurring in others, but they are not yet formally chronicled.

What happens when high demand meets resistance? As if the dearth of competent marketing and business development professionals wasn't bad enough, there is the problem of marketers and business developers themselves resisting the opportunities being offered to them. Some marketers don't want to grow their competencies, and, unfortunately, this attitude only foments further marginalization, exacerbates leaders' uneven expectations, and adds heaps to the functional disconnectivity that already exists in professional service firms.

By way of illustration, in January 2007 I gave a speech to a professional association on the topic "The Evolution of the CMO." I was halfway through my points about how marketers need to step up their skills in quantitative analytics (qualitative, too, but I wasn't there yet), when an audience member raised her hand and said (I paraphrase), "I don't want to do more work —I already have enough to do!"

I replied that I believe marketers need not do *more*, but instead need to take their roles in a new and different direction. She replied (no paraphrase), "I told my boss when he hired me eight months ago that I would not do any math. He agreed. Hey, I know what I'm doing, but I won't do any quantitative stuff."

I was astonished at her remark, and I still find it unbelievable. I wasn't the only one. After my speech, other audience members came up to me to express their amazement at her claim, and they told me they think her myopic attitude would ultimately limit her career as a "marketing expert."

I'm convinced that her firm will, sooner rather than later, be beaten by its competitors. With a CMO who is that stubbornly blind—regardless of the question about math skills—how can they win?

It doesn't take a genius to see what's going on here. It's called unrealistic expectations, and it's culturally embedded in many PSFs and B2Bs. Everyone ends up disappointed. This mutual disappointment eventually becomes part of the firm's cultural DNA, and feeds the cultural cycle— high turnover of marketing and business development talent, exaggerated and unrealistic demand for better talent, more dashed expectations and more turnover.

Leadership development experts would rightly remind us that the problem of unrealistic expectations does not exist in professional service firms alone. Nor is it solely the purview of marketing and business development functions. Of course, they are right. In their 2006 book *Sink or Swim! New Job. New Boss. 12 Weeks to Get It Right*, authors Milo Sindell and Thuy Sindell outline numerous pitfalls that newly hired professionals should avoid when starting a new position. One of them is particularly relevant in the professional and B2B service marketing and business development arena: an eagerness to quickly demonstrate capabilities and results, but failing to first define how the firm's leaders perceive and measure success.[30]

I've seen it happen all too often: PSF marketers and business developers fail at achieving the wrong goals. Revenue generators may ask, "Why didn't we get more people at that seminar?" when, in fact, low attendance may have had nothing to do with tactics used to invite attendees and more to do with the off-base content or poor timing of the seminar. Or perhaps there were a good number of attendees at the seminar, but they weren't yet ready to pull the trigger on hiring the firm for an engagement.

It's the classic blame game. In one way or another, many a service marketer and business developer has felt or heard the criticism: "You didn't increase our revenues." This is an egregious example of the pressure under which these good people work, with so little control of the "product" or the strategies adopted to market the firm. Professional firm marketers and business developers are partially at fault here, because they allow their firm's leaders to take an incomplete look at the marketplace, or let them plunge ahead with assumptions and strategies that worked "last time." If the marketing strategies aren't working, there's something wrong with the assumptions or facts to begin with, or with the marketing strategies themselves.

You can see the expectations gap forming right away, and with entirely too much negative personalization. PSFs and B2Bs rely on marketers for more and more implementation to achieve goals that are unworkable, too vague, too broad, or simply wrong. They are overly focused on client acquisition, and give short shrift to other strategic imperatives. They incorrectly assume they are marketing to the best targets and **segments** with the firm's best **service offerings**. When the results are disappointing, the marketer or business developer is viewed as less than personally effective. This outcome must then be added to the realities marketers and business developers already face: they are limited by position descriptions that are too tactical, underprepared to perform critical strategic marketing functions, and hampered by hard-to-find training, development, and education avenues.

Sink or Swim authors Milo Sindell and Thuy Sindell are right. Too many PSFs' marketing and business development pros still don't help their new bosses develop the appropriately strategic goals for the firm, or articulate the appropriate parameters to succeed, not just what the end result looks like. With situations such as these, it's no wonder the metrics and expectations are off. The marketers can't succeed, and they knock themselves out trying.

Shifting Leadership Demands

The sixth cultural challenge facing effective marketing and business development integration in professional firms is at the crux of all the cultural challenges I've addressed in this chapter. It centers on the very definition of leadership in a professional environment, and how one manages a business built on the intellectual capital of high-achieving equals. In the professional firm of yesteryear, "leadership" did not connote "management." Decisions were made by means of a collegial consensus. Today, as a direct consequence of the colossal sea changes in the business landscape, the concept of "leadership" in a professional firm is undergoing seismic shifts. The leaders of professional firms are having to make enterprise-oriented decisions that have unavoidable competitive consequences. They are being asked to set the strategic direction that will represent a compelling enough call to action to motivate professionals.

Some business-management observers wonder if they're up to the task.

It's a valid concern—so much so that Harvard Business School professor Thomas DeLong and his co-authors, John Gabarro and Robert Lees, published a book in December 2007 about professional firm leadership. *When Professionals Have to Lead: A New Model for High Performance* speaks directly to the shifting demands that face the executive managers of professional firms.[31]

DeLong remarked about this issue in a January 2008 interview for the Harvard Business School's "Working Knowledge" newsletter. Observing that "the entire PSF landscape is in upheaval," DeLong wondered whether "old-style PSF leaders are equipped to respond." He continued, "In the past, the work of PSFs was a gentleman's game—and now it's blood sport."[32]

In the "Working Knowledge" interview, DeLong and his co-authors pointed out:

Today's leaders of professional service firms are being overwhelmed by demanding clients, human capital challenges, lack of organizing strategies, and perhaps most of all, unrealistic expectations of the task itself.

There is also an ongoing trend to focus on the development of only the highfliers and ignore a vast number of very competent professionals who are the heart and soul of the firm.

Associates are harder to recruit and keep; competition for clients is increasing from boutiques below and global firms above; the clients themselves are more demanding; and management time is focused on short-term issues rather than long-term strategy.[33]

DeLong goes on to say:

Professionals in professional service firms are reporting greater frustration, unmet needs, lack of shared purpose, poor morale, etc. . . . The professionals entering these organizations have higher expectations and more suspicion that leaders will treat them like cogs in the wheel. So leaders in PSFs have been calling for a new way of thinking about leadership in their organizations.[34]

The book outlines a leadership model that comprises four dimensions, applied in combination: setting direction, gaining commitment to the direction, executing on the direction, and setting a personal example.

I agree with DeLong's and his co-authors' spot-on identification of the extensive economic changes currently facing PSFs and B2Bs. And I'm elated that the executive managers of professional firms can now turn to two recently published books—this one and David Maister's 2008 book *Strategy and the Fat Smoker*—for insights on how to lead people effectively in working toward mutually beneficial goals. Maister also co-authored with Patrick McKenna a solid exploration of managing professionals in their 2002 book, *First Among Equals: How to Manage a Group of Professionals*.[35] It's absolutely vital that PSF and B2B executive managers better grasp the underpinnings of leadership and the behavior aspects of organization dynamics.

Not surprisingly, though, these books focus on how to lead *professionals* (revenue-generating practitioners). They do not concentrate enough on the vitally important marketing, business development, and administrative sides of the enterprise—those professionals whose work is essential to the practitioners' ultimate success and the clients' perception of the organization's value. Nor do they address the organizational barriers that impede the twin growth engines of marketing and business development.

Another cultural dimension of the issues of management and leadership should also be faced squarely: some professional firm observers (and perhaps even some executive managers themselves) assign a negative meaning to the word *management*. Indeed, they tie the very idea of management to "those bad guys." Their mindset can be described like this: professionals don't want to be managed, and leaders don't want to be thought of as managers. Managers are heartless machines whose sole pleasure is to force rigidity and unquestioned obeisance upon throngs of drones who act but aren't allowed to think. For people who think this way, the better model is "leadership."

But what happens to a professional enterprise culturally when it can't acknowledge the merits of management? When it can't acknowledge that it might make sense for the organization to perform according to a set of standards and widely accepted business principles? When it can't comprehend that the function of executive management could likely mean future gains for the enterprise in the marketplace?

It's important to recognize the level of sophistication that the executive managers of professional firms apply to bringing about (leading) significant changes in their organizations—even though it's likely they are in the early stages of their own learning curves. Executive managers should embrace any critical lesson they can about leadership. To be fair, there is a place for cultural osmosis in developing the functions of an enterprise. Perhaps to executive managers the simple act of *leading a conversation* about increasing the functional effectiveness of marketing and business development feels like a proactive organizational change.

My numerous research results appear to corroborate this impression, but I believe executive managers will discover that soft initiatives to change culture aren't enough; they'll drive more effective change if they enact structural solutions in parallel. Tiptoeing around the importance of *management*—effectively running a professional enterprise—never helped any firm make the enormous competitive gains that most desire. Will **PSF** and **B2B** executive managers move assertively to embrace and apply real principles of running a business?

This shift is as big a cultural paradigm change as any that must take place in professional firms. It's the idea that certain structures must be in place for the good of the whole, and that management must function to create, support, and make appropriate changes to these structures as required by the business environment. The leaders of professional firms will *themselves* need to drive their organizations' evolving expectations of the management function. With more shifts surely ahead in the hypercompetitive PSF and B2B marketplace, I predict that executive managers will be expected to introduce and reinforce new norms about what management is supposed to do for a professional enterprise and the results the management function can deliver.

It's a test they must pass.

Time to Get Your Cultural House in Order

In chapter 1, I explored professional firms' structural impediments to effective marketing and business development integration. Arguably, making structural and functional changes is the easy stuff. Shifting a firm from one set of cultural norms and standards to another, even those that help a firm erase its marketing and business development silos, can seem overwhelming.

But the evidence presented in this chapter about how systemic—and harmful—a number of cultural disconnectivity patterns are, and how much they impede the creation of a better model of marketing and business development integration, should be enough to motivate executive managers to don new mantles: chief cultural influencers. They must apply the principles of organizational behavior, change management, and perhaps political strategy to enact the enterprise's cultural transformation toward marketing and business development integration.

In chapter 3, I'll explore some noteworthy organizational efforts PSFs and B2Bs have undertaken to address their structural and cultural disconnectivity challenges. I'll explain how these "good start" efforts have, paradoxically, themselves ignited a new set of disconnectivity challenges, and some better ways in which to address the problem of marketing and business development silos.

Chapter 3

The Paradox of "Doing Things Differently"

Many PSFs and B2Bs have undertaken narrowly focused initiatives to improve their organizations' marketing and business development performance. While commendable, these "doing things differently" efforts too often ignite a new set of marketing and business development disconnectivity challenges.

This chapter explores some of those challenges, and it makes the case that, if managed by a firm's executives with an integration mindset, "doing things differently" still represents an enterprise-wide opportunity to erase marketing and business development silos. It also can fulfill the ultimate goal of gaining market share, growing the "right" revenues, and optimally serving clients.

■ ■ ■

Despite the structural and cultural challenges faced by professional and business-to-business service firms trying to integrate their marketing and business development functions, substantial evidence indicates that they are very capable of changing their marketing and business development processes and cultural norms. "Doing things differently" is alive and well.

But the ways in which many of these improvement initiatives are being undertaken could be a double-edged sword. Because these initiatives are typically championed by professionally brave individual marketing and business development leaders or small groups, and typically *for narrowly defined issues*, PSFs and B2Bs still end up with fragmented, siloed marketing and business development functions. The energy, focus, and goals of the individual programs and their leaders should be lauded, but too many "doing things differently" endeavors to increase the effectiveness of marketing and business development do not substantively address the deep scope of the structural and cultural barriers to real integration.

We'll now review examples of how some "doing things differently" approaches could actually impede a firm's marketing and business development functional effectiveness.

Individuals Paving Their Own Pathways

The first issue is related to one I introduced in chapter 1: the variable scope and often limited responsibilities of the marketing and business development function. There is growing evidence that energetic, persistent marketing and business development leaders are pushing their professional firms to let them define their functions. Who can blame them? Since the earliest days of the service marketing field, it has been largely up to the marketers and business developers themselves to create their own functional purviews, forge their own growth avenues, and build their own skill sets. Today, many marketers and business developers feel they *must* pursue their own pathways. They consider this effort a positive situation for themselves and their organizations.

My own career is an example. When I began working as a professional service marketer in the mid-1980s, I was thrilled to be asked to develop my own job descriptions, or at least to significantly shape them. Today, more than 25 years later, marketers and business developers are still being offered this opportunity. Professional firms should be commended for their flexibility and willingness to be led by self-starters who demonstrate enough professional bravery, passion, and charisma to blaze their own career trails. And each time these self-starters are afforded the opportunity to shape their own growth pathway, their organizations benefit from a renewed look at the function's value proposition.

Here are several other gutsy people who found fresh ways to deepen the strategic importance of their firm-wide roles.

Paul Dunay is the global director of integrated marketing for consulting firm BearingPoint. When Dunay started his online newsletter and blog "Buzz Marketing for Technology," he billed it (and himself) as a source for "innovative ideas for B2B technology marketers." With a careful disclaimer that his online remarks were his alone and not necessarily those of his employer, Dunay increased his own expertise and his stature both inside and outside his firm. He contributed to the positive reputation of the enterprise, which is favorably highlighted each time his broadly distributed intellectual capital is cited.

I profiled *Jim Lanzalotto* in the July 2007 issue of my online newsletter "The Marketplace Master." Lanzalotto joined Yoh Services LLC, a talent and outsourcing staffing firm, in 2000. Using his "stand in front of the bus" approach to change, soon afterward he became its first vice president of strategy and marketing. This functional link—strategy plus marketing—was one of the few I'd heard to be explicitly combined in a professional service enterprise. The scope of Lanzalotto's position was noteworthy, because it underscored the competitive benefits of astutely deploying a broader marketing function instead of the more limited marketing communications conception of the role.[1]

In the September 2007 issue of "The Marketplace Master," I wrote about *Jay Wager*, the senior manager of business development for the intellectual property law firm Wolf, Greenfield and Sacks. Wager joined Wolf Greenfield in late 2005, after the firm decided to integrate its business development management and its marketing. Even with the firm's "on paper" mandate and the help of his senior colleagues, Wager had to blaze a new trail of thinking and action on business development throughout the enterprise.[2]

I featured *Ed Kasparek*, a senior vice president at the building engineering firm Thornton Tomasetti, in the June 2007 issue of "The Marketplace Master" because of his multiyear efforts to change his firm's business development processes. Kasparek was a wonderful example of how a doggedly persistent revenue-generating practitioner can change a firm's internal culture, integrate its technical purview with marketing and business development, and lead the entire enterprise toward greater marketplace effectiveness.[3]

The resourcefulness of these professionally brave individuals underscores the advantages of working within service firm cultures that have not yet formed standardized perceptions of their marketing and business development functions. And these "doing things differently" pathfinders also draw attention to their organizations' flexibility, willingness to evolve, and marketplace savvy. Indeed, we want our professional firms to be living, breathing, ultimately malleable entities.

But individual pathways and narrowly focused initiatives carry a risk of creating functional barriers. If these enterprises allow individually developed marketing and business development position descriptions, or respond to an individual's new marketing and business development pilot, without a formal framework for cross-functional or enterprise-wide integration, they're in danger of creating more disconnectivity. Consider what happens if the "doing things differently" champion leaves her firm. Does the function she created stick around even if she doesn't? All too often, the individual leaves, and the functional progress that the organization had achieved leaves as well.

Potentially worse, many of these piecemeal initiatives begin as pilots endorsed by the executive committees or special task forces of PSFs or B2Bs, and are often only for limited deployment at the geographic, line-of-business, or industry level. In concept, pilots make a lot of sense. But ultimately, unless a firm's executive manager keeps his eyes on that pilot's change management process or integration trajectory, these professionally brave marketers and business developers and their emerging initiatives could actually exacerbate their firm's functional silos.

Consider what happens if a business unit manager is allowed to launch a region-specific positioning platform and it gets out of synch with the positioning of the rest of the firm. Did executive managers fully evaluate the integration potential of the platform as a whole, enough for it to help the entire firm move ahead? All too often, because the pathway was paved by one individual or small team and organizationally accommodated on a situation-specific basis by executive managers, the answer is no.

Individuals Forging Friendships

Another example of the challenges of "doing things differently" is related to what I call the "Friendship Model" of marketing. Inevitably, especially in the absence of executive managers holding marketing and business development functions accountable for achieving results with other functions, energetic and forward-thinking individuals start to forge their own friendships and informal working relationships to make progress and become more productive.

Remember the "administration collaboration" study I described in chapter 1? It confirmed that the vast majority of marketing, business development, and administrative working relationships are informal ones that typically commence among proactive individuals who have enough professional bravery to try different models of working together.

I've seen this happen many times when PSF and B2B marketers and business developers strike up friendships with professionals in IT, human resources, legal, or other functional areas of the firm. Marketers know their jobs will go more smoothly, say, on the redesign of a CRM system or interactive social media campaign, if the program's processes are worked out with the IT department ahead of time. And I have found numerous examples of human resources professionals seeking out their marketing and business development friends to help craft recruiting messages or campaigns to capture talent.

But in view of the competitive services marketplace, I wonder about the narrow focus of these singular initiatives. Are these "good ideas"— friendly partnering and warm relationships—good enough to help a firm gain a substantial market share, grow the "right" revenues, and optimally serve its clients? I don't think so. And even though the executive managers of professional firms may informally encourage intrafunctional collaborations, most firms don't take the additional step of *requiring* functions to co-develop initiatives or to measure them for their collaboration. And typically, these informal team-ups are not organizationally supported by incentives, rewards, recognized shared accountabilities, or co-developed job descriptions. These initiatives are not integrated. It's too easy for people to become triangulated or pulled away from important pursuits. No matter how strong some of these cross-functional collaborations might be, they break down. Friendships have to be started anew if a professional leaves a firm, or if a friendship cannot be forged in the first place.

The Friendship Model, then, while personally satisfying to those involved (and teamwork, loyalty, and cooperation is a must in the workplace), doesn't work by itself for the enterprise as a whole. Without a vigorous structural and cultural framework for integrated marketing and business development, this approach is simply not enough. Without an overarching executive management agenda for integration, "doing things differently" initiatives can't be harnessed properly. They can't help the organization gather the marketplace traction it needs to make gains or to serve clients optimally. In this context, "doing things differently" can simply disguise the real picture: functional disconnects that deter the firm from competing as effectively as it could.

Managing "Doing Things Differently" with Integration as the Goal

"Doing things differently," if managed with integration as the goal, carries enormous potential for organizational gains.

Kate Kirkpatrick, who was elevated to the chief marketing officer position at the architectural firm Gensler, is a classic example of an astute self-starter who shaped her career growth—with the guidance of executive management—while driving successful marketplace gains for her entire firm.

At SMPS's national conference in August 2007, I co-presented a session on enhancing the marketing function's leadership potential in architecture, engineering, and construction firms. My co-presenter, Kate Kirkpatrick, recounted her journey toward her firm's senior management team.

She began by doing her homework about practitioners' general perceptions of her function. She reviewed the findings of a 2004 Booz Allen Hamilton/Association of National Advertisers survey of CEOs. In that survey, a full 75 percent of respondents agreed that because of newly competitive markets and the pressure to innovate, marketing is more important than ever. But when the survey's CEOs were asked about their perception of marketing's priorities, less than 50 percent believed that what keeps them awake at night are at the top of marketing's agenda. They pointed out that "marketing is not aligned with the CEO's agenda," and instead they focus "on tactical issues such as maintaining branding guidelines, sharing best practices, and counseling divisions." They wanted marketing to provide measurable outcomes and a clear return on investment, but they felt that marketing's metrics were not up to the task.[4]

Kirkpatrick then interviewed leading Gensler practitioners, who believed in marketing but whose comments still echoed the Booz survey: "No matter how many marketers we hire, you guys don't get out of the reactive mode" (practice area leader). "I figure our marketing staff will turn over every 18 months or so . . . that's just the way it is" (office director). "Strategy is good, but I'd be happy just to have things happen without all the drama and mistakes" (office director).

When she asked Gensler marketers about the challenges they faced in becoming more strategically effective for their firm, she heard responses that were not about practice growth or strategic alignment, but about other types of issues:

- "I think the biggest thing that often stands in my way is time."
- "Sounds silly but my title has been an obstacle—I was hired as a 'marketing coordinator' which I immediately rejected but I still have people introduce me as marketing coordinator and I think with this comes the association and perception of proposal monkey."
- "Time crunches and workload are the biggest challenges."

- "I think part of it is just doing what I think I need to do in the spare time I have and proving to everyone that I am truly capable of being more than a factory worker."

- "I think some of us create [the proposal monkey] name for ourselves though. We can't whine and complain if we're not doing anything to move forward or change our positions."

"It was clear what our marketing function was up against," said Kirkpatrick, during her presentation. "Marketers weren't perceived to have the right priorities and the right toolkits. We were seen as replaceable. And we didn't see what the real problem was—that, as a group, we didn't have the practice knowledge to stand at the same level as our design and client leaders."

Kirkpatrick then related a story about one of the initiatives she used to simultaneously enhance her strategic contribution to her firm and advance professionally. Through initiative, volunteering personal time, and the support of an influential mentor within the firm, she built the knowledge base and relationships within the firm to eventually lead to a significant revenue-generating function. She understood the importance of developing personal expertise within her firm's core business services. Specifically, she took on the role of co-leader of Gensler's workplace practice, the top revenue line of business at the firm, for three years. With a team of principals, she led the development of new services, thought leadership initiatives, and a research program that helped lead to significant growth of the practice, from 30 to 40 percent annual growth over the period.

Kirkpatrick's story and her appointment in 2006 to CMO at Gensler may seem inspiring. But it could not have happened in an organization that was not willing to allow this kind of professional growth to happen in the first place, or without a mentor who believed in her ability to contribute on a strategic level. And it could not have happened without integration as an avenue for achieving the organization's goal. Sadly, the collaborative and shared accountability environment at Gensler does not exist in all professional or B2B service firms.

Kirkpatrick's story highlights the power of integration. Her real contribution occurred when she took on responsibilities that assimilated her into the company on both an individual level and functionally. Thus the management directive for "doing things differently" must have integration as a springboard. Professional and business-to-business executive managers, while welcoming internal entrepreneurship and individuals' professional passion, should filter these initiatives for their potential to improve marketing and business development integration. Anything less leaves the organization vulnerable to yet another layer of disconnectivity.

Chapter 4 will outline a new paradigm for PSF and B2B executive managers to consider: three new structural models and three cultural approaches that foster a new meaning of marketing and business development for the enterprise; allow shared accountabilities, collaboration, and co-leadership of marketing and business development; and make expectations more explicit about how everyone can contribute.

Chapter 4

A Fresh Approach to Erasing Structural and Cultural Silos in Marketing and Business Development

The executive managers of tomorrow's professional firms will be expected to drive broad initiatives to grow their companies. To do so, they will have to reconfigure their organizations' go-to-market structures (talent, tools, processes, and protocols). The critical building blocks for an integrated structural framework include a broader functional purview for marketing and business development and better prioritization of all marketing and business development initiatives to achieve meaningful marketplace growth in revenues.

At the same time, these leaders must make cultural changes to foster the integration of marketing and business development throughout the organization. Critical building blocks for a new cultural paradigm include adoption of an updated, well-assimilated common lexicon about marketing and business development; creation of new formal collaboration, shared accountability, and co-leadership models for marketing and business development; and the practice of making expectations more explicit about how everyone can contribute to marketing and business development.

■ ■ ■

In the early days of the professional and business-to-business service sectors, executive committee members and managing partners held almost honorary positions, more akin to figureheads than actual managers. Professional firms also tended to address marketing and business development effectiveness at the individual, geographic, or practice level.

Now, PSF and B2B service firm executives have a more overarching organizational directive: noticeably increase the entire company's competitive advantage and market share. These leaders are held to higher expectations and are charged with driving the growth of their enterprises as a whole.

But growth has to happen within a marketplace. And so PSF and B2B firm executives must increasingly pursue structural and cultural integration of their marketing and business development functions. Their mandate is to break down internal barriers to optimal marketing and selling, most likely carried out by leading vast initiatives to improve organizational competencies, reshaping organization-wide processes, and creating new cultural paradigms for marketing and business development.

Sounds like a lot of heavy lifting, right? Yet there is strong evidence that a growing number of professional service and B2B executive managers are indeed taking steps to redirect their firms' enterprise-wide marketing and business development approaches. In the 2007 "Doing Things Differently" series in my newsletter "The Marketplace Master," I presented many examples of professional service marketers and executives who had undertaken significant structural and cultural changes in order to compete more effectively.

The executive managers of professional and B2B firms can ensure that everyone has an explicit function in marketing and business development by creating a more integrated *structure* (process, skills, and support) and driving a more integrated *culture*, with a common understanding of terms, collaboration, sharing accountability, co-leadership, and shared expectations.

When executive managers commit to reconfiguring their marketing and business development structures, inevitably they find they must first step back and look at every handoff point along the firm's marketing-to-sales process, at all the capabilities of their staff to perform the tasks required, and at the depth and scope of the administrative infrastructure and cultural norms the firm maintains to support marketing and business development.

Doing so gives managers an opportunity to reframe marketing and business development *compellingly* and to integrate these functions (and people's individual roles) *effectively*. Figure 4.1 offers just such a view of both elements of the Integration Imperative concept. It illustrates how an executive manager could lead efforts to embed marketing and business development into every person's function at a professional firm.

Three Structural Integration Imperatives

The left side of figure 4.1 features three interdependent structural frameworks that, taken together, would effectively integrate marketing and business development throughout a professional or B2B service firm. These are the three structural Integration Imperatives.

The first, the Process Imperative, addresses the left-to-right steps in the marketing-to-sales process. At first glance, it may look somewhat familiar;

Figure 4.1 The Integration Imperative

many professional firms have created their own versions of this framework. With the Process Imperative, though, I suggest that professional and B2B service firms *broaden the scope of their marketing and business development functions, better balance them strategically, make them more discernible to everyone in the firm, and make them more obviously iterative.*

The second, the Skills Imperative, is directed at the bottom-to-top pathway of marketing and business development skills growth. Of course, many professional enterprises have created their own well-recognized career pathways for their practitioners. With the Skills Imperative, though, I suggest that firms *reframe their advancement pathways—for practitioners and nonrevenue-generating staff—to more clearly outline the steps every professional can take toward competency growth in marketing and business development.*

The third, the Support Imperative, frames the lateral working relationships between a professional firm's administrative peers in human resources, information technology, finance, legal, and other operational functions. Many professional service firms already enjoy the results delivered by the friendly, informal working relationships that exist between these support functions and their marketing and business development colleagues. With the Support Imperative, though, I call on professional enterprises to *create more formal avenues for function-to-function collaboration, shared accountability, and co-leadership for marketing and business development.*

Adopting a Broader Functional Purview for Marketing and Business Development

To build a structure for integrating marketing and business development, executive managers will have to broadly redefine their functions. More specifically, they will have to help those under them adopt new perspectives on what the functions could mean for themselves and their firms.

What do I really mean when I say PSFs and B2Bs should "broadly redefine" marketing and business development? Most service firms deploy these functions in a more limited way than they could. For example, in the typical professional and B2B service firms the term *marketing* used to refer solely to building visibility, promotion, and increasing awareness of and communicating about the firm. In some firms, marketing was—and, for many, still is—a back-of-the-house support activity for a firm's sales efforts, with no marketing interface with the firm's clients. In still other firms, marketing actually means selling.

But to be clear, marketing is a one-to-many activity. The optimal scope of marketing in a professional enterprise should be broader, and could even begin to resemble the way in which marketing is deployed in a products company. Take the classic four P's (price, product, position, and place) that are taught at many graduate business schools.[1] Today, most professional service marketers have no responsibility for at least two of those P's: price and product. Shouldn't the senior-most marketer have at least advisory responsibilities, if not the lead, in these two areas? What about market and client behavior research? Client satisfaction? Competitive intelligence?

In products or retail companies, these functions are well established. In the professional service arena, they largely have no formal home, much less a home under the marketing umbrella. Because the professional service arena is growing in maturity and competitiveness, and the business focus and experience of senior professional service marketers are deepening, it's time to update and broaden the term *marketing* and its purview.

These structural frameworks, when implemented in combination with a deliberate effort to change the culture, form a powerful yet flexible foundation that breaks down a professional service firm's marketing and business development barriers. The result? Professional firms can more effectively grow their market share, increase the "right" revenues, and provide greater value to their clients.

Better Prioritizing All Marketing-to-Business Development Initiatives to Achieve Meaningful Marketplace Growth

Earlier in this book, I outlined abundant evidence that PSF and B2B service firms overemphasize acquiring clients or retaining them without enough focus on growing their book of business with strategically appropriate clients. The chase to bring in new clients can be thrilling. And retaining an important client relationship can be enormously satisfying and bring important revenue stability to a professional enterprise. Nevertheless, without an appropriate effort to grow the firms' revenues from those clients, PSF and B2Bs are simply treading water in the marketplace.

The structural frameworks of the Integration Imperative more effectively harness the professional organization to achieve *meaningful* growth in revenues, market share, and client added value. These frameworks enable every person, working within any function, to make meaningful contributions toward that meaningful marketplace growth. Rather than being distracted by the all-too-inevitable micro issues (without denying the immediacy or importance of those issues), executive managers can return again and again to the frameworks of the Integration Imperative for a high-level check of how everyone is doing at overcoming internal barriers to building the company and adding unique value to clients. Managers must ask themselves:

- "How are we doing with our marketing-to-business development process?" (Here they could consider the left-to-right aspects of the Process Imperative.)
- "How are we doing at growing everyone's marketing and business development skills?" (Here they could consider the bottom-to-top aspects of the Skills Imperative.)
- "How is our organization doing at linking all roles, even administrative, to achieve our marketing and business development goals?" (Here they could consider the lateral aspects of the Support Imperative.)

There's been enough public discourse about strategic focus, internal teamwork, and calls for a PSF or a B2B to go to market as a "one-firm firm." Without a road map, achieving these goals could be immensely complex and perhaps even unattainable.

In the past, executive managers had to start from scratch to overcome internal functional barriers to a strategic focus, streamlined internal working relationships, and a "contribution" mindset. My idea here is simple: give executive managers a set of high-level directional (yet customizable) frameworks—process, skills, and support—that would enable them to instill new functional connections among the people in their organizations. Using the templates I present in-depth in the following chapters, people will be able to follow distinct pathways to improve their contributions to marketing and business development *individually*. The organization thereby improves its marketplace effectiveness *collectively*.

Cultural Change Management: The Glue for New Structural Frameworks

However compelling they might look on paper, new structural frameworks, process maps, and skill-level benchmarks won't be enough to erase the marketing and business development silos found in so many professional firms. They need glue: changes in the organization's culture. Fortunately, cultural change is not viewed with the same trepidation that it might have been even a decade ago. As this book's research findings, examples, and case studies demonstrate, the idea that change can even be positive is increasingly accepted, even when it occurs relatively quickly. During a 2008 meeting, one of my CMO clients said, "People used to say it takes 10 years to change a culture. Now they're saying it takes two to three."

But cultural change cannot be haphazard or led casually. To influence the change that best serves the enterprise, PSF and B2B executives will have to formally embrace principles of change management. The structural frameworks of integrating marketing and business development will have to be supported mindfully, with clearly outlined cultural principles and desired outcomes. Professional firm executives will have to craft well-defined cultural integration outcomes.

Three Cultural Integration Imperatives

The middle of figure 4.1 features a set of three interdependent cultural principles that, taken together, will effectively integrate marketing and business development throughout a professional and B2B service firm. I refer often to these principles throughout the rest of this book.

The first cultural principle is to articulate the new meaning of marketing and business development for the enterprise. It addresses a particularly vexing hurdle to integration: definitions of the terms *marketing* and *business development* vary widely from individual to individual, firm to firm, and sector to sector.

Not surprisingly, one's understanding of a term leads directly to one's expectation about the role and function of the job. And this is no small matter. Adopting an updated lexicon and assimilating it throughout the enterprise can be a pivotal point for a PSF or B2B striving to effectively integrate marketing and business development.

Moreover, a common lexicon is critical to introducing people to a firm's newer and more expansive way of perceiving marketing and business development. It's also vital in reducing the unmatched expectations that too often are found among the practitioner populations of PSF and B2B firms. Indeed, a lexicon effectively addresses an expectations disconnect. Because PSF or B2B practitioners do not receive much instruction in service marketing during their academic or professional preparation, they typically assign great weight to what they learn from their past professional journeys. As people move from firm to firm, they bring with them their individual experience and understandings of what marketing and selling are. They then inevitably create their own lexicons.

From their own lexicons, they build expectations about what's going to happen in their interactions with marketers and business developers and about the results they and their firm should realize. Even with the best of intentions, too often these practitioners assume they understand what their marketers and business developers mean when they use terms from their own lexicons. The misunderstandings that occur often lead to perceptions that marketers and business developers are not performing to expectations.

Take, for example, the term *return on investment* when applied to the number of people one might expect to accept an invitation to a seminar. Based on their knowledge of the quality of the invitation list (a "cold" list of people who are largely unaware of the sponsoring firm versus a "warm" list of loyal clients and influencers), most professional marketers understand what return they should expect from the seminar invitation list being used. But a lawyer or an executive search consultant might not. Bingo — because they simply misunderstood the meaning of the term *return on investment* when applied to an invitation list, practitioners' expectations may not be met. The first internal barriers are erected.

Misunderstandings over terminology and uneven expectations arise with professional service marketers and business developers as well. In preparing to write *The Integration Imperative*, I encountered this variability time and again when I interviewed my informal advisory group of senior-level PSF and B2B marketers and executives about the book's content. During those interviews, I learned the extent to which each person had different perspectives and definitions for many of the terms I used.

After the first few interviews, I decided to define my terms before describing the issues and models of the book. Once we were on common ground, my interviewees were able to offer substantive guidance. If misunderstandings of terms occur among deeply experienced senior marketers, you can only imagine the extent to which they occur between this community and their practitioner colleagues. Or when marketers and business developers move from one B2B or professional service sector to another.

If no one ever changed jobs, we wouldn't have to create a common lexicon. Everyone would thoroughly understand terms, and expectations could be held consistently. But that's not what happens in real life. Marketers move to new positions at other firms. Practitioners come and go. And, inevitably, in the early stages of their jobs, new marketers have to communicate about and reframe the understanding of their functions.

Don't get me wrong. I'm not calling for a monolithic, static perception of marketing and business development. But reframing our understanding of PSF and B2B marketing and selling is a natural step in the evolution of the field. We have to thank the many individual professional and business-to-business service firms and marketing and management executives who have issued their own authoritative definitions of marketing and business development words. Their perspectives eventually do influence their colleagues' understanding of terms and their expectations about the functional purview of marketing, **sales support**, and business development roles. It takes time, but it substantiates the wonderfully dynamic nature of the service marketing arena.

In chapter 9, the case study of Perkins+Will is an excellent example of a firm that embraced this cultural principle. The organization's executive managers created a new lexicon, and renamed the enterprise's go-to-market and client service orientation. For the people of Perkins+Will, integration is an ongoing, almost holistic, commitment.

The second cultural standard I'll underscore throughout the book is that of increasing formal avenues for collaboration, shared accountability, and co-leadership on marketing and business development. Structural models by themselves are not enough to help professional firms optimally integrate their marketing and business development functions. Too often, these firms create gorgeous structural frameworks that don't outline formal pathways for collaboration, accountability sharing, and co-leadership between practitioners and nonrevenue-generating staff. I think they should. Culture—harnessed and led—is once again the critical glue in reinforcing productive organizational change.

Sure, professional service firms *do* encourage their people to collaborate or share leadership with their colleagues. When I was a marketing director in both large and small professional service firms in the 1980s and 1990s, my performance reviews regularly included acknowledgment of my collaboration with practitioners. It's that way today in the majority of professional enterprises, but typically these pathways are obscure and unevenly available. They aren't expected, just hoped for.

For many executive managers, this situation would be good enough. I contend it isn't, especially if they want their employees to help the firm achieve substantive market share gains and overcome disconnectivity. Executive managers should create formal frameworks for collaboration, shared accountabilities, and co-leadership between practitioners and nonrevenue-generating marketers and business developers.

Informality is a good idea for successfully building the market share of a professional business, but it is not good enough. Under the Friendship Marketing model, as I call it, marketers and business developers make progress with practitioners primarily by currying favors instead of being able to depend on accountable colleagues. Because many marketers and business developers live in a world of dotted-line relationships—if this meager amount of formality exists at all—they've learned valuable techniques for negotiating cooperative arrangements with their practitioner colleagues, and even other marketers or business developers.

Imagine a visionary marketer—an idea champion—who has just created an exciting initiative for helping her firm gain market share. This idea champion genially asks a distant marketing counterpart for help, perhaps making a "what's in it for you" pitch. She asks the person she has in mind, then his boss, then his boss's boss. She might downplay the real commitment she is seeking in case the person realizes just how much effort is really needed. She promises to sing her helper's praises to his supervisors, or at least take the heat for him if his boss gets cranky. She checks in often, to see if her helper is making progress.

You get the idea. Under this Friendship Marketing scenario, the idea champion can never be certain of the helper's real interest in meeting his commitment. She doesn't have real influence to direct an outcome. Priorities shift without warning, and too often away from the idea champion's project. The Friendship Marketing model consumes an inordinate amount of time and energy, and requires cajoling, wheedling, and convincing. It also requires herculean follow-up and, often, frequent resetting of deadlines because the work is unofficial or not formally mandated.

Professional service and B2B marketers and business developers know this scenario only too well. Even the most esteemed firms rely on the Friendship Marketing model. A friend told me recently (I'm paraphrasing): "I wish I could count on the work I'm having to *convince* people to do. All this asking and favor-building; all this monitoring, negotiating, and coaxing. It's a huge waste of time and energy. Wouldn't it be better if I could hold people accountable?"

A powerful example of this second cultural principle is the case study in chapter 11 on Randstad, a global temporary and contract staffing company. In the case, marketing and financial professionals used collaboration, shared accountabilities, and co-leadership principles to transform their unofficial teamwork into formal structures that substantially increased the company's human and financial productivity. Now these cultural standards are hardwired.

The third cultural paradigm is that executives should make their expectations about how everyone can contribute to marketing and business development more explicit. I've already addressed one of the important building blocks of shifting people's expectations: creating an organizational lexicon about the new meaning of marketing and business development. But a new lexicon will not be enough to embed marketing and business development into everyone's function, and it certainly won't be enough to help executive managers outline new expectations for individual contributions.

In what other ways could executive managers make their expectations more explicit about how practitioners, marketers, business developers, and other administrative professionals should contribute to marketing and business development? Internal communication techniques are a possibility. Many PSF and B2B service firms have made great strides in using internal communication when a particularly important internal "expectations" message arises. In these situations, executive managers often turn to marketers to craft their message and distribute targeted information, which is often about changes in collaboration arrangements, new accountabilities, and revamped leadership structures. Not surprisingly, afterward internal communication becomes an ongoing element of marketers' functional responsibilities.

But, like the creation of a new lexicon, formal internal communications techniques won't be enough to break down internal barriers to integrated marketing and business development.

Executive managers also must apply a potent new kind of cultural glue: reviewing and integrating job descriptions, checking and integrating reporting relationships, and reframing performance management guidelines to ensure that people understand how they are expected to work together in new ways toward meeting the organization's revenue, market share, and client added-value goals. Just by communicating that an initiative like this is under way, executives also signal that a culture shift is under way. But rather than simply applying lip service, executive managers are rebuilding the enterprise's expectations from the inside out.

A good example of this third cultural principle is the case study in chapter 11 about R.W. Beck's integration initiative. At this forward-thinking firm, a seasoned human resources and change management professional worked alongside its marketing and brand management leader (and the firm's other executive managers) to reconstruct an entirely new and deeply integrated performance management program. Talk about gaining marketplace traction!

What Will Be Required from Tomorrow's Professional Firm Executive Managers?

Today, the stakes for effectively managing a professional firm are high. Tomorrow, they will be higher. Today's professional service executive managers have to possess stellar **rainmaking** track records and marketing acumen. In the future, it won't be enough for professional enterprises to elect or hire as their firm's leaders those senior practitioners who possess the most consensus-oriented styles or well-rounded personalities. They also will have to possess demonstrable skills in *managing a professional enterprise*.

The school of thought on "management as a true profession" has been evolving over the past decades. Rakesh Khurana and Nitin Nohria, professors of business administration at the Harvard Business School, have written about this topic for years. But they aren't the only ones exploring this concept. Several service sectors have already begun to endorse academic preparation and training in the principles of managing service enterprises. For example, the health care field has identified a set of recognized management competencies for doctors, nurses, and other practicing clinicians. The completion of advanced management degrees or certification is often a direct stepping-stone to leadership positions. In professional or B2B service firms, too, it's no longer a rarity to find executive managers who have augmented their professional credentials with an MBA.

But professional and B2B service firms, especially the cleverest competitors, will soon begin demanding for their leadership the next critical iteration of this concept: *experts* in service company management.

Tomorrow's most successful service company executive managers (and, it follows, those who will be most preferred by their firm's equity owners and shareholders) will lead their service firms using a well-recognized code of management stewardship, including ethics. A "best practices" set of competencies and standards for expertise in managing these enterprises will begin to emerge, become refined, and gain acceptance over time.

I believe these acknowledged best practices will inevitably include at least some variation on the Integration Imperative's structural frameworks and cultural norms for leading a professional firm toward gaining market share, growing the "right" revenues, and adding value to clients.

In Part II of the book, I delve more deeply into the specifics of the three structural imperatives. Throughout the rest of the book, just as culture permeates an enterprise, I'll weave in my observations about the three cultural approaches I've described here. PSF and B2B executives will use these customizable structures and cultural foundations as change management tools in effectively integrating marketing and business development throughout their enterprises.

Introducing the Integration Imperative

A New Professional Service Marketing/Business Development Paradigm

Read this section . . .

- If you're curious about how PSFs and B2Bs could embed marketing and business development into *everyone's* job without generating massive chaos,
- If you want to consider a few structural models that could integrate marketing and business development functions,
- If you want to ponder the cultural aspects of increasing people's shared accountabilities, collaboration, and co-leadership on marketing and business development, or
- If you'd like to review the benefits that a professional or B2B service firm could realize if it integrated its marketing and business development functions.

Otherwise, feel free to skip to Part III.

■ ■ ■

The Integration Imperative is simple: to achieve marketplace success (beyond mere serendipity, that is), professional and business-to-business service firms must embed marketing and business development into every person's job (although each person would have his or her own role). To overcome the disconnects that exist in the marketing and selling processes of today's PSF and B2B firms, their executive managers need to devise both structural and cultural solutions.

The bottom line: clients are looking for those professional and B2B service firms that demonstrate this kind of integration.

The chapters in Part II outline three structural frameworks and three cultural paradigms that could effectively integrate marketing and business development throughout a professional organization, and they highlight the reasons why integration ultimately benefits the firm and its clients.

Chapter 5 depicts a model for integrated marketing to business development handoffs. In chapter 6, you'll learn about a model for growing the skills of a firm's revenue-generating practitioners and nonrevenue-generating marketing and business development professionals.

Chapter 7 describes a model for integrating marketers and business developers and a firm's other administrative professionals. Chapter 8 outlines the many benefits of adopting these Integration Imperatives for PSFs, B2Bs, and their clients.

Chapter 5

The Process Imperative

This chapter describes the Process Imperative. This imperative outlines a way to broaden the purview of the marketing and business development function, fosters a more discernible pathway for the process, enables the handoffs from one step to the other to be more strategic than tactical, better balances a firm's marketing and business development priorities, and better matches a client's actual buying cycle. The key points of the Process Imperative are summarized in table B.1 in appendix B.

■ ■ ■

Many professional service firms employ some kind of stepwise process to help their revenue-generating professionals sell the firm's services. Often, such a process is depicted visually (perhaps as a lovely two-dimensional chart) showing the steps along the firm's pathway. But whether portrayed visually or not, these somewhat task-oriented guidelines focus on the tactical marketing and selling steps that many professionals undertake in order to win a client engagement.

The steps typically (and traditionally) begin with a potential client's inquiry or response to the firm's direct outreach or visibility-building activities. These tactics are often called **lead generation** activities. Increasingly, PSFs track the source of their inquiries for further evaluation: Did this lead come from a Web site link or search engine? Was it a response to an article, speech, or other lead generation activity initiated by the firm's practitioners or marketers?

Once a lead has been identified, the firm launches its selling process: it determines the decision maker; introduces the firm to him or her; tries to discover the match between the decision maker's needs and the firm's current solutions (or customizes the firm's services to meet those needs); builds a trusted relationship; and takes the often numerous steps toward winning a proposal. The simple "racetrack" visual developed by design and construction company strategist David Stone and shown in figure 5.1 depicts this concept.

In the majority of professional service firms, it's up to the experts themselves to define their best targets and segments, initiate marketing

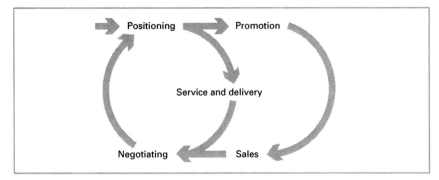

Figure 5.1 The Stone & Company "Racetrack"

communication and direct marketing tactics to generate and pursue their own leads, and sell their services and then deliver the services those clients just bought. In this model, the experts are the marketers, sellers, and service deliverers, all rolled up into one person or small cadre of leaders.

In a growing number of professional service enterprises, nontechnical or nonrevenue-producing marketers and business developers have entered the picture. In this model, the marketers generate a firm's leads and then hand those leads to their business development colleagues, who follow up with those leads and work to develop a solution that the leads buy. Then— voilà—the leads become clients. Later, business developers work (sometimes with account or relationship managers) to sell more services to those clients.

If the firm employs the seller-doer model (and many firms do, even if they also employ nonrevenue-generating marketing or selling professionals), it's not uncommon for it to ask these individuals to develop an individual marketing or selling plan. These individual marketing-to-sales plans are then dovetailed into the firm's overall marketing-to-sales plans.

Does the Marketing-to-Sales Process Help Build the "Right" Revenues and Gain Market Share?

As it is now, too many firms work hard to capture revenues that too easily disappear, or to win clients who do not represent inherently strategic relationships or are likely to grow in loyalty. Too many firms are stuck owning a static share of the market; they can grow only if they acquire or merge with another firm. And too many firms labor to increase their marketing and selling effectiveness, while using processes whose scope is too limited and whose handoff points are too disconnected.

What's needed is a strategy process model for optimizing the marketing-to-business-development pipeline in which a firm's leaders can monitor progress on achieving priorities and recalibrate the organization's tactical processes as needed to achieve the appropriate goals. What's needed is a strategy process model that focuses on functions, thereby allowing the firm's executive managers to more astutely detect marketing and selling collaboration breakdowns, handoff disconnects, or marketplace shifts. And what's needed is a model that is flexible enough to work, regardless of the selling model the firm uses.

I call this model the Process Imperative. It outlines how marketing and business development can be reconfigured into five iterative, stepwise, integrated, and strategic functions. These steps, which I've summarized using an acronym, "DARBI," are depicted in table B.1.

Defining and Identifying the Professional Firm's Most Strategically Important Clients

For this step in the Process Imperative (the "D" in the DARBI acronym), the function of marketing and business development is to segment the market, target the "right" clients, and determine which clients to pursue, respond to, or avoid, and then to determine pricing.

Many professional firms hastily tell themselves they've already done the work needed to identify and define their most strategically important clients and targets. But let's take a closer look at what I really mean when I say "define and identify strategically important clients." In my book *Marketplace Masters*, I described a firm's Looking Out activities, which involve formal research, trends analysis, or forecasting the enterprise's external business environment, client needs, and competitor activity. (For a more visual depiction of how a firm's Defining step aligns with its Looking Out activities, see table B.1 in appendix B.)

Armed with this vital Looking Out context, a professional service firm can then more easily define its ideal client, through the following steps:

- **Segmenting** *the market*—evaluating the characteristics of potential client groups that could match up with the firm's growth strategies, including their need for the firm's service offerings and expertise base, the likelihood they will respond positively to the firm's awareness and business development approaches, and their shared philosophies and attitudes. Some easily identified segments might include public versus private sector, American versus Asia Pacific geographic presence, or a member of the aviation industry. Other segments could focus on demographics such as revenue range or company size, represented on the FTSE 100 index, or "more than 5,000 full-time employees." Keep in mind that segmentation does not just look at the present-time characteristics of the firm's potential client groups; it also reviews them for the future (in what ways is this group likely to be evolving as our marketplace shifts?).

- *Targeting the "right" clients and their decisions makers*—choosing the groups of clients a firm most wants to serve. Once the firm's potential segments have been identified, targeting fosters yet another layer of strategic assessment of those segments that could best allow the firm to achieve its strategic goals. In this activity, the professional enterprise determines which client groups it will directly pursue, which groups it will respond to if approached (and under what circumstances), and which groups it will not pursue or would decline to respond to if approached.

- *Employing the most appropriate pricing models*—setting a price for a firm's services. Many professional service firms price their services on the basis of a time-and-expense method that is closely tied to their competitors' or their industry's time-and-expense pricing traditions. Some firms employ pricing models that align with the client's perceived value of the service being offered. And there are many other pricing methods besides the two mentioned here. A good pricing model helps a professional service firm achieve its desired growth goals and matches the pricing expectations of the firm's most strategically appropriate clients.

These "defining" initiatives should be undertaken using more formal and **longitudinal research**—on clients, loyalties, markets, and behavior—than many organizations employ now. This function should be managed in-house by a person recognized as the firm's leader of marketing, business development, or both. Even if the company must outsource the research aspects of this process, it should be prominently communicated, and well understood that this process is important and is an ongoing responsibility as part of the firm's overall growth strategy exercises.

Professional enterprises also should undertake formal pricing research as they do their targeting and segmentation analyses. How many firms are doing this today? How well does the client's pricing mindset match a firm's purported value proposition? How well tied is all this to the client's unmet needs? The bigger questions here are: How much money is being left on the table? How much less help is a client getting than what he needs? How much more of the "right" revenues could a firm capture if it undertook the "define and identify" work?

In view of the fluidity of the marketplace, firms must conduct this kind of marketplace definition endeavor more often than most do. The effort does not necessarily require a lot of heavy lifting. For example, in identifying the most loyal clients, one might heed Fred Reichheld's call for companies to ask the Ultimate Question: "On a scale of 0–10, how likely are you to recommend Company X to a friend or colleague?"[1]

Acquiring the Professional Firm's Most Strategically Important Clients

For many professional firms, the function of "acquiring the firm's most strategically important clients" commands their entire go-to-market focus. For these firms, acquiring clients features implementation of a set of quite tactical tasks handled first by marketing personnel, and then lobbed over to practitioners or nonpractitioner business development professionals. For many firms, this activity boils down to not much more than an annual review of recent client engagements—mostly of those clients who paid the firm the most money. (Often, the earliest signs of fragmentation in marketing and business development are manifested in the "acquiring clients" processes.)

The "acquiring" function should instead encompass a deeper, more strategic marketing-to-business development process. It should be broader, too. Client acquisition should feel more like a seamless connection between parties and less like a bloodthirsty hunt. The client acquisition phase should be part of a professional firm's broader growth strategy, but only after the firm has undertaken a robust exploration or reexamination of its marketplace, crafted a forward-thinking value proposition that anticipates clients' needs, and carefully prioritized its potential relationships with clients who can effectively help the firm grow.

The "acquiring clients" phase of the Process Imperative, represented by the "A" in the DARBI acronym, is summarized in table B.1 of appendix B. Not surprisingly, it aligns well with a firm's Digging Deeper organizational competencies, a concept I first introduced in my book *Marketplace Masters*. (For a more visual depiction of this alignment, see table B.1 in appendix B.) A professional firm utilizes its Digging Deeper competencies when it conducts client data mining, aligns its marketing strategies with its culture, develops and implements account planning and relationship management programs, and measures its progress using client-oriented metrics to further calibrate its strategic focus. These Digging Deeper competencies also involve a firm's embrace of competitive differentiation, positioning, and branding strategies.

All these Digging Deeper competencies should feature prominently in the processes used by professional and B2B service firms to acquire clients.

What tasks should be implemented under this "acquiring" construct? For marketers, activities include direct and indirect outreach to establish a firm's value, attractiveness, and credibility. If the defining aspect of the Process Imperative was previously well deployed, marketers can much more effectively acquire clients who are naturally drawn to the value proposition the firm has to offer, and who are more likely to be attracted to the firm's brand promise and find it credible.

An additional—and critical—task for marketers is to protect the firm from copycats, or to guide the evolution of the firm's value propositions toward a favorable uniqueness in the eyes of targeted prospects and clients. PSF and B2B practitioners often express skepticism about their abilities to articulate how their firms differ from those of their rival service providers. This concern underscores yet another reason why they need to more deeply integrate their marketing and business development functions. In particular, if a firm has effectively conducted a "defining" phase of the Process Imperative through market and client perception research, and if it has astutely explored the landscape of competitors, it can then be much more effective in protecting itself from copycats prior to the "acquiring" phase of the Process Imperative.

Let's say a firm's service offerings are entirely copyable—and many are. In that case, a firm's service delivery capabilities might be favorably unique. So might any number of other bases of differentiation that rivals can't replicate. Often, it's a firm's marketing professionals who call the question on protecting the firm from copycats. But a PSF or B2B doesn't need to have nonrevenue-generating marketing professionals on its staff to address this important strategic issue effectively. It's less likely to do so, however, if it continues to pursue client acquisition as a tactical activity.

As they broaden their functional purviews, astute marketers understand that this copycat protection work must begin *prior to* the development of external messages. As they move from a role of pure implementation to one of internal advisor, these marketers bring to practitioners important insights about their enterprise's service offerings and service delivery techniques. They ask practitioners probing questions about the firm's narrow focus and the sustainability of its marketing and growth strategies with the "right" prospects and clients. If the firm itself is copying its rivals, it becomes clear immediately. They help steer practitioners away from mimicking competitors, or taking on clients or business that don't fit the firm's core strategy.

From this springboard, the function of business development works to successfully win engagements with the "right" prospects and clients. The emphasis here is on "successfully." For far too long, the function of business development has been conducted without a more contextual mindset. Too many business developers, operating without the strategic road map they could have from a well-integrated marketing and business development function, end up simply going through the motions of setting appointments, hosting meetings, making follow-up phone calls, and the like. (No wonder so many revenue-generating practitioners say they hate selling.)

If the "acquiring clients" phase could be conducted as part of the Process Imperative, business developers would be better armed with more strategic knowledge about their targets and prospects. They would have a better sense of the behavioral buying patterns of those targets and prospects. They would have a better understanding of those targets' perceptions about alternative service providers. And they would have a better comprehension of how attracted those clients might be to the firm's brand promise, or how loyal they have been to the firm.

Retaining the Professional Service Firm's Most Strategically Important Clients

For this step in the Process Imperative, the function of marketing and business development is to foster increasingly significant firm-client relationships and retain current engagements with targeted clients. (Represented by the "R" in the DARBI acronym, this function is summarized in table B.1 of appendix B.)

Winning repeat client engagements presents a challenge, but it's a surmountable one. In some sectors, many years might pass between engagements. Thus "retaining" a client means different things to different people. For architects, engineers, and construction managers, a retained client might be a school district that awards projects on elementary school construction over an extended period of years, with significant gaps between projects. For accountants, a retained client might "return" annually or for periodic troubleshooting.

The overly tactical "acquiring clients" mindset currently held by many professional firms is mirrored in the "retaining clients" mindset. Certainly, it's appropriate to retain clients whose revenues eventually become a significant portion of the firm's gross profits. But "gives us a lot of money" should not be the only criterion for client retention, and yet for too many professional firms, it is.

Currently, many professional firms approach client retention as solely the purview of business developers, and not enough as part of a more strategic integration with marketing. In the "defining" and "acquiring" phases of the Process Imperative, marketers explore client loyalty, which gives the firm a clearer understanding of which clients it *could* best retain and which clients it *desires* to retain. (Indeed, how often have you heard of professional firms that labor year after year to retain the revenues of clients they consider necessary evils, whose cultures are a bad fit?)

Like the "acquiring" phase of the Process Imperative, the "retaining" phase is aligned with the Digging Deeper competencies that I outlined in *Marketplace Masters*. (For a more visual depiction of this alignment, see table B.1 in appendix B.) Especially in the development and implementation of account planning and relationship management programs, the Process Imperative creates a potent structure to consider client retention from a far more strategic basis than many firms currently employ.

In contrast to the current block-and-tackle approach used to retain client revenues, in the Process Imperative framework, client retention is better considered from the strategic marketing perspective: Would it behoove our firm to retain these clients, and, if so, why and how? What will happen to our firm in the future if we do retain these clients? Have we thought about strategies beyond retention (toward even further building our book of business with these clients), and, if so, how will these strategies inform our approaches to client retention? In what ways do we want our relationship to evolve, and how will this evolution affect the overall growth strategy of our enterprise? These and other strategic marketing questions could be established as retention criteria and often reviewed.

The Process Imperative also affords a better consideration of client retention from the business development perspective: Based on the match between our service offerings and this client's future needs, is it appropriate for us to pursue retention with this client at this time? If not now, when, and under what circumstances? How has this client's purchase decision-making channel evolved since our previous engagement? These questions and others could become part of a professional firm's frequently reviewed retention criteria.

Client retention, deployed with a Process Imperative construct, lends itself well to improving an enterprise's strategies for growing its practitioners' and nonrevenue-generating professionals' skills. For example, newer or less experienced associates could be paired with counterparts on client teams, or less seasoned marketing professionals working with clients' marketing teams for award recognition or thought leadership output.

The retention of strategically appropriate clients, if considered with integrated marketing and business development functions, presents other advantages as well. For example, many professional firms operate their practices as nearly independent entrepreneurial businesses, housed under the same roof. Imagine what could happen if these disconnected business units thought about client retention in a more integrated manner. Where one practice could not retain a client, another might be able to. If professional firms began at the client retention phase of the Process Imperative, wouldn't the next phase—increasing the firm's book of business with each client—provide a stronger springboard for **cross-selling**?

Building the Professional Service Firm's Revenues with the Most Strategically Important Clients

For this step in the Process Imperative (the "B" in the DARBI acronym, as shown in table B.1 of appendix B), the function of marketing and business development is to increase each current client's use of the firm's entire service portfolio and expand its penetration into that client's "share of wallet."

The majority of professional firms undertake their marketing and business development processes with an eye toward client acquisition, although a growing number are also deploying marketing and business development for the purpose of client retention. Unfortunately, in the go-to-market models used currently by most professional firms, the question of eventually building revenues with strategically important clients is never asked. It certainly is not asked by many firms that go to market as a group of loosely integrated practices. And for firms that go to market with siloed marketing functions and business development initiatives, the "building revenues" question is not asked either, because the integrated structures and cultural mindsets required to grow a client's share of wallet simply don't exist.

The "building revenues" aspect of the Process Imperative, however, brings with it exciting strategic considerations in ways all the other Process Imperative steps do not. What follows are a few of the reasons why.

First, the notion of building revenues offers professional enterprises a strategic opportunity to take a critical look at their own service portfolios. If they look at their service portfolios objectively, and in context to the marketplace, some questions inevitably arise: Are our services trending toward commoditization? How copied are they? How unique is our service delivery of those offerings? How valuable do our targeted clients find our service offerings? What could we do better? What should we stop doing altogether? Even if, in answering these questions, a firm determines that a particular client is *not* a candidate for a strategy aimed at building revenues, these questions about a service portfolio are powerful ones.

It's the rare professional or B2B service firm that includes service portfolio management as part of its marketing function—or anyone else's purview for that matter. If professional firms employed the Process Imperative, the management of service portfolios could formally become part of their strategic growth plans. In the hypercompetitive environment facing most professional firms, formalizing the function of service portfolio management simply makes good business sense.

Second, any type of discussion of building revenues allows examination of a firm's capacity to innovate. Most professional firms incorporate at least some level of customization of their service offerings in order to best solve their clients' problems. But formal innovation typically gets short shrift. If the goal of building revenues could be part of a broader set of integrated marketing and business development functions within the Process Imperative, PSFs and B2Bs could make more strategic determinations about where their businesses are going and how their firms can survive and grow.

The building revenues element of the Process Imperative aligns with the Embedding Innovation organizational competencies outlined in *Marketplace Masters*. (For a more visual depiction of this alignment, see table B.1 in appendix B.) These competencies lend themselves well to structural frameworks, such as building a classic R&D process (most consumer products companies are doing this) or developing technologies that support new services (many professional enterprises are doing this to generate new revenue opportunities). Some of the Embedding Innovation competencies lend themselves well to cultural initiatives — in particular, the idea of using incentives and rewards to encourage innovation.

Even if a professional firm decides *not* to formally construct an innovation engine, the very act of examining its intentions about innovation leads to better decisions about building revenues with strategically important clients. The "building revenues" phase of the Process Imperative formally permits this examination and decision making.

A third opportunity to build revenues relates to a firm's internal organization to cross-sell, both culturally and structurally. As one of the more complex marketing and business development initiatives in professional firms, cross-selling has too often been reduced to a series of tactical tasks. Ford Harding has devoted the bulk of his consulting career and thought leadership output to the best practices of rainmaking in professional service firms. In the August 2008 issue of "The Marketplace Master" Harding rightly pointed out how often professionals misunderstand what cross-selling is, why such a misunderstanding is important, and the trouble they thus have making it work optimally. In this guest column, Harding discussed the cultural paradigms that best support cross-selling (and building revenues with a firm's most strategically important clients). They include communication, trust and respect, responsiveness, and reciprocity.[2]

These cultural paradigms, and the structural frameworks a firm puts in place to facilitate cross-selling, are vital to the marketing and business development effectiveness of any professional firm. But a professional firm needs an overarching market-share growth rationale to build revenues with strategically important clients. Executive managers who employ the Process Imperative are more likely to succeed at growing their firm's share of a client's wallet, because they will have determined in advance the firm's strategic priority to build revenues. They will have made their decisions *in the context* of the other elements of the Process Imperative.

Moreover, because the Process Imperative fosters better functional integration of practitioners and their administrative, marketing, and business development colleagues, the big marketing and selling picture becomes more compelling. Instead of grumbling about being forced to cross-sell (and still usually avoiding it), practitioners will be able to experience more exciting outcomes such as helping their firm gain market share or outpace competitors, feeling less vulnerable to client defections, stretching intellectually by developing more innovative client solutions, and feeling more supported by internal teammates whose creative energies are better harnessed.

Increasing the Perceived Value of the Professional Firm to All Audiences

For this phase in the Process Imperative (the "I" in the DARBI acronym, as shown in table B.1 of appendix B), the function of marketing and business development is growing the firm's overall brand value and thought leadership equity and building broad awareness of the firm and its favorable reputation.

Programmatically, the job of increasing the perceived value of the firm to its constituents has traditionally fallen under the purview of marketing. The work of increasing the perceived value of the firm has largely centered on broad awareness-building initiatives in public and media relations, sponsorships, and advertising. For business developers, the activities aimed at increasing perceived value have also included entertaining clients at sporting events or golf tournaments. Many professional and business-to-business service firms also throw into this mix their brand strategies and thought leadership publishing programs. It would be very easy to think of the "increasing perceived value" aspect of the Process Imperative as a repository for all of today's most well-known marketing and business development vehicles.

Instead, the "increasing perceived value" constructs and cultural paradigms, if undertaken as part of the Process Imperative, offer professional firm executive managers an opportunity to more effectively harness and integrate their marketing and business development strategies. Here are three reasons why.

First, the "increasing perceived value" phase is clearly separate from the other elements of the Process Imperative. Each of the four phases already described (define, acquire, retain, and build) focuses directly on the firm's most strategically important clients. Client companies and their decision makers are the ones who give money to the professional service enterprise. For professional enterprises, the intended outcome—of "increasing the perceived value of the firm"—is receiving money for delivery of their services. This outcome is distinctly different from that for the other audiences toward which a professional firm directs its marketing energies. They include a professional firm's employees, suppliers and vendors, alumni, and even referral sources and other influencers. Of course, these non-client audiences are as important, but in a way that is less directly revenue-oriented.

If assigned priority in this manner, the activities directed at increasing perceived value, when directed by marketing and business development professionals, can more optimally support the other four phases of the Process Imperative. The expected outcomes are not to receive money and to directly deliver the firm's services. Instead, they may be to stimulate referrals, to increase the pool of candidates for hire, or to deepen the loyalty of suppliers.

In some sectors, efforts to increase perceived value have already become important elements of a firm's professional service marketing functions. In particular, selected firms in management consulting, law, and accounting have enjoyed measurable success in increasing their revenue and market share by formally marketing and developing business with alumni. In addition, a growing percentage of marketing programs now feature internal communications programs directed at employees.

Second, by creating a distinct spot in the Process Imperative for increasing the perceived value of the firm to all audiences, executive managers can more effectively communicate their belief that marketing and business development are everyone's responsibility. This is effective harnessing and integration at its best. Consider the procurement officer who now has a clearer notion that part of her job is to promote the firm's brand promise to the firm's vendors. Or the comptroller who now has a clearer notion that part of his job is to personally demonstrate the firm's brand promise to his accounts receivable counterparts at the companies with which his firm does business. Or the data entry associate who gets it that accuracy truly does increase the firm's favorable reputation.

The third reason why the "increasing perceived value" phase of the Process Imperative optimally harnesses and integrates a firm's marketing and business development functions is that this phase lends itself well to the growth of thought leadership equity. Later in this book, I will talk in greater detail about the Skills Imperative, but it's worth mentioning now, because thought leadership—the output of a person's intellectual capital —is not only developed in the context of clients. It is also developed in the context of other audiences—a firm's vendors or alumni, for example. The "increasing perceived value" phase, like no other in the Process Imperative, provides an avenue down which every person can grow his or her career and skills in a way that benefits the firm and all of its audiences. And because marketing or business development pros will be on hand to harness and direct this market-focused skills growth, a firm can become integrated even more effectively. (For a better idea of what I mean, see the detailed charts featured as tables B.2, B.3, and B.4 in appendix B.)

Chapter 6

The Skills Imperative

*The Skills Imperative addresses the marketing and business develop-
ment aspects of an individual's career advancement pathway and
working relationships in a professional service firm.*

*This chapter, and its accompanying templates in appendix B, outlines
the skills growth that a professional service firm should expect and
can support for revenue-generating practitioners (such as an accoun-
tant, engineer, lawyer, or management consultant) and nonrevenue-
generating marketing and business development professionals. It also
explores opportunities for collaboration, shared accountabilities, and
co-leadership on marketing and business development.*

■ ■ ■

By and large, professional service firms do very well at delivering value
to their clients. Most are excellent at supporting their revenue generators
(those people whose services actually make the firm's money) to become
more productive.

Just as many professional service firms employ stepwise process models
or nicely polished visuals to depict their marketing and selling tasks, so too
have many developed fairly defined stages through which their practitioners advance professionally. The titles assigned to these career levels differ
from industry to industry, but the idea remains the same: a person joins a
firm, successfully completes certain expected tasks, is promoted, and rises
in seniority within the firm.

The firm's executive managers set the benchmarks for their professionals to advance, and monitor each person's progress. In private firms, the
professional may eventually be offered a share of equity or voted into
partnership. These kinds of career advancement pathways also apply to
senior-level practitioners who join a firm from the outside. Many firms
depict these career advancement pathways visually, through a table or
chart that outlines the steps toward the next promotion.

I would like to see professional service firms move beyond practitioner-
exclusive growth pathways, creating competency pathways for professional
growth for everyone, even their support staff. By using a competency

model instead of a seniority or tenure model, professional firm executive managers can be clear about not only skill levels, but also expectations about integrated collaboration and shared accountabilities among a firm's revenue-generating practitioners and its nonrevenue-generating marketing and business development professionals.

A competency professional advancement model outlines clearly each person's responsibility and type of contribution in successfully implementing the firm's marketing, selling, and client service processes. It makes clear what is a **centralized marketing** function and what is not, and outlines for practitioners exactly where they should collaborate and share accountability and for what task.

I call this model the Skills Imperative. As summarized in tables B.2, B.3, and B.4 in appendix B, the Skills Imperative outlines an individual's career pathway as indelibly integrated with marketing and business development. And it highlights a professional service firm's explicit guidelines for skill growth regardless of whether the individual is a revenue-generating practitioner or administrative, marketing, or business development professional.

The Skills Imperative for Revenue-Generating Practitioners

Management consultants, executive recruiters, engineers, IT consultants, lawyers, among others—these are the practitioners whose expertise is being directly bought and "consumed" by the clients.

In contributing to marketing and business development, the skills growth and career advancement pathways of practitioners should be constructed to help them grow their abilities in two specific ways: first, by cooperating with and supporting the firm's *centralized* marketing and business development initiatives, and, second, by collaborating, sharing accountabilities, and co-leading **expertise-oriented marketing and business development**. Both paths offer vital ways to contribute to the firm's eventual market share and revenue growth.

What do I mean by *centralized*? Some marketing and business development functions are best managed or coordinated "centrally," that is, by an individual or focused team, on behalf of the broader enterprise. Functions that are optimally centralized include firm-wide targeting and segmentation, public and media relations, Web site management, brand management, account and relationship management, and the client relationship database.

Centralized marketing and business development makes sense because it clearly benefits the broadest assortment of individual experts who work at the enterprise. A combined database, a company-wide brand identity, a single media relations voice—centralizing allows, and even requires, every single person to focus on building his or her own intellectual capital and on optimally serving his or her clients. It's obvious. And the notion of centralized marketing and business development works, no matter what a firm's size or geographic reach. As soon as a firm grows from one person to two, it becomes vital to adopt marketing and business development strategies that benefit the enterprise rather than its individuals.

But *expertise-oriented* marketing, business development, and client service contributions are best implemented in a decentralized fashion. These activities stem from the individual's (or smaller group's) intellectual capital and direct client contact. But they can be easily supported and leveraged by the firm's internal communication avenues (a centralized function). Examples include publishing, speaking engagements, firm-sponsored seminars and events, sponsorships, business development appointment setting, relationship building, proposals, and, of course, project delivery.

Forging expertise-oriented marketing and business development pathways makes enormous sense for the professional enterprise. Consider the ever-evolving marketplace—clients' needs evolve; competitors make gains. So, too, should a practitioner's expertise. A professional firm must outline the promotion pathway for its revenue-generating people—the business world's answer to natural selection. And a professional's expertise growth must be tied to something bigger than the ability to bring in revenues (although that's critical). Practitioners need business and marketplace benchmarks for their skills growth, something directly connected to anticipating the needs of clients and to running a successful company. Without these benchmarks, their promotion pathway can become insular—that is, too similar to competing in a popularity contest or completing an arbitrary set of fraternity pledge tasks.

Table B.2 in appendix B offers a new look at how a professional firm could map out the growth of a practitioner's career and tie it to both expertise-oriented and centralized marketing and business development.[1] This model could be adapted to the discrete lines of business or practice areas for any professional sector, whether public or private. At each growth stage, I include specific examples of marketing skills levels or expectations. These skills growth charts could also be incorporated into performance review guidelines.

A detailed version of the skills growth matrix for marketing and business development professions appears in table B.3 and is described later in this chapter.

The Skills Growth Stages for Revenue-Generating Practitioners

To illustrate the Skills Imperative for practitioners, I will describe three typical stages in a practitioner's career growth: the newly minted associate, a midcareer practitioner, and an owner or senior-most (but practicing) executive manager. For each stage, I'll outline the ways in which PSFs or B2Bs could map out expectations for a person's skills in marketing and business development, external status, approach employed in marketing and business development, and externally perceived level of importance of the vehicle chosen.

Let's first imagine the skills level associated with the first rung on the practitioner career ladder—say, a research associate in a management consulting firm. For expertise-oriented marketing and business development, a research associate would be expected to collaborate with and to serve as part of a marketing and business development team. For centralized marketing and business development, a research associate would be expected, for example, to help gather local marketing and business development input into the creation or update of centralized marketing and business development strategies and tactics. A research associate's externally perceived status and recognized expertise would be minimal. His marketing and business development approach would be mainly reactive. His marketing and business development "level" would be targeted at entry-level marketing and business development opportunities, or those with very small or local distribution (tiers 3–4 in table B.2).

Now, let's look at the skills level of a midcareer senior associate in a management consulting firm. For expertise-oriented marketing and business development, a senior consultant would be expected to combine collaboration with mentoring in developing trusted relationships with clients, engendering strong confidence and credibility with outside publics, and building a good marketing or business development portfolio. For centralized marketing and business development, a senior consultant would also be expected, for example, to serve on internal committees to develop and shape strategies and their implementation and cooperate with the firm's marketing and business development professionals, acting as eyes and ears for the appropriate implementation of centralized marketing initiatives. Externally, she would be perceived as a recognized industry expert. This approach to marketing and business development would favor proactive measures and embrace appropriate opportunities. A senior consultant's marketing and business development "level" would be targeted at well-regarded but midlevel marketing and business development opportunities as well as smaller or regional distribution vehicles (tiers 2–3 in table B.2).

By the time this practitioner becomes an owner or executive manager of the firm, skills and expectations have peaked. For expertise-oriented marketing and business development, an executive manager is expected to continue to collaborate, but emphasize mentoring. She would be an industry influencer, thought leader, and rainmaker, and would develop new service offerings or service delivery approaches. For centralized marketing and business development, she would be expected to cooperate by, for example, providing input and advice to senior marketing and business development professionals on the creation and dissemination of firm-wide differentiation, positioning, and branding strategies, or providing support to marketing and business development professionals when needed (i.e., convincing colleagues to participate in centralized marketing projects). She also would be expected to champion compensation and rewards to support firm-wide marketing and business development strategies. Externally, she would be recognized as a "guru." Her marketing and business development approach would be highly proactive, and targeted toward the most highly regarded, most selective, and most widely distributed opportunities (tiers 1 and 2 and up in table B.2).

It's terribly important for the executive managers of a professional enterprise to reinforce the distinction between the "cooperate" and "collaborate, share accountability, and co-lead" pathways for marketing and business development skills growth. Although it's tempting to assume the terms are interchangeable, they are not. I chose them very intentionally.

The Skills Imperative calls for practitioners to "cooperate" on centralized marketing and business development functions. For these centralized functions, a firm's practitioners should not lead. They should rely on the expertise of their marketing and business development colleagues, who are professionals in these fields. Although practitioners should weigh in and add their voices to the enterprise's eventual adoption of, say, differentiation, positioning, and branding strategies, they should trust the wisdom of their marketing and business development leaders and advisors, whether in-house or outsourced providers. If the practitioners do not feel they can trust the expertise of their marketing and business development leaders, then they have not hired or supported the skills growth of the right people (there is more on this in the sections to come).

The Skills Imperative also calls for "collaborating, sharing accountability, mentoring, and co-leading" on expertise-oriented marketing and business development. For this pathway, by the time a practitioner reaches the senior consultant level, he or she should have fairly well-polished skills in researching the evolving environment of the client and the client's marketplace, developing cutting-edge service solutions, and business writing and speaking. Having a good marketing and business development portfolio means having measurable and tangible success in building the firm's thought leadership in its marketplace. Examples are publishing articles and making presentations in ever more selective publications and speaking venues, and creating new research agendas that showcase solutions the firm can then sell to its clients. All of these thought leadership initiatives push the outer edge of the individual's and the firm's collective intellectual capital.

Examples

These expertise-oriented initiatives are perfect avenues for internal mentoring among practitioners and for practitioners to work with their marketing and business development colleagues.

Take the hypothetical example of Ron, who works for a management consulting firm that has a nonrevenue-generating marketing and business development function. Ron has just been hired as an entry-level management consulting research associate. He is pleased to be approached by senior members of his practitioner team to assist with their practice area's annual research project. In team meetings, Ron is encouraged to make suggestions about improving the research questionnaire. Once the questionnaire is deployed, Ron works with more senior colleagues to analyze the data. From there, Ron helps draft the research report, subsequent articles, and speech slides for his senior colleagues. With guidance from his senior colleagues, Ron himself publishes some of the findings in the local newsletter of the professional association he's been encouraged to join. As for the firm's centralized marketing and business development, Ron attends the practice's annual business planning meetings, and he is encouraged to offer his views and to volunteer to contribute to upcoming initiatives.

As Ron is promoted to consultant and then to senior consultant, he continues to work closely with his practitioner colleagues, and increasingly with the firm's marketing and development team. By this point, Ron is well known internally for his leadership on certain cutting-edge pilot projects. He's been the lead author on a small but laudable number of published articles, which received broader distribution than those on which he worked as a research associate. Ron has also been the lead speaker for regional meetings of his professional association, as well as for the associations of some of his key clients. On each expertise-oriented initiative, Ron has worked with his practitioner mentors and his organization's marketing and business development leaders to ensure that he has pursued cutting-edge thought leadership. In every instance, Ron finds that his collaborations have pushed him toward more industry expertise and client credibility. He's even begun giving advice and assisting some of his firm's newer research associates.

Ron is now well positioned to be elected an equity shareholder. He is regularly sought after as a lead speaker at annual meetings of his clients' national trade groups; he is asked to lead many of his firm's most critical research programs (he plans to author several nationally important white papers); and, increasingly, the firm's senior-most marketing and business development professionals themselves are working with Ron to help create and sell truly forward-thinking client solutions.

Ron has now been an equity shareholder of his firm for several years. His name is well known among the firm's most important clients, and his reputation attracts other strategically important prospects. For his own professional association, Ron leads some of the committees that will shape the future of his profession. Ron has published a book, and he is in demand as a keynote speaker. He is sought after internally to help shape his firm's future marketing strategies.

Here is an example from the "Effectiveness" study of how the Skills Imperative might work in a law firm. This example was provided by Patrick Lamb, who was then a partner at Butler Rubin Saltarelli & Boyd, a

Chicago-based litigation boutique with a national reputation in the core practice areas of reinsurance and complex business litigation.[2]

At the time, the firm was spending 4 percent of its gross revenues on its total marketing budget. It tracked the number of disputes brought to the firm, the size of these disputes in terms of revenue, and the percentage of work each client gave the firm.

Under the firm's personalized marketing plan, in year 1 every partner was given a certain number of base points (a guaranteed income) plus discretionary points. Butler Rubin's executive managers placed four to seven of the base points at risk as a potential "bonus" (the four to seven point range was chosen because it had proven to be enough of an incentive). Partners not making measurable progress on their annual marketing plans could not win these bonus points, and thus risked losing $30,000–$40,000. In year 2 of the marketing plan, if a partner did not qualify to receive at least half of the bonus points potentially available, the gate to the discretionary bonus was closed. This failure represented a potential six-figure monetary loss. If the partner did not perform in year 3, he or she would not be able to remain with the firm.

Lamb was quoted in the study as saying, "Culture change requires both a stick and a carrot. The carrot alone did not work for us. When we added the stick, we were able to accomplish a lot." The Butler Rubin example is a good one for two reasons. First, it required law firm partners to sketch out their intended marketing and business development plans. Everyone knew—and could depend on—each person's intended contribution. Although Lamb's comments don't serve as explicit evidence of a career advancement pathway, it's obvious what executive managers expected, and that these expectations rose incrementally. Second, Butler Rubin's structure—in which each person created a personal marketing plan tied to achievement hurdles—lent itself well to both expertise-oriented and centralized marketing and business development.

Expectations for incremental professional growth, and a firm's formal support for it, are also becoming more prevalent in accounting firms. One of our "Effectiveness" study respondents remarked, "Our managers are required to network." Networking depends on marketing and business development initiatives, and this respondent's remark implies that by the time they are required to network, managers have gained enough networking skills to conduct the appropriate initiatives successfully. As another example, in 2007 I was engaged by a top-tier U.S.-based accounting firm to help it launch its new networking program for partners. The firm created a process for accounting partners to follow and internal communication assistance to help partners as they worked toward success.

This accounting firm's program also featured a training component that was designed to support partners as they gained skills incrementally, and was tied to their achievement of specific stages. With the new networking program, the firm, for the first time in its 80-year history, made explicit its expectations that practitioners would collaborate and share accountabilities with the firm's extensive marketing and business development staff.

It's up to the executive managers of professional firms to create the structure and culture that make this kind of skills growth possible. The vast majority of professional firms "get it" that practitioners must increase their competence in selling business. Many firms have a very well-defined compensation and rewards framework for business development. And even if they don't offer their own training programs in selling, many firms offer their practitioners the opportunity to attend outside classes.

I'd like to see executive managers take the same approach toward the skills growth pathway for their practitioners. By driving their firm to use at least some version of the Skills Imperative, executive managers can better direct the growth of their practitioners' intellectual capital to stay abreast of clients' needs and ahead of competitors. Executive managers can also more effectively direct their practitioners to support the firm's centralized marketing initiatives. As they typically do with business development, they would offer rewards and incentives (which represent structural support to encourage progress toward meeting the firm's marketing expectations).

By means of explicit skills growth goals and advancement pathways, every individual would be better able to succeed personally and professionally in integrating marketing and business development.

The Skills Imperative for Nonrevenue-Generating Marketing and Business Development Professionals

Executive managers can lead their firms toward greater market share, revenues, and value for clients if they undertake a second critical aspect of the Skills Imperative: creating formal frameworks for collaboration, shared accountabilities, and co-leadership between practitioners and nonrevenue-generating marketers and business developers.

Now we will consider how the same model I introduced earlier for practitioners could be used to map out the career advancement, skills growth, and shared accountabilities of marketing and business development professionals. This template, which appears in table B.3 of appendix B, could be adapted to any size professional enterprise, regardless of sector or corporate structure and incorporated into performance review guidelines.

The three typical stages in a marketer's or business developer's career growth are the newly minted professional, the midcareer professional, and the chief marketing or business development officer. I'll outline the way a professional firm could map out expectations for skills, the external status that should be captured by each level, the approach to be used, and the level of importance of the vehicle employed.

The Skills Growth Stages for Marketing and Business Development Professionals

Let's consider the skills growth of a management consulting firm's new marketing coordinator—someone who is at the very beginning of her career. For expertise-oriented marketing and business development, she would be expected to collaborate as part of a team on tasks such as proofreading press releases or proposals and assisting with sponsored events. For centralized marketing and business development, she would focus on implementation by, for example, updating contacts databases and monitoring the firm's local adherence to brand image standards. Her perceived external status would likely be minimal; she might attend local meetings of her firm's industry association. She would also have minimal exposure to her internal clients (the management consultants)—such as taking notes at business development meetings. Her marketing and business development approach would be mainly reactive and aimed at entry-level opportunities.

Let's assume this coordinator has grown her skills and has been promoted to the level of director. For expertise-oriented marketing and business development, she would focus on managing projects such as media relations strategies or geographic sales strategies, managing some aspects of the firm's innovation initiatives, or establishing a relationship with key clients. For centralized initiatives, she might manage an upgrade of the firm's Web site, manage research for proposals, or lead vendor selection for the firm's new brand strategy. She would have achieved clear externally recognized expertise among her industry's marketing and business development peers, perhaps serving on a committee of the management consulting industry association. She would have strong exposure to her firm's management consultants. Her approach to her function would blend a proactive outlook and opportunism, and would be targeted at well-regarded but midlevel marketing and business development opportunities. For example, she might start her own blog or speak on business development at regional association meetings.

By the time this marketing director becomes a chief marketing or business development officer, she would be expected to be an equity owner and perhaps a member of the firm's executive committee. For expertise-oriented marketing and business development, she would lead the firm's entire expertise-oriented marketing and business development program, ensuring the best integration possible. Examples might include overseeing and guiding practitioners' integrated pursuit of thought leadership and selling strategies, or leading the firm's market, client, and competitor research, and initiating new strategies where none had existed before. She would have relationships with a broad cross section of the firm's key clients and prospects. She would lead the optimization of the firm's service portfolio and service delivery. For centralized marketing and business development, she would lead, ensure the continuous improvement of, and initiate new aspects of the firm's entire centralized marketing and business development program. She would serve as internal champion of integrating the firm's expertise-oriented and centralized marketing and business development initiatives.

By this time in her career, she would be an acknowledged service marketing guru—a voice of influence among her peers in the industry. For example, she'd be widely sought after for contributions to books and high-end articles, and she'd be a well-known speaker on professional service marketing strategies. Her marketing and business development approach would be highly proactive, and targeted to the most highly regarded, most selective, and most widely distributed marketing and business development opportunities.

The Optimal Function of Marketing and Business Development

In discussing the skills growth of marketing and business development professionals, I have chosen to employ the terms "lead" and "mentor" quite deliberately, because when it comes to marketing and selling intellectual capital, practitioners are able to grow their firms' market share and revenues more effectively if they cede some control and leadership to their marketing and business development professionals.

I am not saying that architects, executive search consultants, or IT consultants (to name a few) are not—or cannot learn how to be—expertise-oriented marketers and business developers. I'm simply making a point about the *optimal* function and structural placement of marketing and business development. Even for smaller enterprises, these functions are too important to be led only by part-time practitioners. Certainly, there is the argument that client-facing practitioners are closest to the market. But for expertise-oriented, "one-to-many" marketing strategies, it's time for these initiatives to be led by professional career marketers and business developers.

This point also applies to centralized marketing and business development. For these activities, because they are "one-to-many" oriented, I recommend that professional marketers and business developers take the lead.

Chapter 7

The Support Imperative

This chapter outlines the Support Imperative, a framework that enables the most advantageous functional integration of a professional firm's marketing and business development with its other important administrative functions. This chapter makes the case that if executive managers formalize their expectations for marketing and business development collaboration, shared accountabilities, and co-leadership in these areas, these functions can offer more compelling contributions to a firm's achievement of its growth goals than they do currently. The details of the Support Imperative are outlined in five tables in appendix B.

■ ■ ■

Human resources, information technology, legal, finance, training, facilities management — these and a few other functions, together with marketing and business development, comprise a professional or B2B service firm's administrative operations. Like many of their counterparts in other industries, such as manufacturing or retail, professional firms often think of their administration as "back of the house" or support functions.

A sizable number of professional service marketing and business development professionals accept this characterization of their functions. Not surprisingly, though, if one's function is considered in such a marginal way, it can easily be perceived as making a less than valuable contribution to the fortunes of the enterprise. It is no wonder, then, that an increasing number of PSF and B2B marketing and business development professionals are trying to increase their functional value by partnering with their colleagues in human resources (HR), information technology, finance, legal, and more.

As I prepared to write this book chapter, I sought input from some leading services marketers, business developers, and business consultants about how well marketing and business development functions integrate with a professional firm's administration functions. Typically, especially in very large firms, the answer was a collective "Very well!"

Anecdotal evidence supports this enthusiasm. Today, many of my clients nod affirmatively when I mention the general trend of trying to consolidate the activities of support functions, and connecting them to the overall firm strategy.

I can recount many specific real-life examples, too. In a recent conversation with me on the topic of professional service firm administration and marketing integration, one national-level marketer characterized his working relationship with his firm's human resources group as warm and cooperative. He described instances in which members of the HR team asked for his help on developing language for recruiting brochures, and, of course, he made time to help them out. I heard from another regional marketing leader about the good relationship he had with his firm's chief human resources officer, who made it an occasional practice to attend the firm's internal marketing team meetings. An accounting firm marketing leader told me she and her IT counterpart had a fantastic relationship; the IT director didn't mind at all when this marketer stopped by her office unannounced. They brainstormed regularly on issues in which marketing and technology intersected. There's also evidence emerging from other sectors that influence the professional and business-to-business service arena (telecommunications, in particular) about new best practices for partnering between administration, marketing, and sales.

I have seen similar enthusiasm for teamwork and internal partnership manifested by the executive managers of professional firms, but not nearly so visibly, perhaps because the executive management function of professional service firms is itself quite young. Most executive managers are still learning about their roles and functions. One might reasonably ask exactly what *are* the optimal structures and cultural norms for the executive management function in a professional service firm? Arguably, executive management itself is an administrative function.

David Maister, author of *Strategy and the Fat Smoker*, said it best in a January 2008 "Management Consulting News" interview about his book:

> Managers are good at holding everyone else accountable, but it's the rare firm that has articulated clear performance skills and standards for its managers, and has built in systems to hold them accountable for performing the role effectively. The book has some suggestions as to how this can be done. The reaction of most professional firm managers has been one of horror—"You mean you're going to ask people how well they think I'm doing in my role?" Well, yes—why should you be excluded from accountability?[1]

Now that statement truly makes the point about integration, doesn't it? For most administrative jobs, it is made clear exactly how individuals should perform the job for that particular function. But even with the increasing use of performance management systems that encourage general cross-functional cooperation, these functions are not typically cast in the light of client value or marketplace gains.

But isn't it simply good general business practice to ensure that every professional—even support staff—has a formal job description outlining how they can better integrate their contributions to marketing and selling effectiveness?

Of course, it is. But until now, the executive managers of professional firms have not developed a formal structure that addresses this question.

I advise professional firms to adopt—and adapt—the concept I've labeled the Support Imperative. The Support Imperative suggests guidelines for an administrative person's leadership, co-leadership, or assistance with critical steps along the marketing and business development process. (Tables B.4 through B.9 in appendix B provide a visual summary of these guidelines.)

Guidelines for Contributions to Marketing and Business Development

Executive managers can employ the Support Imperative in two ways. First, they can recast administrative functions for more active collaboration, sharing of accountabilities, and co-leadership on marketing and business development. Second, they can review each step of the Process Imperative and make explicit the ways in which each support area can be integrated with marketing and business development processes.

An Administrative Function's General Contributions to Marketing and Business Development

Here we consider ways to reconfigure each administrative function to generally contribute to marketing and business development in ways that are obvious or unambiguous. The executive managers of professional service firms should expect their marketing and business development function to lead the organization in two iterative ways by

- Developing and managing the implementation of revenue, client, and market share growth strategies and tactics for direct and indirect marketing and business development for the firm, practices, service lines, industries, geographies, and individual practitioners.

- Measuring the effectiveness of these strategies and tactics and incorporating findings into the development, management, and implementation of future strategies and tactics.

Beyond this leadership responsibility, marketing and business development professionals should co-lead or assist in general marketplace growth initiatives with their administration colleagues. For example, marketing and business development could co-lead with human resources on the development of skills training programs for all professionals. Marketing and business development also could assist HR in developing change management initiatives designed to increase the firm's marketing and business development effectiveness.

Similarly, marketing and business development functions could co-lead or assist other administrative functions in any firm-wide initiative that generally contributes to optimizing centralized and expertise-oriented marketing and business development strategies and tactics.

Executive managers should make a similar review of general ways in which a professional service firm's well-recognized support functions could contribute to optimal centralized and expertise-oriented marketing strategies and tactics. For example,

- IT functions could take the lead in creating, monitoring, and maintaining IT strategies and systems to support the implementation of any and all marketing and business development strategies and tactics.

- HR functions could take the lead in developing, monitoring, revising, and shifting the firm's recruiting, hiring, orientation, retention, and career advancement programs toward building a staff of talented market-driven professionals. HR also could lead in developing, monitoring, and revising job descriptions, reporting relationships, and pursuing collaboration, shared accountabilities, and co-leadership of all marketing and business development–related initiatives. HR could lead as well (with executive managers) in developing, monitoring, and revising all marketing and business development–related training programs and internal cultural change initiatives.

- Finance functions could lead in developing, revising, and monitoring financial analysis tools to support marketing and business development strategies and tactics. Finance could also co-lead with marketing and business development the creation, monitoring, protection, and maximization of all marketing and business development budgets.

- Legal functions could take the lead in ensuring that the professional service firm is legally protected in all of its marketing and business development strategies and tactics.

Other nonrevenue-generating administrative functions, like facilities management or professional development, also can be reconfigured to generally contribute leadership or co-leadership to the enterprise's achievement of marketplace gains.

An Administrative Function's *Specific* Leadership Contributions to Marketing and Business Development Processes

There are specific ways that administrative functions can contribute to a professional firm's go-to-market processes, as I outlined in my discussion about the Process Imperative. In mapping out this part of the Support Imperative (see tables B.5 through B.9 of appendix B), I looked at each Process Imperative step to identify unambiguous ways in which each administrative area might share accountabilities or co-leadership with marketing and business development.

In some firms (especially smaller ones), practitioners carry part-time administrative responsibilities; in other firms, administrative functions are implemented by nonrevenue-generating professionals. To ensure that the Support Imperative would work for any PSF or B2B, I looked at *what should be done* to more effectively grow market share, increase the "right" revenues, and provide more value to clients, *not who's doing it now*. I also looked at each Process Imperative step that the function of marketing and business development itself could lead, co-lead, or assist.

From these considerations, and for executive managers who desire specificity regarding the potential changes in their administrative professionals' scope of activities, I developed a set of detailed templates for the way administrative functions could lead, co-lead, or assist with each step of the Process Imperative. These potential contributions could be adapted to any size professional enterprise, regardless of sector or corporate structure.

My objective in developing these detailed templates was to unveil the obvious: a professional firm's administrative functions can be integrated into marketing and business development, if executive managers make it clear what they have in mind. Integrating administrative support into a professional firm's go-to-market processes may be as simple as outlining the activities and responsibilities desired, inserting those desired activities and responsibilities into the administrator's job description, and measuring the individual's performance of those activities.

Marketing: The Designated Driver of Integration

Even though executive managers are the overall leaders of PSFs and B2Bs, the senior-most leaders of marketing and business development should co-lead with them as the drivers of integrating the Process Imperative, the Skills Imperative, and the Support Imperative. Together, they should be on constant lookout for techniques and strategies that could more effectively harness every function to achieve a positive marketing and business development outcome.

Where might such opportunities exist? What follows is an actual example of how a marketing leader integrated his function with finance. This example, from my April 2008 "administration collaboration" survey, offers compelling evidence of the benefits of applying formal structures (in this case, dashboard reporting) and cultural methods:

> The bi-monthly Marketing Meetings that I established for each of our Practice Groups six years ago have evolved (via my invitation) to regularly include our CEO, CFO and COO. These meetings are now designated as Practice Group Business meetings and are viewed as an integral part of our planning and management toolkit. They are still managed by the Marketing Department.
>
> I also created a monthly Marketing Report over seven years ago. This report has evolved over the years to the point where it has become a true "dashboard" for the firm's status. This 7-page Executive Summary, still managed by Marketing, includes Bookings and Revenue Goals and current Status; Projects Awarded and Lost YTD and for the previous month; the Firm's Hit rate (by #'s and $); Current Receivables; Marketing Activity YTD and for the previous month tracked by number of proposals and $ value; 5-Year Market Sector Performance Trend by $ and % booked; Bookings and Revenue and Profitability Summary shown by Team, Practice Group, and Firm Totals; and a Schedule Reminder of In-house and External meetings and events for the next two months.[2]

This particular firm built a strong springboard from which to pursue further integration. Beyond this step, though, what should this firm's senior-most marketing leader do? Perhaps she could develop a new tracking structure with the firm's leader of human resources to create a dashboard that monitors the achievement of performance benchmarks in publishing thought leadership articles, white papers, speeches, and research. Or, as described in the R.W. Beck case study featured in chapter 11, she could co-create with her executive managers and HR colleagues a new skills growth and performance management program that ties career advancement to the achievement of objective marketing and business development goals. Or she could develop her firm's customized version of the Support Imperative template.

The following "administration collaboration" survey comment describes how another professional service firm has taken steps to integrate its administrative functions with its marketing and business development functions. Take special notice of the informal "work closely with" and "collaboration" language.

> In the last three years, we have reallocated our efforts towards activities that most closely benefit and serve our clients' needs and expectations. Our Practice Development and Business Development and marketing personnel are all part of the same organization and work together. We have a strong working relationship with our Finance department personnel and worked jointly with Finance and IT to design Information Systems that allow us to better understand our clients and share information on a more timely basis.
>
> We also work closely with HR and Recruiting in hiring, evaluating and counseling staff. What we have done is not novel or new. It is a radical application of common sense that needs to be applied each day. We could not succeed without collaboration, the cultural glue, and we have succeeded.[3]

This respondent pointed out that the firm's marketing and business development function had already worked with IT counterparts to "better understand our clients and share information on a more timely basis." What might be the opportunities for further integration here? Perhaps it would be, as in the previous example, to create a well-recognized dashboard that tracks shifts in client buying patterns for particular services or links loyalty research findings to retention and cross-selling results.

Chapter 8

How the Integration Imperative Can Benefit Professional Firms — and Their Clients

When the executive managers of professional and business-to-business service firms assess the viability of leading their organizations through significant changes, they rightfully ask themselves whether that endeavor will significantly advance their goals — and their ability to help clients advance theirs. (Anything less than "yes" is an unacceptable waste of resources.)

This chapter describes how the Integration Imperative's structural models and cultural approaches offer professional and business-to-business service firms advantages on two fronts: internal and external.

■ ■ ■

Executive managers continually assess the threats and opportunities that face their enterprises. Whether it's with their partners in a privately held enterprise or their senior colleagues in a public company, their mandate is to weigh the benefits and risks of investing resources in making changes that might help achieve the organization's goals. At each decision juncture, executive managers consider the trade-offs of investing in the improvements they contemplate: if we undertake *this* effort and commit *those* resources, will it make a positive difference in our revenues? Our market share? Our advantage over competitors? And of course, the biggest question: will the effort we're contemplating benefit our clients?

There are multiple and compelling benefits of establishing the structural frameworks and leading the cultural changes I've outlined in *The Integration Imperative*. They can be simply grouped, though, into two areas. The first benefit generally addresses the firm's internal advantages, and relates to its own growing revenues, expanding market share, prevailing over rivals, and recruiting and retaining talented people.

The second area focuses externally, on those benefits that clients can directly observe from firms that have embraced the structural models and cultural approaches of the Integration Imperative. These benefits center on the greater probability that clients will enjoy better value propositions—and service delivery—and that they will simply find it easier and more enjoyable to do business with firms that have adopted the Integration Imperative, instead of with firms that haven't.

The Internal Benefits of the Integration Imperative

The internal benefits of the Integration Imperative loom large.

Integration knocks down the functional silos in marketing, business development, and client service.

On the most tactical level, the Integration Imperative addresses the many functional and cultural disconnects that have crept into the marketing and business development programs and individual working relationships of most professional service firms. It reveals how well an enterprise is (or more likely, isn't) focusing on real market share growth. It encourages executive managers to make deliberate decisions about how they would like their firm's professionals to prioritize their marketing and business development engines and client service methods. It focuses executive managers on reviewing, redefining, and reidentifying the firm's most strategically important clients. Each element—Process, Skills, and Support—requires a fresh look at its juxtaposition with the others.

Its cultural elements, outlining a firm's newly shared accountabilities and more explicit expectations about how everyone can contribute, provide executive managers with an early warning system when new disconnects crop up. By adopting the Integration Imperative, executive managers can have the benefit of a new springboard from which to lead their organizations toward real marketplace progress.

Integration is comprehensive.

The tactical level is only the tip of the iceberg. On the structural side, the combined three imperatives—Process, Skills, and Support—effectively address the broadest aspects of every person's involvement in growing the firm. These imperatives are comprehensive, featuring a marketing and business development role within every function. If you are a particularly visual person, think of the imperatives this way: the Process Imperative addresses the left-to-right orientation of the marketing-to-business development handoffs; the Skills Imperative addresses the top-to-bottom orientation of practitioners and their nonrevenue-generating colleagues; and the Support Imperative addresses the diagonal orientation of administrative professionals working across functional lines.

The Integration Imperative is, in fact, something of a three-dimensional construct, because the imperative's cultural underpinnings bring its functional elements to life. The three imperatives — as structures — provide clearly delineated pathways for deeper and broader processes, professional skills growth, and administrative support. They create the scaffolding, if you will, for everyone to be held accountable, in more visible ways than ever before, for the organization's marketplace success. And there are more expansive opportunities for purposeful collaboration. By using the Integration Imperative, professional and B2B service firms can avoid implementing marketing and business development in a piecemeal fashion.

Integration improves innovation.

From a purely management perspective, the Integration Imperative benefits professional enterprises because it stimulates a new focus on innovation. Especially regarding the skills required to market, sell, and serve clients, it calls the question on how well the firm supports the growth of intellectual capital. It also directs PSFs and B2Bs to spend more time examining their best value propositions for their clients, both for the present and for the future. (We already know that, traditionally, professional firms have underfunded innovation endeavors.) The combined structural and cultural Integration Imperative engines will give executive managers a formal framework for more astutely managing their firm's intellectual capital and service portfolios.

The Integration Imperative also brings new opportunities to make substantive marketplace gains and to compete as effectively as possible. Even if the constructs or cultural principles are embraced incrementally, they offer professional and business-to-business service firms renewed clarity on the marketplace.

Integration is demonstrable.

Because they are organizational structures, the three imperatives are easily demonstrable. They can be shown, discussed, reviewed, and refined as the organization's needs change. Executive managers and individuals can easily see both the big picture and the smaller steps of each imperative.

Executive managers also would find it fairly easy to clarify the organization's goals related to those skills that could enable the enterprise to achieve tomorrow's marketplace gains. Whether it is practitioners, marketers, business developers, client service professionals, or administrators, the structural frameworks of the Integration Imperative are easily identifiable. Individuals — with their teammates and supervisors — can benefit from an open view of each other's pathways toward greater expertise and career advancement goals.

The Integration Imperative is also demonstrable from a cultural perspective, although it must be backed up by functional frameworks. For example, executive managers who wish to articulate a new meaning of marketing and business development for the enterprise could publish a customized firm-wide glossary of terms. If they wish to increase collaboration, shared accountability, and co-leadership, they could demonstrate their commitment to these cultural principles by directing the preparation of revised job descriptions or reporting relationships, a new set of staged bonus opportunities, or modified performance management guidelines.

Integration is flexible.

The three imperatives are flexible. Under the Process Imperative, executive managers can easily assign or change priorities from one function to another. For example, year 1 in a strategic plan may require a focus on *retaining* strategically appropriate clients. Another year may require an emphasis on *acquiring* strategically appropriate clients. (Some firms even assign percentages — adding up to 100 percent — or weights to these steps, and adjust them yearly.)

The stepwise competencies and career advancement pathways of the Skills Imperative are also malleable. For example, a real estate service firm wants to incorporate a new facilities management capability. The executive managers of this firm can retool their skills growth goals for marketers and business developers in order to help them work toward gaining a business purview and added acumen about this new service offering. This is also true for the Support Imperative; it is possible to tweak shared accountabilities and co-leadership between administrative functions.

Another aspect of the flexibility of the three imperatives is their applicability to any professional service firm, regardless of its size, annual revenues, or geographic reach. Just like any structural framework, these models are scalable. In small firms that have only a few partners and no marketing director, fee earners perform the functions themselves. In large firms that have nonpractitioner marketers, business developers, or client relationship managers, the functions can be carved into smaller chunks, reporting up through the organization to the chief marketing, business development, or client service officer. Any of these functions could become more effective in building revenues and serving clients by measuring improvements in their collaboration with their outsourced or internally managed administrative functions.

For sectors in which client engagements are implemented through a variety of roles (project managers versus principals in charge, as in the architectural, engineering, and construction sectors), the Integration Imperative's functional guidelines are still assignable to people in different roles.

The Integration Imperative also works across professional sectors, regardless of each sector's historical approach to marketing, business development, or client service. For those professions that traditionally have eschewed a strongly overt approach to selling, the Process Imperative provides an appropriate foundation to approach selling through a relationship management orientation. Also, if a particular sector relies on its own traditional role for marketing or business development, the Process Imperative affords a renewed exploration of more effective deployment.

Integration is measurable.

As organizational constructs, the Process, Skills, and Support Imperatives lend themselves well to quantitative and qualitative measurement. They also encourage strategic prioritization of resources. For example, in dealing with their firms' go-to-market processes, executive managers, marketers, and business developers already employ a wide variety of tactically oriented quantitative measurements. They track the number of leads, number of proposals, and how these relate to the number of projects they've won. They may also measure the loyalty scores of clients they'd like to retain.

The Process Imperative encourages them to add to the list of measurements, including pricing sensitivity levels, changes in client buying behavior, clients' attraction to brand promises, or the depth of influence that alumni have on those who make purchasing decisions. For the Skills Imperative, for example, executive managers can assess how much they have reduced the turnover of their marketing and business development professionals. In another example, executive managers can evaluate the levels of accountability sharing between practitioners and the firm's nonrevenue-generating professionals. For the Support Imperative, executive managers can track the achievement of project goals as administrative professionals and marketing colleagues co-lead on specific internal assignments.

A measurement examination of the Skills Imperative enables a frank discussion about the perceived value of marketing and business development to the professional enterprise. For too long, and perhaps because of the way in which they've disconnected marketing and business development from practitioner functions, professional firms have been critical of the impact of marketing. If they put in place well-integrated skills growth pathways for both practitioners and their marketing and business development colleagues, executive managers can avoid the unfortunate practice of reducing marketing or business development staff during economic recessions. Return-on-investment benchmarks would already be in place, tied to the increasing responsibilities of the marketing and business development professional. Moreover, return-on-investment expectations would no longer be shouldered mainly by the nonrevenue-generating professionals of the firm.

The Support Imperative suggests compelling ways that each administrative function can add value to a professional or business-to-business service firm's marketing and business development strategies and tactics. And it's no more challenging to include these guidelines in a person's job description, reporting relationships, or performance management review than what they already have now. It's just an updated way to drive the business forward.

Just the act of taking a good look at a firm's administrative functions gives executive managers a valuable opportunity to reharness and reshape these support functions so they are more dynamic partners throughout the firm. Reengaged administrative professionals can benefit the enterprise not only by more effectively managing their function's costs, but also by ensuring that expenditures connect with marketplace results.

Integration is customizable.

The Integration Imperative templates I've featured in appendix B are not how-to cookie-cutter models; rather they are designed to be guidelines.

Executive managers can add or collapse steps in the Process Imperative, tweaking the handoffs to suit their particular enterprise goals. In the Support Imperative, they can shape the mix, level, and depth of shared accountabilities.

Customization is particularly beneficial when considering the Skills Imperative. In the Skills Imperative, executive managers can individualize the competencies and career advancement pathways that best suit their firm. Many professional service firm managers have already embraced responsibility for helping their practitioners improve their selling skills, and have developed customized training programs so that practitioners can develop business and cross-sell the firm's services. They should do the same for their marketing functions, regardless of whom they ask to undertake those functions. They should do so for client service functions too.

Marketers and business developers will also have to continue to make the case for learning customized new skills that could deepen their strategic impact on the firm. "I don't know how to analyze quantitative data statistically, and I know this skill would be valuable to the company. Will you reimburse me for taking a class to gain this expertise?" The same idea applies to any kind of expanded skill set a marketer or business developer should bring to a professional enterprise—and that maps well against the Process and the Support Imperatives.

Such a request for new skills is best made in the context of taking on new job responsibilities. We've already seen how many professional or B2B service marketers and business developers map out their own growth trajectories. But such mapping should be done in collaboration with the firm's executive managers and, if available, in partnership with a professional association that has laid out the career pathway to some extent, much like the Society for Marketing Professional Services did with its certification program.

The Skills Imperative also would be valuable to professional firms because it thwarts the temptation to advance a career through a quantity benchmark rather than a quality benchmark. Too often, professionals in marketing and business development—and their executive managers—fall prey to the temptation to add more and more tasks to the list of responsibilities. Even if the added job scope is more strategic and value-added in nature, professional service marketers and business developers too easily give in to the "I can do this, too" mindset. The Skills Imperative offers an objective way to address the quantity versus quality issue, in a way that also allows a discussion of equity ownership by marketers or business developers.

Customization also applies to the Integration Imperative's cultural norms. Although I talk about the "professional service sector" in broad terms, I am mindful of the wide differences between each particular industry within it, and the varying levels of marketplace maturity in which each industry conducts business. Nevertheless, the three cultural standards of the Integration Imperative allow each enterprise within each sector to cast its own organizational imprint. The Integration Imperative's cultural guidelines can be adapted to any enterprise, no matter its history, founding philosophies, or tenure in the marketplace.

Integration improves marketing and business development effectiveness.

In summary, the internal benefits of the Integration Imperative are compelling. It's no accident that marketers and business developers continually seek ways to increase their functional effectiveness. And it's no accident that the executive managers of professional and B2B service firms characterize their quest for market share growth in terms that sound like the fruitless and never-ending search for the Holy Grail.

The structural models of the Integration Imperative, combined with its compelling cultural principles, may in fact be the logical and potent context that everyone has been seeking. Not only does it present the tactical benefits of erasing marketing and business development silos, but it also, on a strategic level, frames a new forward-thinking meaning for marketing and business development. It allows growth for every individual and the greater possibility of participating in profits or shared equity. And it promotes new working connections between people and functions, fostering a new sense of purpose and teamwork to achieve growth to which all have contributed. Even for large enterprises, the Integration Imperative offers the exciting advantages of entrepreneurism.

The External Benefits of the Integration Imperative

Now we will focus on the external benefits—those that clients perceive—of a PSF's or B2B firm's embrace of the Integration Imperative. I've gathered new evidence that most professional firms believe their efforts to break down functional silos between marketing and business development result in real benefits to their clients. In the last of my Integration Imperative online surveys (hereafter the "Integration Benefits" study), conducted in May 2008, a nearly unanimous group declared that their clients directly benefit from integrated marketing and business development.[1] The benefits they cited fell into three categories.

Integration helps create a better client value proposition.

According to the survey respondents, the biggest benefit of integration was that it allows them to create a better value proposition for their clients. Respondents said their enterprises develop more innovative solutions for clients when they integrate marketing and business development and ensure market-focused connections among everyone in the firm. The ideas are simply more potent and forward thinking, and the intellectual capital is more compelling and relevant. Respondents also pointed out that integrating marketing and business development functions helps their firms consistently develop, implement, and communicate their differentiation and brand strategies.

Integration fosters a better understanding of client needs.

The second benefit of integration cited by respondents was a "better understanding of clients." By combining structural models and supporting them with cultural principles, these professional firms said they can better anticipate their clients' emerging needs. Integration fosters more direct processes for capturing client feedback. And there's more astute listening to clients, accompanied by more awareness of their choices. Also, referencing their own internal productivity, the "Integration Benefits" study respondents noted that integration could help them "cut down on the amount of imagining that many of us have to do when trying to 'get into the customer's head.'"[2]

Integration promotes better service delivery.

A third benefit of integration was "better service delivery." As one respondent noted, integration fosters a more holistic view of the relationship between clients and the firm:

> A better quality service delivery to the PSF's client is often the end result of a better value proposition or solution for the client. Erasing functional silos eradicates barriers to internal communication at PSFs. If internal

PSF communications are clear and direct, it paves the way for an improvement in communications with the client during project planning, and in [the project's] deliverables.[3]

Another "Integration Benefits" participant remarked, "Erasing the silos prevents the likelihood that marketing will over promise something that the delivery team cannot accomplish." This respondent's remark speaks volumes about one of the biggest disconnects between practitioners and nonrevenue-generating marketing and business development teams. Experienced marketers and business developers in professional service firms will certainly recognize the situation: a senior practitioner returns from a proposal meeting, having promised the prospect an unrealistic level of service delivery. The marketing and business development team is then faced with an untenable choice—jeopardizing their honesty, and eventually the company's reputation, by supporting the practitioner's unrealistic promises, or challenging the authority of the practitioner, forcing him to renege on promises he made to the potential client.

By offering the benefits of clearer accountability and co-leadership connections between practitioners and their marketing, business development, or administrative colleagues, the Integration Imperative helps professional and business-to-business service firms avoid this kind of situation.

The two remarks just noted also touch on the advantages presented by the Process Imperative, with its emphasis on client and account management. Respondents commented:

Erasing these functional silos, when properly done, improves communication within the PSF, leading to a clear focus on targeted clients and services. With Marketing and BD functions on the same page, the firm's energies are directed toward the client in a way that can benefit both the bricks and mortar and financial outcomes of any project.

Marketing and BD are also services to clients and should provide the direct feedback loop needed to tell us if clients are satisfied; if we are making good on our promises; if our marketing claims accurately reflect our performance and the client's experiences.

Marketing and business development are meant to support client service. Both functions work together to better understand what clients want and need and communicate that understanding to lawyers.[4]

The Biggest Benefit of the Integration Imperative

Many professional firms are undertaking improvement initiatives like the Integration Imperative in order to better serve their own interests and those of their clients. In this chapter, I've outlined the many ways in which the structures and cultural principles of the Integration Imperative can benefit professional and business-to-business service firms. Each singular point stands on its own.

But the biggest benefit lies in the hope, enthusiasm, and plain old-fashioned energy that's created when executive managers give their organizational backing to efforts to connect people to a market-focused purpose. Clients feel these benefits as well. I've interviewed hundreds of clients in my work with professional and B2B service firms. They tell me they are deeply impressed by—and prefer to work with—service companies that demonstrate their commitment to excellence in business and marketplace practices.

Moreover, clients *want* to work with service firms that work toward marketing and business development effectiveness. They know real integration when they see it—and they prefer it, especially over the alternatives.

The next section describes how the Integration Imperative is being implemented in 11 professional and business-to-business service companies, from small to enormous, representing nearly a dozen sectors. The stories are compelling, even if some of the firms I've presented have yet to demonstrate quantifiable marketplace results. In each case, there's a sense of purpose, forward momentum, and an anticipation of mutual benefit.

The Integration Imperative Can and Does Work!

Read this section . . .

- If you benefit from reading about how real firms from a variety of professional and business-to-business service sectors realized their marketing and business development functional silos, and decided to work toward erasing them,
- If you find it helpful to read about how professional firms created their marketing, business development, and client service integration structural frameworks and cultural paradigms, or
- If you just like reading stories.

■ ■ ■

Part III

The three chapters in this part feature 11 stories about how real professional and B2B service firms have worked toward greater functional collaboration, shared accountabilities, and individual competencies in each of the three Integration Imperative areas.

I chose each story for its uniqueness, the demonstrated deliberateness or formality of the program used by the firm, and its broad implementation (that is, there were no rogue initiatives that did not merit senior management endorsement). Overall, I looked for firms whose stewardship of marketing and business development featured very deliberate steps toward erasing functional silos. Their integration efforts also had to embrace both cultural and structural elements.

The Process Imperative features five case studies (chapter 9), the Skills Imperative four (chapter 10), and the Support Imperative two (chapter 11). The mixture of these case studies is intentionally broad—by sector, size of revenues, the firm's life cycle, and its focus on a domestic or global marketplace.

Each story focuses on four key areas: the marketing, business development, and/or client service integration challenge; how the firm addressed the challenge; internal hurdles or unanticipated obstacles; and the results or lessons learned.

Chapter 9

Cases: The Process Imperative

The five firms whose cases are featured in this chapter illustrate how broadly the Process Imperative is being adopted across professional sectors. The fact that five stories are included for this imperative (more than for the other two imperatives) lends weight to the notion that professional firms are pushing hard to break down their marketing and business development silos. From executive search consulting, law, and architecture to accounting and information technology services, each story depicts the variety of solutions professional firms are utilizing to more effectively connect marketing and business development and to more optimally meet clients' needs.

■ ■ ■

Using Service Offerings as the Catalyst to Integrate Global Marketing and Business Development Initiatives

Korn/Ferry International is one of the world's largest executive recruiting firms. It used its broad array of services as a lever to integrate marketing and business development functions and to broaden the firm's overly heavy focus on recruiting as a revenue generator. In doing so, the firm better prepared itself to compete against emerging competitors, and it shifted clients' perceptions of its work from transactions to a valued partner.

• • •

Executive recruiting firms have a unique perspective on the human talent within the world's economy. It's an exciting — and daunting — perspective, especially when considering the influence wielded by the senior-level candidates who pass through a prominent search firm's portals. This may be especially true of top-tier firms such as Korn/Ferry International.

Founded in 1969, Korn/Ferry is currently number one in global market share among executive recruitment firms. In helping its clients attract, retain, and develop senior managers, the firm maintains a worldwide presence. It has nearly 2,600 employees in more than 80 offices in 40 countries in the Americas, Asia/Pacific, Europe, the Middle East, and Africa. (Korn/Ferry went public in 1999 and is traded under the symbol KFY.)

Korn/Ferry's main service offerings revolve around recruitment: executive recruitment, corporate governance and CEO recruitment, and outsourced recruiting. Even though recruitment is the big *kahuna* in its portfolio, resulting in 2007 fiscal year global fee revenue of $653.4 million, Korn/Ferry's services also include management assessment, executive coaching and development, **onboarding**, leadership development, board and team effectiveness, executive compensation, and succession planning.

Skeptics might sniff, "How could these folks be challenged on integrating their marketing and business development? Arguably, they did what they needed to do long ago in order to achieve number one status."

And yet when I went looking for excellent examples of professional service firms that are working proactively to erase their marketing and business development silos, I recognized Korn/Ferry as an enterprise that *leans into* its future marketplace challenges.

Executive recruiting firms know all too well about marketplace challenges. They've been through the jarring rough rides of wildly variable economies. (Business observers will remember the early years of the new millennium when the executive recruiting arena suffered steep financial losses. Remember the *BusinessWeek* article "The Incredible Shrunken Headhunters" from March 2002?[1]) I picked Korn/Ferry as a case precisely because of the proactive steps it took after the executive recruiting sector emerged from the early 2000s downturn. The company's executive management worked on productivity to such an extent that in 2008 the firm produced one-third more revenue than it did in 2007, with significantly fewer people. And it still exercises that kind of proactive approach. Its executive managers recognized that the firm's service portfolio was overweighted toward prominent recruiting assignments in good times, leaving revenues (and profits) too vulnerable to the swings of the marketplace.

Korn/Ferry's executive managers, in considering the level of strategic importance to assign to their decision to focus on the company's go-to-market functions, knew they had to undertake this effort while they were in a position of strength and before they felt the marketplace start to kick and gyrate again. They decided to use Korn/Ferry's strong array of services as a lever to integrate marketing and business development functions, and to broaden the focus of the firm's professionals, many of whom were concentrating too much on recruiting as a revenue generator.

Korn/Ferry's integration approach is forward thinking because the company acknowledged the importance of retention and revenue building with clients (including all the initiatives related to becoming their trusted advisor), as opposed to continually stoking the firm's client acquisition engine.

Leading the Charge for Functional Integration

Korn/Ferry's long tenure and prominence as an executive recruiting and talent management company have been accompanied by the firm's commitment to diversifying its service offerings, in particular with two additional service lines. Futurestep, specializing in middle management professionals, was established in 1998 as Korn/Ferry's scalable, outsourced recruitment subsidiary. And Korn/Ferry's Leadership and Talent Consulting unit, created in 2000, offers behavioral assessment and talent developmental tools to help clients align their leaders with their company's strategic goals and culture and maximize the effectiveness of their talent.

Korn/Ferry executive managers chose Mike Franzino, who came on board from rival Heidrick & Struggles in September 2007, to improve the firm's internal go-to-market functional capabilities, lead its global accounts program across all industries, grow its Global Financial Markets practice, and serve on the firm's Operating Committee.

Irreverent and energetic, Franzino speaks with a bold clarity that unveils the obvious. "Search attracts the world's self-proclaimed entrepreneurs," he said during our first interview. "The problem is, they never met a search they didn't love." With a mindset like this, Franzino declared, too many executive recruiting professionals end up neglecting the most important foundation of their firm's revenue—the relationship with the client. Franzino feels—and this viewpoint highlights his vision to improve Korn/Ferry's go-to-market strategy—that too many recruiting professionals have failed to position favorably all of their firm's key services, those arrows in a quiver that could be used to gain access to clients with greater value-added offerings. By failing to do so, they have sacrificed an opportunity to broaden those relationships.

Mike Distefano, Korn/Ferry's chief marketing officer, echoed Franzino's thoughts: "This is where our real differentiation came to light: embedding our offerings, and making them better connect with our strong focus on executive recruiting. Previously, we had offered our services separately, as 'stand-alone products.' But we started to see a rise in our clients' needs for more embedded services. We suspected we could more broadly serve our clients, from whichever service they had originally hired us for."

Shortly after he joined the company, Franzino confirmed that Korn/Ferry did indeed have opportunities to integrate its marketing and business development functions around a broader array of traditional recruiting offerings, in particular its Futurestep and Leadership and Talent Consulting businesses. Franzino recognized that Futurestep and Leadership and Talent Consulting could not be imported wholesale into every client relationship. From one service offering to the next, for example, the firm might have different definitions of "the most strategically important client." And it might go about introducing those services to clients differently from one to the next, and seek to retain those clients or build business with them in varying ways. Franzino explained:

> The concept of having two non-search related services to augment our recruiting offerings is a powerful one and, I think, an attractive value proposition for our clients. But we hadn't yet vetted a strategy around how to integrate those non-recruiting related services into our client relationships. It might be tempting to ask our executive recruiting professionals to simply introduce these services to every one of our clients and then wait to see what happens. As a generic approach, this policy might have merit, but there's a flaw in that logic, because the service offerings of Futurestep and Leadership and Talent Consulting don't play well universally across all of our clients' functions, geographies, or industries. For instance, the head of investment banking at a large financial services client probably doesn't have a need for Futurestep. But if we were talking to the Global Head of Human Resources at that same company, he or she might have a real interest in both. Or, if we were talking to the head of Operations and Technology at that company, he or she might have a real interest in all three of our offerings: Futurestep, executive recruiting and Leadership and Talent Consulting.
>
> There's a necessary limitation to each particular client's purview. And because you only get so many swings at the plate, you can't rely on the individual relationship. You have to think more broadly about marketing and selling services based on their differing levels of attractiveness and need, and their necessity to different client businesses, industries and geographies.

Using this conceptual framework, Franzino could see that the functional side of Korn/Ferry's executive search business was not organized to reflect the marketplace that the company serves. Beginning in April 2008, as part of his charge to refine Korn/Ferry's go-to-market strategies, he began calling for the firm to use its executive recruiting business as the primary driver for its two other revenue engines, Futurestep and Leadership and Talent Consulting.

This new line of thinking is strategic, not tactical. It does not require Korn/Ferry professionals to implement a new set of marketing and business development steps. Rather, it requires executive recruiting professionals to reorient their thinking about issues that keep the client up at night, and to think about these issues from the client's functional, industry, and geographic perspectives. This new approach requires Korn/Ferry professionals to have a strategic understanding of the client's perceived risks and business challenges.

Franzino explained:

> This initiative is about creating a structure that is user-friendly for our recruiting consultants to market and develop business with our clients. We have to think about how clients keep us top of mind. Clients can do that better if we bolster our functional capabilities. For instance, we already have a Chief Financial Officer practice, and we are developing a Chief Marketing Officer practice. If we have a dedicated functional practice area, say in General Counsel searches, it helps our people do a better job of creating internal teams and building up an internally recognized expertise base.

Evolving a Brand

Starting earlier but continuing in parallel to Franzino's work, Korn/Ferry's executive managers decided to evolve and better integrate the company's brand. Distefano recalled:

> We wanted to erect a brand identity that would envelop all of our three revenue engines. We conducted a global study with a prominent strategy consulting firm, and followed that with brand research with an equally prominent branding company. Our brand, "The Art & Science of Talent," was formally launched in 2007.

Distefano is uniquely qualified to bring his own integration methods to Korn/Ferry's marketing and business development initiatives. He began his career in the financial services sector, which allowed him to bring to Korn/Ferry a holistic view of the marketing function. Appointed as Korn/Ferry's chief marketing officer in July 2007, he was able to help the firm look at its marketing function, and he then recommended ways to better integrate it with business development. His idea was to empower Korn/Ferry with a consistent, scalable, and productive business development strategy that simultaneously captured the essence of Korn/Ferry's people and brand. He wanted to make it easier for the consultant to deliver that essence to clients.

In order to better support the consultants, who drive the lion's share of the company's responses to clients' needs, the organization strengthened Korn/Ferry's centralized knowledge management access point. They called this initiative "The K/F Advantage." "This is our training center and best practices repository for assistance and consultant support," Distefano explained. "When we launched 'The Art & Science of Talent,' we also launched 'The K/F Advantage.' This is where the brand is stitched together."

Overcoming Professional Service Traditions

Franzino knew the Korn/Ferry integration initiative would require a deliberate change management effort. Even though Korn/Ferry's new go-to-market strategy would not require a momentous change in the firm's marketing and business development processes per se, Franzino recognized that the mindset change would be significant.

Because executive recruiting is the firm's largest revenue driver (accounting for more than 80 percent of Korn/Ferry's revenue and some 90 percent of its profit margin), Franzino expected that he would have to not only outline a series of new functional approaches, but also work on winning his colleagues' hearts and minds. "Change is tough. I knew we'd have to sell this idea around the world. We knew it would be about giving them real examples about how this new approach could help them raise production, drive higher margin revenue for the firm, and bring more value to clients."

Franzino encountered two internal obstacles to the early success of his integration program. Both had to do with perspectives long held in a professional service environment.

The first hurdle was to change people's minds. As in other professional service firms, Korn/Ferry's professionals are its source of revenue. They sell their expertise, and they are rewarded for their contributions to the company's marketplace success. Also as in other professional service enterprises, tradition is hard to break, especially if the firm's executive recruiting consultants start believing that a new approach might take money out of their pockets. Franzino knew he would have to make a strong case for the merits of integration and its ultimate advantages for both the company and its clients:

> I wanted to get our people to think as broadly as possible about how we pick our clients. I suggested they consider choosing clients in a way that's similar to managing a stock portfolio—like an asset allocation model.
>
> In a well-diversified portfolio, you don't pick three automotive stocks and leave it at that. In this example, what happens if you wake up in the morning and read in the newspaper that your top two clients have merged? What do you do? This situation shows us why it would be wise to utilize a "portfolio management theory" of clients. You allocate your clients across industries, size of companies, and other criteria. The whole thesis is to keep yourself in front of a wide variety of clients that fit your overall portfolio of clients. It's smart to have a well-diversified client port-folio of strong strategic fits.
>
> And in the recruiting arena, a strong strategic client fit inevitably requires a look at their own recruiting strategies. We can't represent every single company in a particular sector, especially if they recruit from others in that sector. In cases like this, we'd choose a different firm, per-haps an up-and-comer that recruits from firms that have higher league table standing.
>
> But it's also the reason why we need to integrate the way we market and sell our other service solutions into our client relationships. By consider-ing a broader array of our functional capabilities, we not only provide greater value to our clients, but we also create robust annuity-like institu-tional relationships with them.

Franzino's second obstacle was measuring success. He feared his col-leagues might too easily fall into a diabolically simple measurement trap. Certainly, it would be painless for Korn/Ferry recruiting consultants to cele-brate the revenue growth of Futurestep and Leadership and Talent Consult-ing, regardless of what happened to the firm's executive recruiting services.

But Franzino believed these metrics, if considered in a vacuum, would eventually open up an internal schism over Futurestep and Leadership and Talent Consulting, and eventually drive revenue independent of executive recruiting services. Instead, he believed revenues for all three service offerings should rise at the same time, or at least in the same proportion. "The real benchmark is, 'How many million-dollar-per-year clients do we have, and for how many of those clients are we generating revenue in all three businesses?'"

Prove It to Me!

How many professional service firms have embarked on enterprise-wide marketing and business development initiatives comprised of potentially advantageous processes and protocols? How many times have business or industry observers seen the same thing? How many initiatives with fancy names or acronyms that are endorsed by the CEO are shepherded by a high-level committee of internal luminaries, only to eventually fade away into obscurity, or worse yet, become the fodder for jokes in the hallway?

Most veterans of senior management circles, regardless of a company's industry, can recount a critical lesson learned in promoting a new functional structure and establishing a new cultural mindset. It's the modeling of the executive managers, whose examples set the tone for any initiative's success.

It's not rocket science. And, luckily, Mike Franzino knew how to lead a charge. "If I am talking about recruiting to my colleagues, then I am out there executing the work. If I am guiding my colleagues about new integrated ways to market and sell our services to clients, then I am out there in front of those clients, marketing and selling Korn/Ferry's integrated services to them. So, when I ask somebody to make calls at four in the morning so they can jump-start a project on the other side of the globe, or if I ask them to check their voice mail on Saturdays and Sundays, or if I tell them to get on a plane, they won't think twice about it. They know I do the same things."

It also takes perseverance, commitment, political savvy, and a tangible show of early results. Franzino and his senior teammates had to demonstrate how Korn/Ferry could benefit in recognizable ways: higher revenues, bigger client relationships, more satisfied clients, more freed-up time for consultants, and plum assignments.

Franzino and Korn/Ferry's senior executives had to win a kind of leverage throughout the company. Franzino and his team did this (and continue to do this) through an extensive traveling road show around the company's global offices. Franzino introduced the new integration approach to local office heads, geographic heads, and practice leaders to ensure they were out there, as he says, "singing off the same hymn sheet." In particular, Franzino spearheaded by example the Financial Services practice's embrace of the new approach. Along the way, he was mindful of changes in market conditions and the complexities of working on local conditions within a global environment.

"The work we've undertaken sets the stage for a compelling future," remarked Distefano. "In five to seven years, we expect to be competing against a different set of companies than we have in the last 40 years. Our work will no longer be viewed as simply a transaction about filling up seats in a client's company. We'll be the valuable partner our clients turn to when they think about their talent."

How One Marketing Department Became a Full-service Internal Marketing Agency

Holland & Hart is the largest law firm in the U.S. Mountain West. It simultaneously restructured its marketing function into an internal branded service agency, reconfigured the firm's marketing and business development processes, carved out exciting new professional growth pathways for marketing team members, and exceeded lawyers' expectations for value.

• • •

Earlier in my career, when I was a marketing manager for a global consulting firm, I led a team of 10 people whose roles were defined by narrowly focused tasks. Today, marketers and business developers are succeeding in their efforts to broaden and deepen their assignments. Simultaneously, though, they have also raised their managers' expectations for extraordinary performance (translated: "Make our firm more money or get a bigger share of the market than we could have achieved without your increased strategic participation"). Unfortunately, they are still required to deliver this extraordinary performance through the tactics-oriented, transaction-focused way in which most PSFs and B2Bs market and sell business.

Typically, it's up to professionally brave executive managers, with their senior marketing or business development colleagues, to compel their organizations to make incremental changes. It's rare that one finds a professional enterprise that completely rebuilds its marketing organization and its go-to-market processes.

But when a firm commits to making broad, sweeping organizational changes, as did the law firm Holland & Hart, the result can be eye-opening. Even more gratifying for the PSF and B2B executive managers reading this book, Holland & Hart has demonstrated that it is possible to manage both the cultural and structural aspects of integrating marketing and business development processes and functions across the firm.

Since its founding in 1947, Holland & Hart has grown into the largest law firm in the United States Mountain West; its annual revenues are in excess of $190 million, and it has more than 900 employees. The firm's more than 415 attorneys work in 15 offices in Colorado, Wyoming, Idaho, Montana, Nevada, New Mexico, Utah, and Washington, DC. They, together with the rest of the firm's employees, work to provide legal services to individuals and companies of all sizes throughout the United States and the world.

Although its legal service offerings are broad, Holland & Hart enjoys special recognition in specific practice areas. For example, in the 2008 *Best Lawyers in America*, the oldest peer review publication in the legal profession, it was ranked the number one law firm in the United States in environmental and natural resources law.[2] Also, many of the firm's attorneys were recognized in the 2008 listing of *Chambers USA: America's Leading Lawyers for Business*.[3]

Of particular relevance to this story, Holland & Hart also displays a notable commitment to its employees. "In addition to providing quality legal services to our clients, we are committed to maintaining a dynamic and satisfying work environment, and encouraging the professional and personal growth of individuals in the firm," said the firm's managing partner, Larry Wolfe.

We Are Succeeding — Help!

This story begins in April 2001, when Holland & Hart hired its new "marketing guy," Mark Beese. Although the firm had had a formal marketing organization since the 1980s, Beese was charged with building a new department from the ground up. In his first six weeks on the job, Beese hired six new team members.

Problem solved, right? Wrong.

By November 2001, Beese's group was overwhelmed with implementing attorneys' requests for what they had long been accustomed to getting: lots of marketing program implementation. Worse, however, was that even though their requests for tactical assistance were growing, it was clear that Holland & Hart attorneys viewed the firm's marketing assistance as optional. "We were order takers," said Jennifer Kummer, one of Holland & Hart's marketing managers. It wasn't unusual for Holland & Hart lawyers to send some of their marketing service work outside the firm.

Beese and his new teammates recognized they were at a critical juncture: although they were successfully fielding a growing number of opportunities to work with attorneys to market the firm, they were facing significant challenges to better manage their attorneys' expectations. And would there be any time left to carve out long-term growth pathways for themselves? Help!

That fall, Beese kicked off the first of a series of annual marketing retreats during which his team asked itself important questions. The first area of self-examination was the marketing team's internal clients—its lawyers. Marketing group members asked themselves: What do our internal clients want from us? How can we best deliver value to our internal clients? The second question centered around the marketing group's own professional goals: What do we want out of our work? What do we want to achieve personally?

Over the course of the next seven years, Beese and his marketing teammates successfully initiated four critical shifts, each of which played its part in creating an extraordinarily effective marketing–business development integration machine.

Restructuring Marketing into an Internal Marketing Services Agency

In the early fall of 2001, Beese and the marketing team members decided they would organize themselves into a new structure—as an internal marketing services agency. Their goal was to earn the attention of their most enthusiastic "clients" by offering a broad spectrum of classic marketing services, including event planning, marketing and client research, advertising and public relations, client database management, writing, graphic design and layout, and a variety of training programs.

Their second goal was to consolidate the firm's use of marketing services. "We began calling ourselves account reps, and aligned ourselves by departments that were well recognized by the firm's attorneys," said Beese. Initially, there were two account reps. One marketing manager handled marketing services for the firm's litigation practice; another managed marketing for all the natural resources– and corporate-related practice needs. Soon, through their own proactive internal communication, as well as the positive word-of-mouth endorsements of happy "clients," the team added more accounts. A third account was added, focused strictly on business and intellectual property clients. "We created account plans, and proactively brought these plans to our attorneys," Beese pointed out. "When they asked us for help, we responded in a highly focused manner." Soon, an increasing number of practice groups wanted to try the new model. A chain reaction had started.

Demonstrating the Power of Brand Loyalty

By February 2002, Holland & Hart's marketing team had renamed itself *Imaginate*. Team members embarked on an internal campaign to build their visibility and brand awareness as the firm's very own internal marketing services agency. They developed their own Web site, created branded T-shirts, and developed trading cards featuring teammates' faces and biographical information.

Flash forward to September 2005, when Beese and his marketing team had become so successful in the eyes of their fellow legal service marketers that Holland & Hart was named one of the top 50 law firms for marketing and communications by *Marketing the Law Firm*, published by Law Journal Newsletters, a division of American Lawyer Media.[4] This outside recognition, combined with the marketing team's success in working with more and more Holland & Hart attorneys, helped the group demonstrate a very important point: branding and brand management can indeed encourage client loyalty.

Evolving Marketing from "Doers" to "Advisors"

Also in the fall of 2001, Beese and his teammates decided to work on changing their lawyers' perceptions of them from "doers" to "advisors." Beese explained:

> We realized we wanted to be utilized as thinkers. We knew we could get our clients to consider us as thinkers if we were excellent at *doing*. Once

we had our clients' trust, we start acting like consultants. We started asking them to consider new approaches, and we gave them new advice they'd never heard before. They said, "Oh, I had no idea you could do this." We didn't ask permission to make this shift; we just did it. Now we are being asked, even expected, to consult.

Adding Integrated Services to the Marketing Department's Portfolio of Offerings

Even from their earliest thought of evolving themselves into an internal marketing services agency, Beese and his colleagues had always considered both marketing and business development as the rightful scope of their functions. The firm's leaders, however, struggled to understand the difference between marketing and business development. Often, attorneys used the terms interchangeably. What's more, attorneys had never really thought of business development services as part of their marketers' repertoire.

In October 2006, managing partner Larry Wolfe developed and distributed a survey to the firm's partners. He wanted to know what his fellow partners needed and expected from the marketing department. From the findings, Wolfe delivered in November 2006 what the *Imaginate* team soon fondly began calling "The Memo." For Beese and his colleagues, "The Memo" generated enormous new insight: the firm was asking them to be more strategic and to do more to help grow the enterprise. Emily Hager, a Holland & Hart marketing manager, recalled her reaction: "In so many words, our firm gave us a new mandate. They wanted us to 'up our game.' Even though the partners didn't explicitly ask us for help with business development, we recognized that was what they were asking for."

At times, Beese believed, the marketing team had been providing business development activities since 2001. But Wolfe's partner survey and subsequent feedback memo required a proactive and creative response. And so, in preparation to deliver their formal response to Wolfe in their own January 2007 memo, the *Imaginate* team members made the critical decision to add business development services to their agency's portfolio of offerings. They spent the rest of 2007, and early 2008, readjusting the group's service approaches.

The *Imaginate* account representatives settled on the following suite of integrated marketing and business development services:

- Identifying and researching top client prospects
- Identifying and researching industry associations, speaking opportunities, and publishing opportunities
- Creating a "who knows whom" matrix to connect attorneys with clients, prospects, and other attorneys
- Developing integrated marketing and business development plans
- Preparing marketing materials that support both business development and marketing activities

Keeping the Focus on Results

An early challenge was to understand and use familiar terminology that would mean something to the attorneys, and add momentum to the shift toward the marketing team's broader strategic purview. "When we convey how our skills have expanded and grown, we talk about deliverables," said marketing manager Brittaney Schmidt. "We don't name our roles as 'your marketing manager' or 'your business development manager.'" In doing so, the *Imaginate* team telegraphed its ongoing shift away from tightly bounded "roles" and toward more process-oriented, stepwise "functions." The emphasis was on action, movement—and value-added results.

The marketing team's embrace of broader service offerings also required its members to educate themselves. They scoured anything published on selling professional services. They attended Legal Marketing Association and Legal Sales and Service Organization education sessions. And they continued working with their outside leadership consultant to help them effectively evolve attorneys' perceptions of their newly integrated functions.

Meanwhile, *Imaginate* team members faced the continuing challenge of successfully managing their fast-growing workloads. Almost immediately after announcing their new capabilities, they realized they had to control the ways in which they delivered their services. Beese decided to arrange the group's deployment according to interest areas, ability, and the required deliverables for projects. For example, when a request involves both marketing and business development services, it is called an "account." Every other request is labeled a "project." Beese explained, "The projects and accounts list is always changing. New initiatives pop up, and some go dormant. Everywhere, though, we are seeing more activity."

The group began to embrace classic project management principles. Because team communication is a must, Beese initiated two types of meetings. The first type, held once or twice a month, is a project meeting with the whole *Imaginate* staff. Individuals share information on projects that affect other people. For the second type of meeting, Beese meets with marketing managers once a month to share initiatives that are under way with each account group, to share best practices, and to reallocate resources as necessary. It was important, all agreed, to make priority decisions based on well-understood criteria.

Lessons Learned: Managing Your Success Takes Vision

Each time it rearranged itself into a new organizational structure and each time it offered newly integrated services, the marketing team embarked on proactive communication with the firm's department chairs, practice leaders, and partners. Taking ownership of their new functional purview, account reps attended practice meetings to talk about their new services and delivery approach.

Each time the group added and integrated marketing and business development services, despite the inevitable naysayers or avoiders, a strong percentage of Holland & Hart practice group leaders became prominent evangelists for the new model. The result? Almost before they were ready, Beese and his teammates had to ramp up their delivery capabilities. Again and again, they were reminded they had to pay close attention to balancing their clients' demands against their own resource capacities. Managing client expectations will always be necessary. Managing your success requires an outcomes-oriented vision for the future.

Not surprisingly, Holland & Hart attorneys continue to push for progress on integrating their firm's marketing and business development. By the spring of 2008, Wolfe and his partners had so fully embraced the *Imaginate* team as business development advisors that they began asking the team to act as personal business development coaches for new attorneys.

By late 2008, Beese had integrated yet another capability—client service—into his team's functions. With this evolution, Holland & Hart partners and their marketing colleagues arrived at an exciting and competitively advantaged moment: strategically managing their clients' entire buying life cycle, from marketing to buying to consumption of a professional service firm's palette of offerings.

Integrating, for the Clients' Sake

Perkins+Will is a global design firm. It initiated a firm-wide internal study to break down the internal silos that were impeding the firm from optimally addressing clients' broader design needs. This significant internal exploration resulted in setting a groundbreaking new direction for the firm's future marketplace journey.

• • •

When clients purchase professional or business-to-business services, they do so because they have chosen not to perform themselves the services they require. Most consumers of complex services are willing to trust their service providers; they don't need to see the machinations behind the scenes. However, most PSF and B2B clients do place a premium on the delivery of excellent client service.

In the area of architectural services, competition among rivals is keen. Many architectural firms, mindful of their reputations among peers and admired clients, jockey for plum assignments, work hard to create optimal design solutions, and enthusiastically vie for appropriate awards recognition, all within very narrowly defined industries (such as aviation, health care, and higher education) or recognized solutions (such as interior design or landscape architecture).

And so architectural firms are faced with twin forces—the mandate for ever-increasing excellence in client service and the reality of uncomfortably narrow industry and expertise concentrations. These dual forces put enormous strains on architectural firms to grow market share and make gains in revenue and value-added growth for clients. Talk about being forced into a box (a metaphor architectural firms understand only too well).

Only a handful of architectural and design firms consistently manage to achieve acknowledged excellence in these two areas. Perkins+Will is among them. Established in 1935 by Larry Perkins and Philip Will, Perkins+Will quickly captured in its early years national and international respect for its design accomplishments in education and health care. It soon expanded its focus into corporate, commercial, civic, higher education, science, and technology work, and became well known for its broad-based work in interior design across these sectors. In more recent decades, Perkins+Will has added capabilities in branded environments and planning and strategies (in which the firm develops recommendations to connect clients' strategic objectives with their people, processes, and place).

In 1999 Perkins+Will was recognized by the American Institute of Architects as "Firm of the Year," and it continues to be highly ranked by industry publications, including *Engineering News-Record, Interior Design Magazine*, and *Building Design+Construction*, as well as specialty publications focused on health care, education, government, and residential design. By 2008 Perkins+Will had completed projects in 49 states and 43 countries, and was delivering its services through 20 offices across North America, Asia, Africa, the Middle East, and Europe. In 2007 its 1,200 employees generated nearly $330 million in revenue.

It's no accident that Perkins+Will has achieved such success. Since the firm's founding, its leadership has insisted that all professionals strongly focus on client service. Nevertheless, even design professionals fall prey to functional disconnects.

Help! I'm Stuck Inside the Matrix!

Like many professional service firms, Perkins+Will is organized internally as a matrix. Architectural services are deployed through various capabilities, including architecture, interiors, branded environments, planning and strategies, and urban design. Each discipline delivers its work through the firm's areas of practice, including health care, higher education, K–12 education, science and technology, and corporate-commercial-civic.

Professional service clients, pressured by escalating business competition, feel growing anxiety about getting their own products to market quickly and efficiently. In parallel with the shifts their clients are experiencing, Perkins+Will's board of directors watch for ways in which to continually build their firm's value to clients and to meet their changing needs.

Beginning in 2006, members of the board and other Perkins+Will leaders began to notice the emergence of a worrisome problem. Almost without knowing it, and with a laudable zeal to provide excellence, the firm's professionals had begun to create some internal organizational silos. Each capability area or practice manifested its own sort of culture, its own well-recognized processes, and its own particular methods of delivering services. The professionals appeared to be concentrating less than they should have been on the ultimate quality of the services delivered in the interest of the clients. What's more, board members realized that the firm was marketing and selling its services in a siloed way, instead of introducing clients to the full range of capabilities the firm offered.

Board members also began to notice a change in the firm's clients, who increasingly were articulating their desire for the seamless delivery of a broad range of architectural services. Manuel Cadrecha, a member of the Perkins+Will board, design director for its Atlanta office, and the firm's national sector leader for its corporate, commercial, and civic work, explained:

> Our clients are not just hiring us to think about architecture, interior design, or brand strategies, for example. They want to engage us for a more holistic approach to solving their needs. They understand the complexity of their challenges. They know we have a lot of expertise. From their perspective, it's simple: they want to get our full range of capabilities delivered to them through easily understood methodologies. They want a friendly, authoritative, easily understood, and high quality solution. We realized that our organization—providing our expertise through a series of entrepreneurial business units—was actually not serving the clients the way they needed us to.
>
> Over the past century, the design profession has become fragmented into a series of silos related to the type of design that is being undertaken —interior design, architecture, or brand, for example. We realized we needed to create an environment that is supportive of holistic design, one that integrates all the qualities of our expertise and delivers them to our clients in a meaningful, timely, and distinctive manner. We realized we needed to redefine ourselves around what we are—a design practice.

The board of directors of Perkins+Will found this realization vitally important to the future of the enterprise. They recognized that they had to take deliberate steps to increase the quality and integration of both the firm's offerings and the way they were delivered. They made a critical decision to address this significant "disconnectivity" challenge head-on, with nothing less than a deep and broad review of Perkins+Will and its approach to its marketplace.

Of all the cases featured in this book, Perkins+Will stands alone in its holistic view toward erasing functional silos. And, of course, its integration initiative encompasses marketing and business development functions; otherwise, I wouldn't have featured this story here. Perkins+Will's integration initiative springs from its deep philosophical focus on the ultimate endgame—optimally serving its clients. Rather than considering a set of tactical fixes to break down the firm's problematic organizational silos (although leaders might ultimately have decided that tactical fixes were all that were needed), Perkins+Will's leaders were determined to look at "everything." Phil Harrison, Perkins+Will's chief executive officer, was also deeply involved in the review, and brought a firm-wide point of view. He summarized the initiative and its true intention: "We viewed this as much more than a marketing and business development effort. Our stated goal was: 'Build a culture of innovation and creativity, delivering client value through interdisciplinary teams working in an integrated model.' Literally, we wanted to reinvent ourselves, to become more than an architecture firm."

It's no surprise, perhaps given its area of professional expertise, that Perkins+Will approached its functional "disconnectivity" problem from a design perspective. But I was also struck by the way the leaders of Perkins+Will were willing to evolve the definition of "design" from a term that describes a patchwork quilt of expertise areas that are somehow related to architecture to a term that signifies a broader capability.

Designing a New Way of Serving the Clients

Once it decided to undertake its integration review, the Perkins+Will board of directors set up a representative subgroup of leaders, led by Manuel Cadrecha, to frame the scope of the work and to suggest a way to make recommendations. The subgroup itself represented a kind of integration model and included leaders representing the capabilities within the firm and different perspectives such as technical, quality control, finance, and marketing.

Interestingly, this endeavor remained nameless in its early incarnation. (Until the effort had a more defined scope and direction, task force members understandably felt no urgency to call it something. It was more important to focus on content rather than a label.) The group agreed to investigate in two general directions. One focus was internal and required an exercise in self-examination to understand how the firm currently delivered its services (whether integrated or not) and to identify what might be some difficulties in delivering them more effectively. The co-leaders of this internal exploration were Perkins+Will's chief marketing officer, Bill Viehman, and the leader of its planning and strategies practice area, Janice Barnes.

The second focus area was external and was led by Cadrecha and Eileen Jones, a principal and the national discipline leader of the firm's branded environments practice. Jones explained:

> We decided to conduct up to ten external interviews with companies in different industries, and to complete the interviews in three months. We asked ourselves what we knew or had read that pointed to organizations already practicing in an integrated and multidisciplinary fashion. In November 2007, we came up with a list, prioritized, and honed it down. We considered companies we could access in a timely manner and finally settled on a set of enterprises, including graphic design firms, brand designers, financial organizations, consumer products companies, business consulting firms and media organizations. Where we could leverage an existing relationship, we did so. In some cases we made cold calls to introduce ourselves.
>
> I sent an e-mail to tell them what we were trying to accomplish and asked them to let me call them. We moved forward from there, and tried to complete interviews by the end of February 2008 (although we did conduct one or two the next month).

The interviews, conducted by Cadrecha and Jones, centered around a set of dialogue-like questions (although interviewees were not led lockstep through each question and not required to answer each). The questions were:

- What business factors led your company to an integrated, multidisciplinary work model?
- What obstacles were encountered in establishing a multidisciplinary process model?
- What made the transition to this model successful?
- What impact does this approach have on culture, including recruitment and retention?
- How does an organization maintain this structure and process for long-term effectiveness?
- How is success measured in this model?
- How would you describe the rising importance of design and innovation as a business strategy?

- What operational processes do you have in place to maintain the integrated process?
- How can we get out of our own way?
- What are some keys to building consensus within the organization?
- What is the best way to manage the internal relationships or existing issues that persist?
- How can we develop a common understanding of "success"?

Their research unearthed about 15 key insights, validating that integrated design is a client mandate and that it's happening globally. The most critical insights follow.

Our customers want to align themselves with partners who mirror their own values and structures. This insight was corroborated in Perkins+Will's conversations with a large consumer packaged goods company. The company reported that it was increasingly looking for partners who show an understanding of the multidisciplinary way its people work. Specifically, when this company's decision makers seek a service provider, they want to ensure that they engage a firm that will not present a fragmented and segmented response. Rather, they seek responses that are complete and seamless in both conception and delivery.

The outcomes of multidisciplinary engagements require a professional service firm to think differently. The outcomes of such an engagement are not necessarily defined by a product—for example, a building—but much more broadly. For example, the framework of a traditional architectural assignment is to ask a client, "What kind of a building do you want?" In the new model as outlined by the interviewees, the question would rather be, "What is the problem you are trying to solve?" CEO Phil Harrison explained:

> We began to understand that we should look at problem definitions and solutions differently than we used to. The research revealed the importance of defining different outcomes—a big mindset shift for us. In the new model of work, we would leverage everyone's expertise to ensure that the *correct* problem is being solved, versus the problem we used to think clients wanted solved.

Professional service firms that are capable of creating and delivering enriched solutions must develop new perspectives on internal processes and talent. The firm's research helped it understand the importance of talent (hiring new types of people) and implementing new internal processes. Regarding new types of people, Jones explained:

> We heard from a couple of people that we would need "T-shaped" people as employees. For example, the vertical position on the letter T would represent the deep and specialized capabilities that people have; their technical knowledge. The horizontal position on the letter T is the contextual or translational knowledge they bring to their expertise. Let's say you were an undergraduate in architecture, but after graduation you became a marketing specialist. This enables you to look at things in a cross-context way; you look at architecture in a bigger, marketplace perspective. The question then becomes, "How can we place that architect in marketing, communications, and other business areas? What do we know as a firm, and how can we translate that across other disciplines, in order to come up with an enriched solution?"

The subgroup learned one other thing about how firms are developing and delivering enriched solutions; it centered around the way they changed their processes. The Perkins+Will subgroup began to understand more about the concept of rapid prototyping, and how the firm might apply the concept to the way it developed creative solutions to client problems. Jones recalled a particularly exciting team epiphany:

> We diagrammed an iterative process model of addressing the client's needs. For example, consider what the field of architecture has traditionally delivered in the past—a beautiful three-dimensional, physical model of a design idea. Now consider a new brainstorming methodology that brings all the firm's interdisciplinary expertise to the table, all gathered around the client's problem. With a process model like that, you can rapidly prototype multiple solutions that are at the heart of the problem, without building a beautiful iconic "thing." You get to a problem solution faster and better, with the client included in the brainstorming, and immediately able to respond to what you are diagramming.

As the interviews concluded in March 2008, the subgroup met with Perkins+Will's leadership group, which convenes several times a year, and involves the firm's board of directors, office managing directors, national market sector leaders (aviation, health care, higher education, and K–12), national discipline leaders (architecture, interiors, branded environments, etc.), and C-level executive managers. The subgroup presented its initial internal and external research and findings, and then framed a discussion of what other business enterprises called "integrated design."

The leadership group gave its approval for the initiative to move toward recommendations to help Perkins+Will improve the quality of its product. From there, the subgroup began to create a preliminary plan about how its discoveries might affect Perkins+Will.

Decision Time!

The subgroup presented its initiative to the Perkins+Will board of directors in June 2008 (and again in July 2008 to the leadership group), and everyone expressed approval. By now, the initiative had gelled to the point that it had a name — the Interdisciplinary Design Initiative.

The thrust of the presentation was a call for the firm to begin leveraging its expertise as *embedded* value rather than *added* value — specifically, to start delivering interdisciplinary design. Jones remarked:

> We decided not to label this work as an "integrated design initiative," because you can be integrated in your approach without being interdisciplinary. For us, the value lies around the multi-disciplines, operating in an interdisciplinary fashion.
>
> This decision influences how we will frame our value proposition too. For example, if you're speaking to a Facilities decision-maker, that's one buyer. The CEO is another buyer, and so is the marketing team. We had already begun seeing requests for more interdisciplinary engagements; now there's huge demand for this new design approach. We may eventually make a choice to pursue only those that align well with us. Or, we may say, "Yes let's take this assignment, but we'll educate the client."

Roll Up Your Sleeves!

Perkins+Will's internal self-examination, checked against the marketplace, has set it on a course to define an entirely new client engagement model and a new work process model. As of this writing, its preparatory work is under way. Not surprisingly, numerous internal changes will be needed to support this new model. For example, the firm will have to realign its human resources approaches to attract and retain new types of people. Its professionals will need to deliver hospitality to clients differently. And the firm will have to figure out how to engage its internal experts in new and different ways. For example, why not engage Perkins+Will's IT team when arranging common dialogues with clients? Why not align Perkins+Will's IT team with clients' IT needs?

The firm is committed to undertaking a significant internal educational process to address the inevitable subset of skeptics who will challenge the new concept, asking what is so different about this interdisciplinary design approach, and hasn't the firm been doing this all along? (The answer is "Well, no, we haven't. Here's what's different.")

One of the early efforts will be to develop and communicate a common understanding of what it means to practice interdisciplinary design. Jones explained:

> When we reached out in our own industry to see how others approach the ideas of "integration," or "interdisciplinary," we found many different meanings, and so many models! We knew we'd need to make these meanings clear to ourselves. Once we do that, it'll be important to make sure our customers understand our terms and how these terms will impact their work with us.

Moving Forward

There is a palpable sense of professional passion streaming through the halls of Perkins+Will offices these days. (Not that this attitude didn't exist before, but I couldn't help but find it remarkable.) There's a sense of future purpose and a clear-eyed commitment to breaking down old barriers and working in a new team-oriented way.

Harrison confirmed the sentiment. "This means we will stop thinking that Perkins+Will is an architecture firm, and start thinking of Perkins+Will as a design firm. In re-envisioning our practice in this way, design emerges as a transformative power, where creativity and innovation are applied through interdisciplinary teams to solve clients' business problems."

This firm is literally redefining itself from the inside out, with an eye toward integrating with clients and embedding its value to them in an extremely powerful way. Who would be surprised if market share and revenue growth don't also come to pass?

Reconnecting Marketing and Business Development with the Business

Moss Adams is the largest regional accounting firm in the western United States. It developed new marketing and business development integration tools that accelerated the process in which practitioners connected marketing to selling and selling to client service. These frameworks and new cultural norms are driving strong revenue gains, even in a difficult economy.

* * *

Early in my career, I heard the aphorism "Don't confuse effort with results." It sounds simple enough, right? But for marketing and business development for professional and business-to-business service firms, it has been a challenge to connect the two. In fact, the majority of these firms' senior marketers and business developers are less than satisfied with the processes they're using to measure their combined efforts. It's still too hard to connect marketing and business development to tangible results.

Even with praiseworthy advances toward more effective evaluation of their go-to-market programs, many partner-driven enterprises still find it too easy to fall in love with thrilling marketing and business development initiatives that don't connect neatly to the organization's overall strategic goals. Increasingly, executive managers are asking: Do these activities actually drive revenues? Do they actually sustain the firm in its marketplace? Do they actually help the firm *grow*?

But what about their marketing and business development programs *can* executive managers control and improve? Their structural integration, of course. When these managers' organizations adopt a Process Imperative approach, they balance their allocation of resources and activities for each part of the process. They pay attention to coordinating the handoffs between the marketing and business development steps.

One firm that has made notable progress in better connecting marketing and business development handoffs is Moss Adams. Founded in 1913, Moss Adams was ranked in 2007 by the *Public Accounting Report* as the eleventh largest accounting and consulting firm in the United States, and the largest headquartered in the U.S. western region. Moss Adams's staff of more than 2,000 (including more than 240 partners) operates from 20 locations in Washington, Oregon, California, Arizona, and New Mexico. Its

2007 revenues were more than $315 million. Moss Adams is organized into more than 20 industry and specialty service groups, including apparel, construction, health care, hospitality and gaming, not-for-profit/government, real estate, and technology.

Who's Sailing This Boat? Us or the Economy?

In mid-2006, a group of Moss Adams's office managing partners and industry group leaders gathered in Phoenix for the firm's annual leadership meeting. Moss Adams chairman Rick Anderson said:

> We have never proven that we can grow this firm in flat economic cycles. Historically, when the economy expanded, we expanded. When the marketplace hit a downturn, we went flat. I want to change that. We are pretty good at marketing, but we need to get a lot better. We are pretty good at service, too, but we must get better.

Attending that meeting was Scott Jensen, who had just joined Moss Adams as its first-ever director of sales. Having previously led regional sales efforts at a much larger accounting firm, Jensen had seen close-up what he believed were accounting firms' propensity to expend enormous amounts of marketing resources that ultimately produced no or a minimal uptick in awareness among potential buyers, or for that matter revenues.

Jensen believed Moss Adams's marketing was in many instances disassociated from the firm's overall business processes. Displaying his trademark straight-talk style, Jensen related to me the gist of what he said to his new colleagues that day in 2006:

> Our people, partners and senior managers too often confused marketing activity for value. They thought that if we put out brochures, if we had ads going out, things would be good. Our people are tempted to have us drum up a lot of marketing initiatives, especially, for example, when they see our competitors aggressively launching huge rebranding campaigns. But we have to be very cautious about feeding our own egos. For marketing to be really good, it's got to be tied to the business.
>
> I'd rather have us be closer to the dollars. Dollars come from clients. I asked my colleagues: "What's the bridge between marketing and service?" We've always said our business is a relationship business. Nobody buys Moss Adams because we have the coolest ads. Sure, they might be aware

of us because we have a cool ad, or because of our brochures, or because they've attended our events. But few people buy our services because of those things.

Interestingly, Jensen had begun introducing his perspective and a new approach to marketing and selling even before he joined Moss Adams:

> During my interview for the job, Chris Schmidt, Moss Adams's president, came in looking sour about something. He said, "So I suppose you're going to tell me we need to redo all our brochures and spend a boat load of money on advertising." I told him, "If that's what you want me to do, we can stop the interview right now, because I don't believe that will bring you the results you want."
>
> Marketing, at its most overarching definition, is broad messages to wide audiences. Sales, at its narrowest definition, is one-on-one messages to narrow audiences. Sales is the bridge between marketing and service, because we are in a relationship business. I told him I wanted to redefine the way Moss Adams links its marketing and selling activities. Schmidt sat up and started to smile.

Three months later, Jensen was in front of his new colleagues, addressing the meeting in Phoenix.

Redefining the Way a Professional Service Firm Links Its Marketing and Selling Activities

Jensen's first order of business was to convince his colleagues that they had to change their behavior. This, he knew, would be a tall order. The firm had just come off of a record year for revenue. Why change? And like many of their professional service brethren in other sectors, Moss Adams accountants had learned to rely on a broad variety of marketing initiatives that they hoped would start the phone ringing with qualified prospective clients. Instead, Jensen wanted to see Moss Adams accountants and business consultants demonstrating their personal involvement in initiating and building client relationships.

The reason I chose to profile Moss Adams is because Jensen and his co-executive managers so astutely blended structural and cultural elements to drive new behaviors. The structural aspect of this integration initiative featured easy-to-understand depictions of the Moss Adams process of marketing, selling, and client service delivery. In fact, Jensen created two visuals (discussed shortly—see figures 9.1 and 9.2), using Moss Adams's culturally accepted terms for recognized steps in the marketing–selling **pipeline** to help his colleagues visualize how they could work together to improve their handoffs from their one-to-many marketing activities to their one-to-one selling activities. He had the professional bravery to boldly label his initiative as one of "integration." He actually used the word "selling."

But Jensen did not start out with a focus on structure; rather, in his early steps he concentrated on cultural change. He decided not to engage Moss Adams professionals in the obvious—a one-time internal training seminar, something the firm had tried in the past. Instead, he embarked on a significant internal campaign to introduce them to an entirely new model of growing revenues and expanding market share.

And so, in the summer of 2006 he began an internal communications campaign to engage each of the firm's office managing partners and industry group leaders in discussions about new concepts of revenue generation. From this, Jensen intended to work closely with the most enthusiastic partners, whom he hoped would then encourage other colleagues to embrace a relationship-oriented selling program.

Jensen and the executive team were prepared for a long change management slog. But serendipity stepped in to help speed things up dramatically. It was during one of these encounters that Jensen created—on the fly—the first of two visuals that soon became iconic centerpieces for Moss Adams's integrated sales and marketing program.

It happened quite by chance during a meeting in the firm's Spokane office. Accompanied by the Moss Adams training leader, Heather Kean, Jensen listened as one of the partners expressed a desire for sales presentation training. Jensen thought this was too limiting, and he marched up to a white board to sketch out his vision of what was more appropriate. What emerged was a rough draft of what eventually became the Moss Adams Marketing and Business Development Continuum (figure 9.1).

On its left side, Jensen's rough drawing illustrated the passive tactical vehicles of marketing ("Messaging"), including advertising and articles. Moving to the right of the drawing, Jensen showed at what points different, more active tactics should be used as the personal connection with the prospect becomes closer. The right side of the drawing was labeled "Revenues."

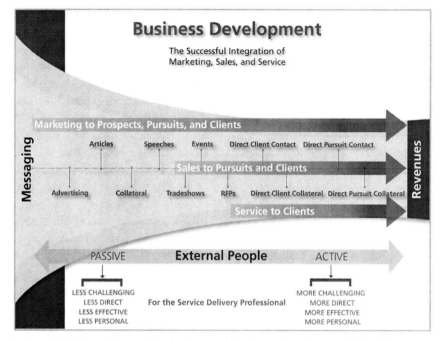

Figure 9.1 Moss Adams Marketing and Business Development Continuum
Source: Reproduced with permission of Moss Adams LLC.

He was surprised when he heard later about the enormous impact his rough sketch had had on his colleagues. Kean explained, "Suddenly, people could clearly see the difference between marketing and sales and service, and the interdependence between these functions. Scott presented these ideas with a clarity they hadn't seen before."

Jensen used a more neatly formatted graphic version of his Marketing and Business Development Continuum drawing as he continued his cultural change journey. This visual tool helped his colleagues realize that marketing, sales, and service all influence each other and must be integrated. Meanwhile, he spent a lot of time on the phone with Moss Adams professionals; he attended internal planning conferences held by various industry groups; and he continually targeted and retargeted new enthusiasts of his vision for integrating marketing, sales, and service functions. He also willingly adjusted his concepts in favor of valid input from partners and the Moss Adams leadership team.

The second visual, now called the Moss Adams Marketing and Sales Process, also emerged by sheer chance. In March 2007, Jensen met with the Moss Adams IT group about the firm's efforts to acquire and implement a new client relationship management system. Jensen wanted this new CRM system to be built not only around marketing and sales, but also around eventually accommodating how the firm serves its clients. The members of the IT group replied that they could not implement a CRM system without understanding Moss Adams's business processes.

Once again, Jensen jumped up to draw on a white board. "I ranted for about 10, maybe 15 minutes. It was boom, boom, boom," Jensen explained. "I tried to help them visualize how marketing and sales and service work together, not against each other, and that while we may not have had a documented process, we did have a process." Like before, this now-iconic visual emerged from Jensen's brain about 80 percent complete.

In the final version (figure 9.2), marketing is placed to the left. It is in charge of initiating and leading broad tactical vehicles to fill the firm's revenue generation pipeline. In the middle is a series of left-to-right stepwise boxes, in a flowchart format, with go/no go decision checkpoints. Along its bottom, the graphic depicts how marketing tactics help move qualified leads through the firm's marketing and sales process, and how these tactics help broaden and deepen relationships, from prospect to client to repeat client.

Internal Communications

In April 2007, Jensen launched a bimonthly internal blog, "My Two Cents." The blog, featuring a Q&A format and written in a conversational style, is designed to keep sales and marketing front and center. Jensen reports that its readership is very high. "I worried about having enough to say but apparently that has not been a problem," Jensen joked. A sample blog entry appears in figure 9.3.

To augment these internal communications efforts, in January 2008 Jensen introduced a quarterly internal newsletter for all Moss Adams partners. The content features a front-page article reinforcing a key concept. The newsletter also highlights recent wins, noting the specific marketing or sales techniques that ensured a win. Extra effort is taken to ensure a demonstrated link between service, sales, and marketing. Changing from month to month, an open page showcases activities and rewards such as a crossword puzzle featuring sales and marketing terms and a sales training

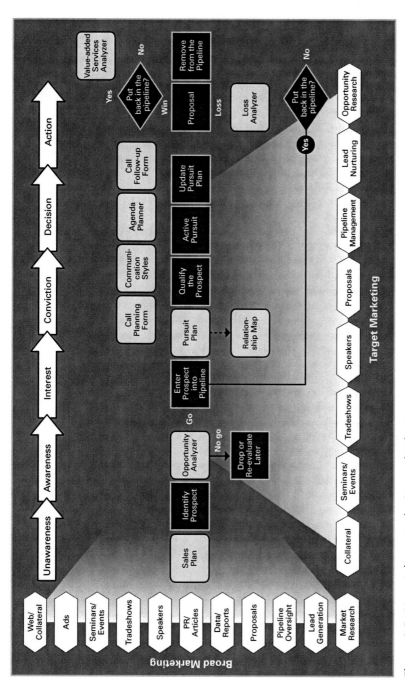

Figure 9.2 Moss Adams Marketing and Sales Process

Sales and Marketing Success

"Scott, have you worked yourself out of this job yet?" Well, that question was a little disconcerting mostly because the answer is "No." Plus, I like being here. There is an associated host of follow-up questions like, "Do you want me gone and why?" Hold that thought—perhaps I don't want to know. That said, you can be assured that my job will be done here when:

1. Partners and staff willingly participate in focused marketing activities
2. The Sales & Marketing Team provides partners and staff training that fits their expertise and experience while also addressing the firm's needs
3. Partners and staff respond positively to the training
4. Client satisfaction surveys and interviews reflect scores that support loyalty
5. Clients offer unsolicited or support solicited referrals for service to their peers and colleagues
6. Partners conduct substantive business discussions with their clients and offer all the relevant services the firm can provide
7. Our consulting (value-added) services are at high levels with key clients
8. We add significant numbers of new clients to the firm despite economic cycles
9. The community and market place knows and respects the firm
10. We explore and develop new services as potential offerings to clients
11. We understand the competition's strengths and weaknesses
12. We continue to create and reinvigorate competitive industry groups
13. We support our brand (reputation with clients and pursuits) with effective marketing staffing and tools (logo, advertising, brochures, Web page, proposals, CRM, etc.)
14. We implement technology to accelerate existing attitudes
15. We understand client demographics
16. We serve only those clients where a mutual beneficial interest exists
17. We serve only those clients where we can clearly develop and sustain client loyalty through premier service
18. We balance and allocate the necessary resources to the functions
19. We plan and align the activities of marketing, sales, and service delivery to support our clients
20. We monitor and reward business development results
21. We routinely update action-oriented plans
22. We celebrate our clients and winning
23. The firm actively supports an alumni program
24. All of the above is happening because noticeably superior client service and growth are part of the firm culture

Perhaps we've just scratched the surface on some of these items and others are a little further along. Give me your thoughts on how far we are to sales and marketing success. What other factors need to be considered? What needs to be emphasized?

Figure 9.3 "My Two Cents" Internal Moss Adams Blog: Sales and Marketing Success, Posted April 2007 by Scott Jensen

alumnus profile. The back page features a personal "words of wisdom" message from Jensen. Distribution is old-fashioned print and mail, to set it apart from the multitude of electronic communications. Jensen's "second-in-command" colleague, Marilyn Monserud, generates the content. "I am gratified when people in the firm say 'Scott's Training' or 'Scott's advice.' But, our success is a team effort. I may call a few plays, but it is the people in the field who get the credit," said Jensen.

Building New Norms About How to Market and Sell

Despite the enthusiasm and clarity generated from his work, Jensen knew he would not be able to rely on beautifully formatted process charts or new internal communications to make his vision come to life. He knew he had to connect marketing and selling to the ultimate prize: service to clients:

> I knew our people got the message that there is a difference and dependence between marketing and selling. They understood that we cannot effectively sell unless we market, and that we cannot market unless we sell, and finally that without superior service, both are wasted. Marketing is too expensive without selling. Selling is too hard without marketing. But when we market, we send messages to the marketplace. That creates a sense of expectation about Moss Adams. When we sell, we also send messages, but the message shifts from a statement to a question.
>
> So, when we market effectively and sell correctly, we establish the basis for serving passionately. Because now our clients know what they believe about us from marketing, and what they expect of us from selling. From there, it should be easy to fulfill those expectations during the service process.

In order to guide his colleagues' understanding of these complex concepts and their embrace of them, Jensen built a cultural change program around four key elements. The first element was training, carried out in a nontraditional way. It came about like this.

In September 2006, Moss Adams rolled out the first in a series of internal training programs. Initially targeting Moss Adams's younger generation (and purposely not its senior management), Jensen and the firm's leadership chose 50 employees who identified with the new vision and who wanted to see change in the firm. He required these 50 people to complete about four hours of pre-program assignments, which he then graded in order to select a group of 25 to take the first program.

The one-day program was then followed by five one-hour phone sessions among classmates and Jensen over the succeeding 10 weeks. During these calls, Jensen coached participants to apply his new techniques with prospects and clients. Jensen recalled, "It was very much like group therapy. On the call, someone would say, 'You know, I ran into a so-and-so challenge the other day, and here's how I addressed it.' From that, others had courage to tell their own stories and to refine their own approaches."

After the first one-day program, Jensen introduced a second set of training programs in October 2006, and followed that with four more sessions in 2007. With each iteration, he broadened the circle of lead adopters and influencers. By 2008, his training sessions were being offered increasingly to senior managers and partners. By the fall of 2008, he had added a negotiations course, which builds off the sales training program. In 2009 an account management course to more explicitly express superior service will be added.

The second element of Moss Adams's cultural change program was the introduction of sales tools or infrastructure, such as the "pre-call planning form," which Jensen introduced in the sales training class. Designed to help accountants and business consultants prepare to meet with a prospect or client, the guide helps Moss Adams's professionals understand, among other things, the purpose of their meeting and the client's preferred communication style, imperatives, and needs. It also lays out some questions for them to address face-to-face with clients. Participants are required to conclude their training sessions with a completed pre-call planning form.

Participants initially pushed back. They viewed the pre-call planning form as just another piece of work to add to their already too-heavy business commitments. Almost immediately, Jensen declared that he wasn't wedded to the form itself. Indeed, it wasn't the exercise of filling out the document that mattered. More important was that the Moss Adams business developer considered the conceptual areas it outlined, and planned appropriately for the upcoming meeting with clients. Other tools introduced over the last two years have included a Call Follow-up, Long-term Pursuit Plan, Sales Plan, Relationship Map, Communications Styles, Loss Analyzer, Opportunity Analyzer, and the third element of Jensen's behavioral change program, the Pipeline.

The Pipeline, which targets group accountability, is a forward-looking plan that helps Moss Adams professionals identify target companies to pursue and then better prepare to build business with those targets. At first, people were resistant to being held accountable. They were comfortable with their previous method (a past-oriented proposal log). Jensen had to resort to absolute logic to point out the value of pipeline planning:

> When people queried me about the value of this tool, I would give them an example. "Let's say your office revenue goal is $30 million this year. It looks like you're going to repeat $25 million. So that means you've got a $5 million gap. And I'm looking here at a proposal log of $4 million. And you won't win all of that revenue, so tell me what steps you will take to go out and get the rest of the business? You're not going to sit around and just wait for an RFP, are you?"

It took Jensen about six months—well into 2007—to achieve real lift-off for this significant cultural change. Along the way, he fueled the firm's desired behavioral change by employing the fourth element of the program: celebration. At each opportunity, he found successes to tout among the firm's partners. From his perspective, "success" was not necessarily a big contract win or a huge engagement. Instead, Jensen highlighted simple changes—those small individual steps that demonstrated how Moss Adams people were adopting his new approach and the favorable results.

Change Requires Commitment

Almost as soon as Jensen's sales training programs had launched, he received feedback that the one-day session was not enough. He immediately increased the training to two full days. This internal obstacle was relatively easy to overcome.

But other internal challenges were related to some of the more arcane norms identifiable with privately owned professional service firms. In particular, Jensen tended to carry himself with the authority and air of collegiality that most accountants and business consultants expect from equity owner peers. But Jensen was not a Moss Adams partner, and he understood that he had to go the extra mile to prove his professional worthiness.

A second, more insidious cultural barrier was associated with many professionals' natural unwillingness to change, especially if they are well paid and fairly comfortable with the way their PSF does business. (Of course, this cultural barrier does not exist in Moss Adams alone.) To vault this hurdle, Jensen relied on the enthusiastic backing of Moss Adams's chairman, Rick Anderson; its president, Chris Schmidt; and the firm's other top managers.

As he kept pushing harder on the flywheel (the firm is a fan of Jim Collins's *Good to Great* book), he found that Moss Adams's practitioners were looking at his efforts and realizing that they could indeed help him: "They started pushing with me." Interestingly, "graduates" of the sales training program formed an informal alumni club internally. Soon, Moss Adams's sales-trained leaders became the go-to guides for professionals who had not yet received the instruction. They began serving as internal ambassadors for the new norm.

"Culture is a long term proposition and our early results are encouraging," Jensen concludes. "Revenue continues to grow even in this slowing economy. Our pipeline is strong, with more than 2000 identified significant pursuits."

Anderson added, "We sold, albeit a bit poorly, before Scott came. He is the impetus for the improvement, and I could not be happier with the progress we have made. In the end, though, it is not one man, but one firm that makes the difference. We now have the training, the tools, the accountability and we are seeing the performance."

Connecting Marketing with the Needs of the Sales Teams

IBM Global Technology Services is the world's largest business and technology consultancy. Through a set of still evolving structural and cultural initiatives, IBM's services division has made substantial progress toward erasing the disconnect between marketing's lead generation activities and the firm's sales pipeline. This work has resulted in better linkage between the firm's service marketing investment and its sales return on investment.

• • •

Generating leads, especially a lot of leads, is always a good thing. But what happens to all those leads after the marketing team has generated them? Where do they go? Who's making sure those fantastic leads are moving from inquiry to booked revenue, and beyond to repeat work and expanded assignments?

Nowhere else is the disconnect between marketing and business development more obvious than in the handoff of leads to the business development pipeline of a professional or business-to-business service firm. Many of us suppose that the smaller the enterprise, the less of a headache this handoff might be. Some people would not even call it a handoff. And yet even in smaller firms the marketing and business development processes and functions are often disconnected from each other.

But what does this handoff look like in large global businesses? Within the complexities of a highly matrixed, far-flung organization, who is responsible for keeping the company's valuable leads moving smoothly through its marketing and business development pipeline? Some larger enterprises have addressed this challenge by adopting a customized version of account management. I applaud this idea, but account management, as a process, doesn't necessarily help PSFs or B2Bs overcome the silos that historically have existed between marketing and business development functions.

And so I went looking for evidence that a huge global enterprise can consider ways to better connect its marketing and business development functions. I was especially keen to find out whether a gigantic company could embark on a "doing things differently" initiative intended to increase the company's marketplace effectiveness.

Enter IBM's Global Technology Services group, the world's largest business and technology consultancy. As of early 2009, IBM (NYSE: IBM) boasted a stable of nearly 400,000 employees operating in 170 countries worldwide and overall annual revenues of nearly $98.8 billion. (The Global Technology Services group's pretax income represented 37 percent of the overall company.) IBM Global Technology Services group offers a range of services that help people link business and technology. Its consultants provide full outsourcing, infrastructure outsourcing, product support, security services, service-oriented architectures, and technology services that help customers be more "green."

Professional and B2B service observers will remember when IBM began its dramatic shift in the early 1990s from being a computer hardware company to a services provider, and the later payoff in revenues from that strategic decision. IBM's executive leaders continue to keep their eyes on marketplace shifts, and in 2007 they declared their intention to participate in the world's growth markets and improve IBM's productivity. How? By ensuring that IBM would become a globally integrated enterprise.

For Mary Garrett, former vice president of marketing for IBM Global Technology Services (and currently the marketing leader of the overall company's sales division), this mandate meant one thing for her group: to better link marketing—and the leads it generates—with sales.

What Have You Done for Me Lately?

Garrett's earliest epiphany on the integration issue occurred when it became clear that marketing didn't know enough about the ROI of its efforts. Global Technology Services leaders needed to understand the cause and effect of the group's marketing expenditures. What's more, the company didn't have the right metrics or the best internal mechanisms to show the sales teams exactly what was being attributed to marketing. Garrett explained:

> I could say the marketing team is wildly successful in generating all these leads, but if leads are not getting into the hands of the sellers, I know we'll have a skeptical sales force that says, "You guys *think* you are successful, but I haven't made my numbers, so why are you doing the happy dance?" We knew the key is to work together so the opportunities that get generated are absolutely the right ones, and are able to get into the hands of somebody that can really work them.

Starting in mid-2007, Garrett and the marketing team conceived some new initiatives to more effectively connect the company's marketing activities with its sales teams' activities. The goal was to more tightly link the marketing investment with the subsequent sales ROI. In particular, the marketing team wanted to improve its pipeline of new opportunities, the associated dollar amount spent to pursue and acquire those new leads, the number of wins the team achieved, and the resulting revenue dollars. Needless to say, these mandates required better tracking capabilities.

Garrett's directive was to ensure both that marketing and sales worked together across the geographic regions of the global teams and that Global Technology Services eventually developed a common approach that everyone could embrace. She knew it was important to quickly secure the support of the senior business management and the geographic heads as a foundation for action. At the same time, though, she wanted to move forward with a "test" mindset, with the expectation that changes to her team's suggested approaches could be made.

By late 2007, Garrett and her team had unveiled the first part of their integration solution: an experimental "Opportunity Identification War Room," piloted in one geography and in one local business line. In the early incarnations of their solution, they brought together the different sources for generating opportunities: sales teams, a representative of the business partners, a Web person, and someone from marketing. Even though they anticipated that the makeup of these sources of opportunities would change according to the situation, in general they decided to focus on three areas:

- Examining the performance of the different sources of opportunity together, with the sales teams. Marketing and sales asked each other, "So, marketing created X number of leads this week. Have they gotten into the hands of the appropriate sellers? How is the group progressing with those leads?"

- Ensuring the most effective distribution of content. The marketing team began to use the War Room to ask, "Do the sales teams know about all the enablement material that is available for them? Do they know what there is to help them with the sale?" Representatives from marketing and sales began to discover that, in some cases, good content had not gotten into the hands of the seller.

- Focusing on communicating *ahead*. Regardless of the different avenues for generating opportunities, everyone agreed that they needed to improve their engagement and participation with each other. For example, members of the marketing team would say to their sales team colleagues, "Are you familiar with the kinds of activities that will be under way in your local region over the next 30, 60, 90 days?"

In the beginning of 2008, from its pilot in one geography and local business line, Garrett and her team rolled out the War Room concept in seven countries. Garrett reported:

> Early on, our best progress was in India. After that, a couple of regions in the UK got started. Then the rest of our targeted regions got underway. It was very early, and we knew that we were going to learn a lot more as we continued to evolve this integration experiment. We knew that what we designed at the beginning was going to change. But we were excited about how well the War Room model was already helping us break down our internal silos.

Designing a Marketing/Sales Integration Approach That Overcomes Both Structural and Cultural Barriers

After the early stages of this integration experiment were launched, five different geographic units signed on to become involved. This level of participation was, of course, both thrilling and daunting, because it initially meant designing five different process approaches to link marketing with sales. Garrett and her marketing team colleagues felt as if they were spinning their wheels a bit trying to get started. They knew it was critical to design a common approach.

Key representatives from marketing and sales got together and looked at the streams of work between the "sides" and how these processes linked together. To make their work more manageable, group members looked at challenges in three general areas:

- What management system will we use to capture and organize marketing and sales business intelligence?
- What content are we going to share?
- How are we going to actually deploy this? How do we get it into action?

By late summer 2008, the marketing team's integration initiative appeared to be less like a formal pilot or experiment and more like "business as usual." No one needed convincing that integration was the answer and that they were on the right track. Garrett's mandate morphed, then, toward addressing the hurdles that needed to be overcome. The emphasis was on—and still is on—*speed*.

In particular, the organization's management system data were not in a format that salespeople found effective. Garrett and her team worked to create solutions that addressed an impediment to optimal effectiveness: creating tools that better articulate the pipeline information in a way that is understandable to a sales rep. Garrett reported, "We still have to get better at the data we share."

But true integration requires both structural and cultural components. Arguably, the structural elements of integration are fairly straightforward. It's like rearranging a line of dominoes so they fall into each other effortlessly. The off-kilter pieces are easy to spot and adjust.

For many other PSFs or B2Bs, however, especially the larger ones, the bigger obstacle can be cultural. IBM Global Technology Services did not have a strong cultural connection between marketing and sales. Perhaps this failing was related to the traditional mindset of most service businesses — that is, to *not* depend on demand generation and to not truly understand how to use marketing. Both sides contributed to the success of Global Technology Services, of course, but they did so from their own silos, and from their own cultural corners.

IBM's sales teams were legendary for their laser-like concentration on achieving the company's business objectives and for loyalty to their line managers. Garrett recognized the possibility that members of the sales teams might consider their marketing counterparts as mere distractions.

But there were other cultural challenges too. In particular, some of the sales team members were skeptical about working with the marketing team, giving rise to questions such as: What do you even do? Why are you here? What value are we getting? Garrett recognized that sellers would need proof that changing their strongly held norms would be worth their time and effort.

As with any effective marketing program, one of the first steps to overcoming these cultural challenges was just getting in front of the sales team members, listening to them, and convincing them to hear marketing's perspective. Garrett explained:

> We wanted to work with the sales line management directly, to participate in *their* forum. We knew it was best for marketing to go to them, rather than expect them to attend our meetings. This accomplishes two things: first, you save setting up an additional meeting. Second, you get the support of the sales executive leadership to tell the sellers that this new integration process is important and is worth paying attention to.

For months, the marketing team listened to sellers' concerns. Then marketing had to decide how best to respond. Some of the sellers' concerns required marketers to alter some of their own processes — for example, adjusting the timing of marketing's development and distribution of client analytics, which the sales group needed earlier in the company's planning cycles than marketing had previously understood. Other efforts required marketing to make a concerted communication outreach to sales, in particular to explain the kinds of marketing activities that would help sellers and show them the potential results. Also, marketers were able to engage sellers in fact-based data discussions centered around the company's sales management tools. These tools helped both sides have much more productive dialogues about the leads in the pipeline.

As they continued along their cultural change journey, marketers asked for help from sellers in the geographies that had already adopted the new integration approach. They asked them to help communicate a message to their counterparts in other geographies. The message was that the initiative to integrate marketing and sales, though not an easy one, was worth it in the long run. The ultimate argument, of course, was the compelling benefits the clients of IBM Global Technology Services could realize from engaging with a service provider that has succeeded at its deliberate efforts to erase its marketing and sales functional silos.

Happiness: Never Having to Justify a Marketing Investment Again

The IBM Global Technology Services group's effort to integrate its marketing and sales functions continues, with ongoing leadership support from IBM's overall business executives. Garrett identified three important lessons learned that have been equal contributors to the early success of the marketing-selling integration effort: "First, get buy-in from your own marketing teams. Have team members collaboratively develop the programs they'll present to their sales counterparts. Second, work with a consistent approach. And third, meet Sales where Sales meets. Go to them. Don't expect them to come to your party. Go to *their* party."

Ultimately, Garrett's goal was simple: "to never have to justify another marketing investment again." The job is nowhere near done, but it's not too difficult to envision the potential outcome. Sales will act on many more of the leads that marketing generates. And then the barriers to effective integration between marketing and sales will begin to crumble. The collaboration between marketing and sales will become a new cultural norm. People will feel informed and included.

I've featured this story about the IBM Global Technology Services group's integration initiative as a way to confirm that even a huge global firm can take steps to do things differently. And even baby steps make a difference.

Chapter 10

Cases: The Skills Imperative

This chapter profiles four firms for their work on the Skills Imperative. These four stories reveal the results professional firms will realize when they develop their people. Executive managers are using a variety of approaches to help their practitioners and nonrevenue-generating professionals build not only integrated competencies, but also standards for collaboration, shared accountabilities, and co-leadership in marketing, business development, and client service. These cases center on professional firms in environmental, engineering, and management consulting; law; engineering and architectural planning, design, and consulting; and real estate services.

■ ■ ■

Giving Marketers a Seat at the Table — and Getting a Leg Up on the Marketplace

Haley & Aldrich is one of the top U.S. environmental, engineering, and management consulting firms. It created a pathway to a "seat at the table" for its nonrevenue-generating marketing leader. This structural framework, coupled with the firm's mindful stewardship of a shared-accountability culture, has contributed to the enterprise's continued prominence in its sector.

• • •

Experts become experts by gathering in-depth knowledge of their subject areas. However, during their formal education many PSF and B2B company practitioners do not learn management, marketing, strategy, or other administrative functions such as human resources or finance. Thus once they form their own professional firms, typically they hire nonrevenue-generating "outside" experts who bring to the table their own deep knowledge. Practitioners functionally divide themselves from these "outsider" nonrevenue-generating professionals. It's no surprise, then, that a firm's executive managers may not consider their nonrevenue-generating senior professionals to be key players in the management of the company.

"Getting a seat at the table" (the executive committee or board of directors, the pinnacle of a firm's leadership) has become a well-known metaphor among professional service marketers and business developers. "Getting a seat" means being recognized by the equity owners of one's firm as a valued participant—a peer—in the strategic and management decisions of the firm.

Giving marketers and business developers a seat at the table is not as unusual as it used to be. But it is rare to find a professional firm that took this step *more than two decades ago*. Even I was surprised when I discovered Haley & Aldrich had done just that.

The Haley & Aldrich story reveals the enormously positive chain reaction produced when a professional enterprise embraces a marketing mindset by integrating marketing professionals and client service practitioners into the firm's senior leadership. Collaboration, an external focus, the adoption of formal processes, dedication to personal growth and organizational learning—all of these factors contributed to Haley & Aldrich's ever-broadening integration mindset. Here's a firm that figured out how to integrate *with its marketplace*.

Founded in 1957, Boston-based Haley & Aldrich began as a small engineering firm offering specialized services in the geosciences. Now it's a firm of nearly 450 employees who generate revenue of almost $100 million from 21 U.S. offices. Its palette of services has expanded as well. Today, Haley & Aldrich delivers an expansive set of consulting services to real estate development, energy, industrial, and infrastructure clients who are facing environmental, engineering, and management challenges.

Through the years, the firm has won many awards. In 2007 alone, it was recognized by several organizations and publications for its excellence in engineering; its contribution to safety, health, and environmental performance; and its achievements in projects related to highways, civil engineering, building design, and site innovation.

Haley & Aldrich's Web site declares that its people are dedicated to producing meaningful outcomes, fostering open communication, and pursuing continual learning and improvement. These principles form the backbone of the story that follows.

Inventing the Future

In the early 1980s, Haley & Aldrich enjoyed a preeminent role in its local market, but the firm's executive managers were concerned that more competitors were emerging. When Sylvia Wheeler was asked to join the firm as its senior marketing professional in 1984, she was charged with raising the marketing awareness of partners, including those who were not eager to take on business development responsibilities.

She came on board with the understanding that she would be considered for ownership sometime within two years. Then, as now, a peer review process determines who is invited to take shareholder positions in the company. In 1986 she became a vice president and an equity owner of Haley & Aldrich.

In 1994 Wheeler became the first nontechnical professional to serve on Haley & Aldrich's board of directors, as well as the first female member elected by the firm's shareholders. (During her four-year term on the board, the firm also welcomed a second female board member, and several women have served as board members since.) Worthy of note was that Wheeler was hired for her experience as a marketing professional rather than being a "homegrown" leader who had patiently worked her way up through the ranks of the company. This was a considerable shift for a company known for building from within.

Wheeler retired in late 2007, and she was fêted at a Haley & Aldrich reception attended by most of the firm's leadership, as well as respected marketers from several architecture, engineering, and construction companies. Many of the speakers made heartfelt remarks about Wheeler's leadership in the field of professional service marketing, her standards for excellence, and her indelible contributions to the firm's respected stature in its industry.

Those are the facts. I've known Sylvia Wheeler for many years, and I can personally attest to her forward-thinking intellectual capital in the field of professional service marketing. But as capable as Wheeler is, this story is instead about Haley & Aldrich's extraordinary blend of culture and structure that welcomed a professional marketer as a company owner and enabled her to be an influential leader in the first place—and about the marketplace benefits the firm realized in parallel.

Bruce Beverly, Haley & Aldrich's CEO since 2000, recalled the firm's approach to marketing in the 1980s, before Wheeler joined the company:

> In the early days at the firm, our marketing amounted to answering the phone because of our expertise, and then responding with a written proposal. At a few particular points in our history, we noticed the phone wasn't ringing. We said, "Well perhaps we should do something differently!"

When people come in with different experiences, it is really a good thing because you learn about what other people do, and their processes. Sometimes, guess what, you find out they are better than what you may have evolved in your own internally focused environment.

Sylvia brought in diverse thinking; she helped us begin to look at what was happening outside.

Beverly's remarks illuminate the unique culture resident within Haley & Aldrich. Wheeler's journey to the firm's offer of a "seat at the table" would not have been possible had the firm not been so strongly focused on competitive success and learning, and capable of harnessing its individuals to achieve goals for the larger group.

For her part, Wheeler certainly understood the importance of "pushing the envelope." Almost from the beginning of her tenure at Haley & Aldrich, she interpreted her marketing role much more broadly than did most marketers, certainly at the time and arguably even now.

Haley & Aldrich's high-achievement culture provided the structural springboard—*strategic planning*—that enabled Wheeler to become one of the firm's management leaders. She explained:

When I was being interviewed by Haley & Aldrich, it was a well established and highly regarded company. The company had a lot of strong personalities who were used to being very successful. They didn't have to compete for work that much.

But the firm's leaders recognized the market was maturing for the services they provided, and that they needed to become more sophisticated in the way they marketed. They recognized they needed a senior marketing professional to work with them as a teammate to evaluate market opportunities and help grow the firm in a more systematic and strategic manner. Over the years, the three CEOs with whom I've worked embraced a market-focused strategic planning process for that purpose.

Wheeler tapped into her colleagues' willingness to look at the outside, and their natural predilection to learn and to evolve. In 1998 she worked with the CEO, an outside consultant, and selected industry advisors to enhance the firm's strategic planning process. Geographic and service expansion had brought in new thinking that required broader participation by the firm's emerging leaders, along with a better understanding of its position in its more diverse markets. Haley & Aldrich began a more rigorous stewardship of its brand, intentionally harnessing its cultural strengths with marketplace opportunity.

Even before he became the firm's CEO in 2000, Beverly began implementing his own "diversity" strategy. He embarked on a self-education process by enrolling in an intensive executive education program and, at every opportunity, attending conferences of industry and client market leaders. From these and other sources, he gained new perspectives on the power of diverse ideas, collaboration and teamwork, goal setting, strategic planning, and systems thinking. Then, he began pushing the envelope further, to dismantle Haley & Aldrich's well-entrenched homegrown norm of tying ownership of the firm to an individual's title or management seniority. Most important, Beverly challenged the company at all levels to reevaluate how the world was changing and to change with it.

Integrating a Company into Its Marketplace

The Haley & Aldrich story of change may seem deceptively simple. Just bring in marketing professionals to participate in key decision-making committees. Just give marketing professionals an ownership stake in the company's success. Encourage your firm's leaders to learn and grow with their clients and markets. Engage in a periodic strategic planning process.

How many PSFs and B2Bs have taken some steps to change—perhaps even steps like the ones I've just outlined—and still found they were just metaphorically treading marketplace waters?

Haley & Aldrich's story is an example for other PSFs about how to integrate a professional enterprise into its marketplace. Beverly explained:

> I consider my role to be one of stewardship of the company. We are always trying to operate our organization like a living organism, where it is continually sensing its position relative to what is happening in the environment, evaluating what is happening and then understanding what it means to ourselves and our clients. We are always taking some proactive steps to adapt to those changes. We're building an organization and people within it who have skills to adapt to whatever comes our way in the future.
>
> Our Company Vision is "To be the company most sought after to integrate technology and human potential to tackle tough issues facing the world." This shared vision is taking us on a long journey. To be the company most sought after, we have to be able to improve our competencies to move this company ahead. For example, next week I am going to the

World Innovation Conference in New York City. This will be the second year I've attended, and last year our firm was the only professional service firm represented. My goal is to learn about innovation, to see how we can improve our competencies in innovating.

In 2008 Beverly extended this leadership agenda: to change how Haley & Aldrich runs itself and how it deploys its strategy. The goal was to operate even more collaboratively than ever before, using the principles articulated in James P. Womack and Daniel T. Jones's 1996 book *Lean Thinking*. According to Womack and Jones, five basic principles characterize a lean enterprise:

- *Specify value* from the standpoint of the end customer by product family.
- *Identify all the steps in the value stream* for each product family, eliminating every step and every action and every practice that does not create value.
- Make the remaining value-creating steps occur in a tight and integrated sequence so the product will *flow* smoothly toward the customer.
- As flow is introduced, let customers *pull* value from the next upstream activity.
- As these steps lead to greater transparency, enabling managers and teams to eliminate further waste, *pursue perfection* through continuous improvement.[1]

To customize these principles to a professional service enterprise, Beverly recruited an expert on *Lean Thinking* and assembled a team that included Denise Coleman, Haley & Aldrich's vice president of marketing (and Wheeler's successor) since 2006, and selected senior managers, corporate group leaders, and business unit leaders. He asked this group to help the firm change the way it implements its strategy, using a customized version of *Lean*'s policy deployment process.

One of the group's goals was to start breaking down the company's internal silos. "Let's say a business unit person doesn't know what Haley & Aldrich's marketing group and other company leaders are doing," said Coleman. "It was our job to find the communication breakdowns, fix them and improve our competence around those processes at the same time."

One of Coleman's near-term objectives was to improve the firm's marketplace sensing activities and subsequent internal communications and response processes around appropriate marketplace opportunities. She compared Haley & Aldrich with other professional service firms in a variety of sectors, and she gathered benchmarking information about e-communications and how they are being deployed. From that, she developed recommendations for how Haley & Aldrich could use internal communication vehicles that feature the least erosion in information between what is learned from the person in direct contact with the client and what is learned by the people who receive that information (i.e., least waste—highest value).

The company also began incorporating its own version of *Lean Thinking* into its already successful methods of client listening. According to Coleman, the firm uses a technique it calls "the art of the strategic conversation with clients," in which people employ neutral ways to delve deeply into what their clients value and what concerns them. From there, they can begin to consider how Haley & Aldrich might meet those needs through new service offerings and business models.

These initiatives—and others Beverly plans for the firm to develop over the next three years—are all conceived as part of Haley & Aldrich's *Lean Thinking* adaptation: let Haley & Aldrich be *pulled* toward where the clients want to take it.

Overcoming a Company's Legacy of Silos

An organization this focused on its marketplace was only able to become so because of its strong internal integration of marketing and business development functions with those of the revenue-generating technical professionals. But for Haley & Aldrich, the road wasn't without its potholes. Beverly described his biggest lesson learned:

> In my tenure as the CEO, I have been challenged on the subject of the marketing group: where is their value and what do they do? Such comments are made because the person just doesn't understand the interdependent nature of marketing and business development. I've tried to consistently give a message of the value that our marketing professionals provide and describe in clear terms exactly what the marketing group is doing for us.

And now with our new strategy deployment process, I'll continue to encourage staff to understand that we are in a collaborative learning process that generates and uses marketing ideas to help our company attain its goals over the next three years, and into the future.

Coleman and Wheeler added to Beverly's lessons learned remarks, pointing out that the firm has done particularly well at positioning the people in the company's business development and marketing support group as business partners. They applauded the firm's senior technical professionals for reinforcing the cultural norm that it is a shared responsibility to work with marketing professionals. Wheeler concluded: "At Haley & Aldrich, there is a strong understanding that marketing is an important business function, and as such, should be a fully integrated cross-functional part of any business, including a professional services business."

Training Attorneys to Market and Sell: Small Steps Equal Great Gains

Baker Donelson is a regional law firm, and one of the 100 largest in the United States. It developed two new personal productivity programs to help attorneys gain a sense of accountability and improve their skills in marketing and business development. The direct result was higher billings for attorneys who participated in the programs.

● ● ●

The vast majority of professional service firms operate as privately held partnerships. For many professionals, whether accountants, architects, management consultants, lawyers, or any others whose intellectual capital is the "product," partnerships are a highly attractive way to participate in running a business. If a relatively inexperienced new hire rolls up his sleeves, puts in long hours, and learns the ropes of the business and the profession from his firm's senior leaders, he will eventually get a shot at sharing in the firm's profits, and perhaps its equity.

But these privately held partnerships also feature a double-edged sword. Internal competition is keen. And indeed, especially where colleagues are encouraged organizationally to work together on marketing and business development, trust can be all too elusive. I'll never forget the moment I realized that "partnerships" don't always translate into smooth personal feelings between a firm's professionals. When I was the regional marketing director of a management consulting firm, I attended a proposal planning meeting with the head of one of the firm's prominent practices. We were discussing how we might assemble a team whose experts could best solve the prospect's problems. I suggested bringing on board one of the firm's well-known professionals whose capabilities would be a perfect match for the potential client. The practice leader's reply was immediate and, I thought, harsh: "I certainly won't invite *him* to my prospective client meeting! I don't trust him!"

I've encountered many variations of this scenario throughout my career. It's a vein of "disconnectivity" that runs throughout every business, but it is particularly dangerous in a professional service environment, no matter what the size of the organization. It doesn't matter what go-to-market processes, protocols, or tools a firm's leaders might require; if people don't want to market and sell business together, or for some reason *can't*, silos inevitably abound. Mergers and acquisitions—a favorite growth mechanism for PSFs—only serve to exacerbate marketing and business development disconnects that already exist.

I was especially intrigued, then, when I heard about the unique marketing and business development integration approach being implemented by law firm Baker, Donelson, Bearman, Caldwell & Berkowitz. Founded in 1888 (yes, you read that right), Baker Donelson was ranked in 2007 by the *National Law Journal* as one of the 100 largest law firms in the United States. The firm's more than 500 attorneys and public policy advisors work in almost 20 offices across five states. Mostly concentrated in the southeastern United States, the firm also has offices in Washington, DC, and Beijing. Baker Donelson's practice areas include public policy, health care, securities, and intellectual property.

Baker Donelson's story is a good fit for this book because it emphasizes helping people identify integrated ways to work together. The firm developed two new programs to help attorneys grow a shared sense of personal accountability for the firm's marketing and business development functions. Instead of requiring a one-size-fits-all process for marketing and selling, Baker Donelson had the professional bravery to help its people build their own new integration processes and grow their competencies in marketing and selling. It also formalized their accountabilities for doing so and tracked their achievement of goals.

Baker Donelson's approach is a great example of the results a professional service firm can achieve when it intentionally makes marketing and selling *every* person's job, even allowing for the fact that each person has a different role to fill.

When Overachievers Underproduce in Marketing and Selling

The hallways of Baker Donelson's offices are crammed with gifted attorneys. These attorneys are regularly recognized among peers and industry observers for their professional stature in nearly every aspect of the law.

From 2002 to 2007, through mergers and acquisitions, Baker Donelson more than doubled in size. Even if the firm had the world's most dazzling process handoffs from marketing to business development, that is a lot of new people who are expected to work together to fill the revenue pipeline. The skills and experience needed to generate leads and grow revenues varied widely among these newly incorporated professionals. They simply didn't know each other well enough to market and sell business together as effectively as they could.

But Baker Donelson's executive committee members believed they faced an additional challenge. The firm's most senior attorneys—even as talented as they were—weren't as productive in marketing and selling as they should have been. "Many of our most experienced attorneys had gotten set in their ways and were not experiencing the same growth in their books of business as they had experienced in years past," commented Jerry Stauffer, the firm's chief operating officer.

It's Personal: "Getting to Know You" to Help Break Down Marketing and Business Development Silos

In 2006 Baker Donelson's marketing and professional development departments (including Laura Hine, chief marketing officer, and Susan Wagner, director of professional development) embarked on a joint initiative to help all these professionals improve their delivery of excellent client service, time management, and business development. Called PracticeAdvance, the program offers year-round training classes to all attorneys at all levels. The monthly sessions focus on how to build relationships with clients, improve individual marketing skills, and become more proactive in seeking new business for the firm. Hine explained:

> By creating PracticeAdvance, Baker Donelson's Marketing and Professional Development departments have invested in the Firm's greatest,

client-focused assets: Baker Donelson attorneys. Participants gain the tools necessary to be more effective, efficient attorneys, in a setting that is comfortable and informal. Discussions of each topic by and between attorneys at different levels of experience are encouraged. The Firm's attorneys are the Baker Donelson brand, and the PracticeAdvance program builds upon the strength of that brand.

Within the first 12 months of the PracticeAdvance program, more than 350 attorneys had participated. After each program, a survey was submitted to gauge the overall response to the program. The comments were incredibly positive. One lawyer stated: "The program today caused me to rethink the way I manage my contacts and the importance of keeping those contacts up to date and staying on top of how often I am interacting with each client, referral source and prospect. Thanks for the ideas!"

In 2006 the firm's new director of client development, Tea Hoffmann (now chief business development officer), went to COO Jerry Stauffer to suggest an extension of the PracticeAdvance program. Hoffmann wanted the firm to capitalize on her strong background of success in increasing people's productivity in marketing and business development (she had already authored a book on the subject; earlier she had run her own consulting company helping legal professionals grow their businesses; and she was recognized as one of FranklinCovey's top trainers in 2007 and once held the only FranklinCovey U.S. training license for law firms).

Hoffmann believed Baker Donelson had taken some critical first steps, but that it was now time for the firm to go beyond its PracticeAdvance program by taking another important step: developing an initiative to enable Baker Donelson attorneys to work together more effectively to market and sell.

She asked Stauffer for funds to take the firm's senior attorneys through her customized version of the FranklinCovey "7 Habits™" and "FOCUS™" programs. They agreed it would be better to make the program voluntary, available first to the most interested attorneys. From Baker Donelson's perspective, Stauffer's goal was to help these selected attorneys develop more business with existing clients. But Hoffmann knew the outcome of participating in a FranklinCovey program could even be more deeply personal.

Stauffer and Hoffmann developed a six-month program called "20 Over 40," and geared it toward senior-level attorneys aged 40 and older. They planned to accept applications from attorneys who wanted to increase their personal and professional productivity. "When the 20 Over 40 program was announced in September, 2006, we thought we would start with only one group of 20," said Hoffmann. "The response was overwhelming. Almost immediately, the participation roster swelled to 78 people, with a waiting list. We ended up creating four groups of about 20 each."

The program, which began in October 2006, featured some clearly defined rules. Participants would not be allowed to miss any more than two of the monthly all-group sessions. And everyone was required to attend a one-and-a-half-day class on how to obtain "focus" and develop goals. Each participant was asked to develop two professional goals and one personal goal in conjunction with a randomly selected "accountability buddy" who was also at the retreat. The goals were then shared with the rest of the group. Each goal had to include a fully developed plan of execution and designated timelines.

The initial "focus retreats" were conducted off-site at state parks so that distractions would be minimal. The training was intense. Attorneys revealed many of their personal aspirations to the entire group, and in most cases many of them were meeting in person for the first time. The bonding experienced by the entire group was perhaps one of the most beneficial outcomes of the entire program.

Once goals were set and openly stated, the accountability buddies were selected, and the participants had returned to their respective cities, progress was measured monthly. Participants had to not only work toward their goals, but also read at least two books during the course of the program and present a "book report" to their respective groups. In addition, they had to attend monthly training and refocusing classes and receive personal coaching from Hoffmann on how to keep on track.

Small Steps Equal Great Gains

Hoffmann offered three examples of the positive impact of Baker Donelson's 20 Over 40 program:

- An attorney who set a professional goal of personally visiting existing clients, for no reason at all, conducted more than 30 visits during the course of the six-month program. In doing so, he opened up 13 new matters and received two referrals for new business.

- An attorney who decided he wanted to launch an International Franchise Association (IFA) networking group for the state of Tennessee worked with one of the firm's marketing professionals to set up a series of events, hosted in Baker Donelson's offices and videoconferenced to other offices throughout the state, to facilitate franchise leaders' discussions about current industry topics and to help them access valuable educational opportunities. More than 30 people came to his first IFA meeting, and only 13 were existing clients. He now offers these sessions once a month to five offices within the firm and averages more than 50 attendees per month. Meanwhile, he has been named the head of the firm's Hospitality and Franchise Industry Service Team, and he has built his book of business to nearly $1 million a year with this new focus.

- An attorney who had recently joined the firm after serving as general counsel for a publicly traded company found the road to rebuilding her book of business more difficult than she had anticipated. Her goal was to build her book and her hours. The program allowed her to meet attorneys throughout the firm and share her expertise. Within a few months, she not only was able to meet her goal of rebuilding her book of business, but also gained referrals from members of each of the 20 Over 40 groups that enabled her to meet her productivity goals sooner than expected.

The results, then, were strongly positive. In their six months of participating in the program, this inaugural group of 20 Over 40 members increased their revenue productivity by nearly $3 million compared with the same six months of the previous year.

Hoffmann also saw the positive effects of the working relationships and shared accountabilities between the firm's revenue-generating attorneys and its nonrevenue-generating marketing and business development professionals. Marketers and business developers gained a better understanding of the business world in which their professionals operated. The lawyers learned how to better support the firm's marketing initiatives. And they gained a greater appreciation of the value provided by their nonrevenue-generating marketing and business development staff.

For example, while most of these talented lawyers knew of the firm's competitive analysis abilities, many had gotten lazy about researching their existing clients and prospects. One program session featured the firm's competitive analysis manager, who did a report on one client or referral of each participant. Working with their accountability buddies, participants were asked to look for one "unexplored" opportunity and develop a plan to explore that opportunity.

But beyond the arguably touchy-feely aspects of "understanding" and "appreciation," participants and their marketing and business development colleagues added new competencies. Then they practiced their newly acquired skills and celebrated their achievements.

The firm's marketing department also received public kudos in December 2006 when it was recognized in "The Second Annual *Marketing the Law Firm* 50: The Top Law Firms in Marketing and Communications" for creating and implementing its two attorney training programs.[2]

At the conclusion of the program, each person received a trophy—a leather baby shoe. It was certainly not a traditional choice to honor the completion of a significant task, but that was the point. The small leather shoe signified not only the small steps that each person had taken, but also the small steps they would continue to take over time: greatly enhanced skills to more effectively generate more revenues with more deeply integrated marketing and business development processes.

Many small steps, taken over time, lead to real progress. All this, simply by asking attorneys to volunteer to be held formally accountable for collaborating on marketing and business development.

"The program greatly exceeded my expectations," said Stauffer. "Not only did more of our lawyers participate than I expected, but the level of genuine enthusiasm and deepening of personal relationships was something truly unique."

Growing a Professional Service Firm . . . Together, One Step at a Time

From a firm-wide perspective, one of Baker Donelson's most significant lessons learned from the 20 Over 40 program was the tight bonding that occurred among members. Even after the program ended, and even though they worked out of 15 different office locations, the first group of attorneys continued to meet and interact with each other to cross-market and cross-sell. On a daily basis, they help each other set goals. Their shared accountability continues.

Hoffmann and her team also learned, the hard way, not to facilitate so many groups concurrently. Indeed, even though the initiative was clearly a success, she felt it could be even more so if she concentrates next on a smaller group. Another lesson learned: the firm decided to run its 20 Over

40 program every other year instead of annually. According to Hoffmann, "The resources required to co-ordinate the program and maximize its potential should be laser-like focused and can cause other programs to suffer. Conducting the program every other year enables our entire department to give each activity the appropriate amount of energy without overtaxing its resources."

Last but not least, Hoffmann was gratified with one of her early decisions: the program did not need to be high glitz. Attorneys were quite satisfied to meet off-site at state parks, for example, rather than high-priced conference venues. In fact, this decision likely enhanced the program's uniqueness and stimulated an unexpected sense of informal camaraderie.

Using a Balanced Scorecard and Informal Mentoring to Integrate Marketing and Selling with Client Service

Ross & Baruzzini is an engineering and architectural planning, design, and consulting firm. It is ranked one of the top 50 engineering and architectural firms in the United States by *Building Design+Construction* magazine. It adapted a big-time performance management tool (Balanced Scorecard) and combined it with an informal "guardian angel" mentoring program.

* * *

As anyone who has ever worked for a professional or B2B service firm eventually learns, the managers of these companies sometimes have to perform excruciating balancing acts to guide their organizations' growth. On one hand, they must ensure the implementation of a jumble of processes to market, sell, and deliver the company's services, and then, through more processes, make sure everyone is appropriately recognized for their contributions. On the other hand, they must do this across a firm's geographies, lines of business, industry groups, and more. With all these moving parts, managing a professional service firm can get messy.

And yet I'd argue that the management infrastructure aspects of the business are the easy parts of leading a PSF. Beyond that, these leaders must also address that squishy cultural area: helping one group of people adapt to another group's learning or communication styles, setting up the best mix of internal working relationships, and figuring out how to best motivate everyone to row in the same direction for the good of all. This culture management arena is the hardest to lead, but it plays a huge role in a firm's ability to gain traction in the marketplace.

Consider the critical importance of instilling in their people a sense of responsibility and enthusiasm for marketing and business development. PSF and B2B executive managers face the difficult reality of building a go-to-market process that works for everyone in the company. They must encourage the most desirable behaviors from people who find them unfamiliar, and in some cases, distasteful.

One firm that's effectively managed this difficult balancing act is Ross & Baruzzini. This small engineering company adopted a big-company management tool, the Balanced Scorecard, as its structural springboard to build market share. At the same time, it demonstrated a great deal of cultural savvy by informally encouraging professionals to collaborate and share accountabilities for growing the firm. Each of its initiatives—whether formal or informal—was intentionally designed to bring technical people into the world of marketing and business development.

Founded in 1953, Ross & Baruzzini is based in St. Louis, in the heart of the U.S. Midwest. It provides its architectural, mechanical, electrical, communication, and security systems engineering services to clients who need to solve their facilities and infrastructure challenges, primarily in the aviation, higher education, government, health care, and maritime industries.

Through offices in St. Louis, Miami, Indianapolis, New York, and Orlando, Ross & Baruzzini's 110 professionals generated nearly $18 million in revenues in 2008. The firm's expertise in mechanical, electrical, and specialized telecommunications systems have helped it to garner numerous awards from leading national and regional design, construction, and real estate publications.

Planning Starts with the Client in Mind

From the mid-1990s to 2001, Ross & Baruzzini grew robustly. Nevertheless, early in the new millennium members of the firm's operating committee began to feel that the company was not firing on all cylinders. As recounted by partner Dave Kipp, "We seemed to be hitting a plateau. Our revenue began to flatten. We found ourselves dependent on too few market niches, which left us with an unbalanced portfolio. And we began to feel that our successes—or disappointments—happened too unpredictably."

The five partners who made up Ross & Baruzzini's operating committee met monthly to review the firm's marketplace progress and to make decisions on key short-term and long-term issues. In 2002 the firm initiated a three-month discussion within this operating committee about the possibility of adapting a tool developed by Robert Kaplan and David Norton (the Balanced Scorecard) to Ross & Baruzzini.[3] Operating committee members wanted to be more explicit and purposeful in making progress on the firm's plans. They decided they could indeed use this tool to align their professionals' everyday behavior to the strategic goals of the enterprise.

They began using the Scorecard that same year. Now each year, centered around the company's July 1 fiscal year, Ross & Baruzzini's operating committee reviews the firm's rolling five-year strategic plan and makes up its annual target plans. This event triggers a top-down goal-setting process that flows through the organization to every individual.

All professionals are required to sit down with their supervisors to review the company's overall annual goals and the goals of their business units. Supervisors may spend an hour with each person, going over the individual's Balanced Scorecard. During these meetings, the professionals lay out their developmental needs and the contributions they will commit to making to the firm. Together, professionals and their supervisors outline, in plain terms that are meaningful to both, each individual's goals and actions and how they align with the firm's overall strategies. The result is a first draft Scorecard. The supervisor and professional may review it again in person before it's sent back "up" to the operating committee.

After the Ross & Baruzzini operating committee takes a last look at the content of all the Scorecards, they are finalized for the year ahead. From there, Scorecards become living documents that are reviewed quarterly at an "All-Hands" meeting with every person in the firm. Ross & Baruzzini's director of human resources receives a large bound book of all the Scorecards and then tracks them to ensure their tactical implementation.

Ross & Baruzzini is decidedly open about this process; anyone can see anyone else's Scorecard. The firm's Scorecard and that of each division is even published on the company intranet.

A Tool for Breaking Down Silos

Like any typical Balanced Scorecard, Ross & Baruzzini's Scorecard features four perspectives: financial, internal business processes, customer, and individual learning and growth. It was embraced early on as a powerful tool to help everyone track their own performance in a static manner. But operating committee members realized the Scorecard's four separate quadrants could easily build silos, not erase them. They were committed to helping their professionals become more market-driven, not less. They wanted the Scorecard to help increase their effectiveness in collaborating and sharing responsibilities for marketing, selling, and delivering excellent service to clients.

To guide the best cultural mindset, operating committee members made several decisions about how they wanted their professionals to think about the Scorecard. For example, they renamed the customer quadrant "client satisfaction." Also, instead of overly focusing on any one quadrant (and falling into the temptation to spotlight the financial quadrant), the firm's leaders began to regularly reinforce the notion that revenues and profits were only an outcome of outstanding execution in the other three quadrants. Kipp explained:

> For us, the Scorecard cycle starts with the client's satisfaction, flows over into learning and growing, from there into internal business processes, and finally to financials. We think of it as a wheel, starting with the client and deriving our professional learning and business processes from that. Financial results are seen as an outcome of doing the other things right. For us, the Scorecard lends itself to encouraging everyone's mindset that business development is their responsibility.

Table 10.1 depicts a sanitized version of an actual Ross & Baruzzini employee's Scorecard. This particular employee was relatively new to the firm, and so this was his first Scorecard.

"There has to be a structural component for our professionals to grow—and eventually disseminate—their intellectual capital to our clients," said Kipp. "A guy could sit in his office writing all day long, but if there's no connection to our clients' needs and no means to get it out, it amounts to nothing from a client perspective. We're interested in leveraging our knowledge to improve ourselves and help our clients."

Ross & Baruzzini president Craig Toder echoed Kipp's comments. "Having scorecard goals set around client satisfaction helped this professional get off to a fast start. He immediately hit the marketplace running, with a lot of impact, more than we usually see."

Client Satisfaction Quadrant		
The strategy for creating value and differentation from the perspective of the client		
Results desired	**Actions required**	**Target date**
Continuity of government thought leadership. Create within select customer communities the perception of the firm as a thought leader and solution provider of choice for Continuity of Government design, planning, and business process improvement solutions and services.	Identify key clients and stakeholders and cultivate relationships.	December
	Create a Ross & Baruzzini marketing recommendation paper.	February
	Identify key regional forums and deliver relevant intellectual material.	Quarterly
	Identify, pursue, and win $M of strategic opportunities.	3d quarter
Increase access to customers.	Identify select bidders lists and add firm to lists.	November
Sales	Identify sales potential of $M.	3d quarter
A&E Critical Infrastructure Protection provider of choice. Build positive name recognition for existing Ross & Baruzzini services with select customer groups.	Identify key clients and stakeholders and cultivate relationships.	December
	Identify key regional forums and deliver relevant intellectual material.	Quarterly
	Identify, pursue, and win $M of strategic opportunities.	3d quarter

Learning and Growth Quadrant		
The priorities to create a climate that supports organizational change, innovation, and growth		
Results desired	**Actions required**	**Target date**
Understand the firm. Learn how to best use and sell the capabilities of Ross & Baruzzini.	Learn Ross & Baruzzini processes and process gatekeepers.	January
	Understand the scope of skill, capability, and accomplishments of the firm.	January
Develop professionally.	Create a professional development plan—one that is based on the needs of our clients.	January
	Start obtaining training that resonates with clients.	January

(continued)

Table 10.1 Balanced Scorecard of a New Ross & Baruzzini Employee

Internal Business Processes Quadrant		
The strategic priorities for various business processes, which create customer and shareholder satisfaction		
Results desired	**Actions required**	**Target date**
An efficient and productive Ross & Baruzzini capture process. Create a market analysis and capture process that allows the firm to realize revenue and growth targets.	Review current processes and procedures.	December
	Through collaboration recommend change as directed by _____.	January
Grow positive market opinion of Ross & Baruzzini.	Develop and deliver market intellectual capital material for the Maritime, Continuity of Government, and Critical Infrastructure Protection markets.	Develop and present material at least twice annually.
	Identify key competitors and potential partners and build within them a positive perception of Ross & Baruzzini.	Immediate

Financial Quadrant		
A strategy for growth, profitability, and risk viewed from the perspective of the shareholders		
Results desired	**Actions required**	**Target date**
Increase the capability of the firm. Identify companies and personnel that if acquired will provide the firm with strategic growth potential.	Identify one company.	May
	Identify two personnel.	January
Utilization.	Approaching 30%	December

Table 10.1 Balanced Scorecard of a New Ross & Baruzzini Employee *(continued)*
Reproduced with permission of Ross & Baruzzini.

Hold On, But Loosely!

For members of the operating committee, the Balanced Scorecard idea was an epiphany. They knew it was absolutely the right structure to guide professionals to better integrate their marketing, selling, and client service. But, especially as they began more broadly implementing it throughout the firm after its 2002 debut, they knew the Balanced Scorecard could not, by itself, provide the cultural underpinning they sought. Kipp explained:

Especially regarding the Learning and Growth quadrant on the Score-card, we realized we needed to approach our professionals' development very differently than would a manufacturing company. For example, we couldn't just command our people to attend a training course.

So we looked at some of David Maister's ideas; he says managers should be more like coaches than bosses, and this felt like a fit for us. We started to play around with the idea of measuring our performance not just in terms of the hard results, but how well we are doing as coaches.

The operating committee thought a formal mentoring program would appear too controlling to employees; they believed it could defeat the spirit of collaboration that could allow the firm to thrive. Although they never deliberately rejected the idea of a formal mentoring program, operating committee members began talking more about enabling a cultural evolution toward informal mentoring.

Starting around 2004, Ross & Baruzzini executive managers began looking for opportunities to give newer professionals a chance to get in front of a client, to make mistakes, and to try and spread their own wings. By setting an example of their own outreach to newer colleagues, they could more effectively encourage other Ross & Baruzzini principals to get engaged in helping the staff grow and develop. The idea was not to be heavy-handed, but to interact when serendipity presented opportunities to do so.

Kipp recalled a time when he and one of the firm's younger associates were on a plane, traveling to a client meeting. During casual conversation, the young man mentioned an interest area that he hoped to develop further. Kipp saw how passionate this young colleague was about the topic, and he saw an opening to help the young man find an outlet for his interest. He said, "I'd love to help you develop your idea. Why don't you scribble up an outline and we can work on it together?" Right there, an informal mentoring relationship began, and it continues to this day.

This relaxed mentoring model has also helped the firm better capture its professionals' ideas on solving clients' emerging needs. "If someone has a passion, a spark about a new client solution, we try to capture that and see if we can find an outlet for it that helps our clients," Kipp said. He continued with a vivid example:

We became known in the marketplace, sometime around 2005, for our unique approach to designing mission-critical facilities—data centers, emergency operation centers, and command and control facilities. We patented and trademarked our service offering, and gave it a brand name —CODE (Critical Operations Design Engineering). Since we formally launched it, we've generated a significant amount of business out of it. We've sponsored some research on it too.

One day in 2007, we were having one of our typical brainstorming meetings, where we ask ourselves, "What's new? What's going on? What's out there in the marketplace? What are our clients thinking about?" One of our principals, Dan Proctor, started talking about domain awareness. He had come from the military, and he said clients are struggling with how to resolve their inter-jurisdictional disputes—their own internal turf wars. On the face of it, they can arrange to build the facilities they need, and bring in the right technology. But if they cannot work together, then it's all for naught. Proctor said, "Clients who are responding to and recovering from natural or man-made incidents that disrupt operations need to move from raw data to actionable intelligence. How do we process that collaboratively, rather than in stovepipes?"

One of the other principals in the room immediately saw the potential for this idea. He blurted out, "critical operations domain awareness—CODA!" Everybody said, "CODA, ahhhhh, got it. We have a CODE and now we have CODA." We said, "Why don't we take this CODA thing and run it out and see what happens." We wanted to give him a way to take his zeal for that activity and bring it to the clients.

Now, Proctor and others are all over the country speaking about CODA. We have trademarked that name. Now we are doing CODA consulting. This new service offering is an example of how our firm, and our clients, benefit by our finding someone's interest, and coaching him to move ahead on his own. It's much better than our demanding, "You must find a new idea. Do it."

Listening Nonjudgmentally

To be sure, Ross & Baruzzini's cultural approach to integrating marketing, selling, and client service is not without its challenges. It takes time, enormous amounts of internal communication, and an ability to tolerate people who resist. By employing, as Kipp called it, a "guardian angel" method, an organization cannot run itself as an autocracy. Instead, as the members of Ross & Baruzzini's operating committee understood, achieving their integration results might take years.

They also learned that negativity is inevitable and that it serves a purpose. In order for the enterprise to progress in the most practical possible way, the organization's executive managers had to be willing to let the doubters express their criticisms. They believed naysayers have merit in terms of keeping the firm and its professionals well grounded.

They also realized the importance of flexibility. Craig Toder summed it up:

> It took us a couple of years to get the Scorecard going. People needed to see that we were serious, and we needed to get significantly better about having fewer and more measurable goals. But still, we don't look at our scorecard as a fixed point or our mentoring initiatives as overly rigid standards; they can change and grow as we do.

And what are the results of this balancing act? Since 2001 — an uncertain year in nearly every industrial market — Ross & Baruzzini has prospered in all of its market niches, added new client types, and increased its contract size and profitability. The firm's portfolio is appropriately balanced and positioned to both capitalize on opportunity and weather downturns. Fueling the change is the idea that every professional can be involved in the acquisition of business and the prosperity of the business. The firm has gradually been able to shed the limitations imposed by an inward focus. It has moved to a balanced posture driven by its clients.

Growing a Global Client Base While Promoting Individuals' Professional Growth

Jones Lang LaSalle is a financial and professional service firm specializing in real estate services and investment management. Through a new internally developed program called START, it built new marketing and business development connections that improved optimal value delivery for clients. Now globally implemented, START also has served as the springboard for other programs designed to increase the company's value to clients, expand its book of business with them, and simultaneously grow individuals' professional competencies.

❋ ❋ ❋

Seasoned observers of the professional service sector are familiar with the saying "herding cats." If you've ever tried to herd cats, you know how nearly impossible it is. Regardless of whether one speaks about management consulting or law, accounting or engineering, IT services or architecture, the adage still applies. The "cats" are the experts, whose collective intellectual capital is the source of the enterprise's revenue. And, in a nearly perverse twist, the more those "cats" demonstrate their entrepreneurial zeal—that is, the less "herdable" they become—the more likely it is that they'll move up the firm's internal pathway to leadership.

"Herding cats" doesn't pose much of a problem for smaller professional firms. But the larger the enterprise becomes, the harder it is to manage the "cats," especially helping them to navigate the delicate balance between providing unique value to their clients and simultaneously helping the enterprise itself to thrive.

It's rare, then, to encounter a very large professional service firm that succeeds at managing multiple mandates at once: increasing the company's value to clients, expanding the firm's book of business with those clients, and growing its professionals' competencies.

Jones Lang LaSalle is a giant, publicly traded real estate services company (NYSE: JLL) that helps its clients to increase their own value through strategic ownership, occupancy, or investment in real estate. In 2007 its global revenue was nearly $3 billion, achieved through more than 30,000 people in 700 cities in 60 countries. From its earliest origins in 1783 London, the company has continued to grow its geographic presence and range of activities. Jones Lang LaSalle Inc., formed by the 1999 merger of LaSalle Partners Incorporated and Jones Lang Wootton, has expanded many times over the years through significant acquisitions, including a 2008 merger with The Staubach Company, a U.S. real estate services firm. The LaSalle Investment Management unit manages assets of approximately $53 billion.

Jones Lang LaSalle is one of the cases featured here because of its compelling commitment to growth. The company combined this commitment with its creation and deployment of formal initiatives to integrate marketing and business development. Moreover, Jones Lang LaSalle demonstrated its astute comprehension of two critical concepts: the *structural* and the *cultural* underpinnings of growth.

With the structural underpinnings of growth in mind, the firm implemented formal initiatives to achieve its marketplace leadership goals. Each of these initiatives is today aligned with the firm's internally famous "G5"—that is, the five priorities for global growth formally announced in

2004 that are intended to drive shareholder value, help its clients succeed, support the company's own long-term performance, and establish Jones Lang LaSalle as the clear industry leader and innovator.

The cultural underpinnings of growth are related to the notion that supporting the growth of individual professionals enhances the likelihood that they would subsequently pursue advantageous growth for the organization as a whole.

Jones Lang LaSalle's commitment to growth is manifested in three ways.

First, with its START program, Jones Lang LaSalle began to globalize its Corporate Solutions business. It developed comprehensive processes and systems, instituted training, and drove global integration of local marketing and business development activities. The result is a powerful network that allows the firm to develop truly global service offerings for clients. The START program also produced other programmatic initiatives, most notably the company's Account Growth Program, which in 2007 began as a pilot project in its Americas' regional Corporate Solutions business unit. This program extends the firm's growth commitment, allowing it to directly focus on building its book of business with strategically important clients.

Second, Jones Lang LaSalle set about to grow the competencies of its own professionals to better integrate its marketing and business development functions, thereby providing more integrated solutions for clients. This "grow-your-expertise" effort is a valuable illustration of how a company can simultaneously help its people grow their skills, outline new formal processes, and clearly establish new shared accountabilities and collaboration pathways.

Third (and related to the second), the company supported the evolution of individual roles and responsibilities to lead new enterprise-wide functions. It is well known, especially when an organization becomes as large as Jones Lang LaSalle, how challenging it can be for a person to break out of a company's well-identified growth pathways. (You've already heard me criticize marketing and business development job descriptions that appear unchanged since the Jurassic period.)

At Jones Lang LaSalle, though, it is possible for individuals to grow professionally, both inside and outside of a formal company-supported training program. This case provides examples of professional skills growth related to the development of the START program and its progeny, the Account Growth Program. In both programs, the company encouraged individuals to create new functions that brought positive results for the enterprise and also fostered new skills and professional advancement avenues.

Integrating Marketing and Business Development Globally in Order to Develop Better Client Solutions

Jones Lang LaSalle's Corporate Solutions unit specializes in providing out-sourced real estate services to corporate clients, including tenant represen-tation and lease administration, facility management services, project management, and strategic consulting. Worldwide, the company's Corpo-rate Solutions unit drove more than $700 million in revenue through its corporate relationships for FY 2007. Despite the company's overall mar-ketplace prowess, the leaders of Corporate Solutions knew they could do better in bringing in profitable growth.

Real estate is quintessentially a local business. Traditionally, real estate services companies have sold their services locally as well. In the early 2000s, Jones Lang LaSalle's business development teams worked within three distinct regions: Americas, EMEA (Europe, Middle East, Africa), and Asia/Pacific. Each region followed the company's generally common processes, but localized them to fit their particular geography. As the com-pany's corporate clients began to operate more globally, their real estate service needs also began to evolve. Jones Lang LaSalle's business develop-ment team members began hearing from corporate clients about how dif-ficult it was to work through the company's siloed business development functions to purchase the global solutions they needed.

Nancy Grimmer, then the head of the Americas' Corporate Solutions facilities management proposal team, began thinking the time was ripe to more closely integrate every regional marketing and business development professional, each of whom represented a variety of business solution units. Having tracked the trends in requests for proposals (RFPs) from clients who needed global or multinational real estate services help, Grim-mer saw opportunities for individuals to work more closely together using common resources rather than being separated by their narrow business unit or geographic niches. The idea was to present to clients a coordinated solution developed by integrated client relationship managers and sales support team members. Encouraged by her boss, Paul Uber, then the exec-utive vice president leading the company's facilities management business development, she pitched her idea for a "business development engine" to

Peter Barge, who had recently moved to the Americas to establish the Corporate Solutions business. Barge was very enthusiastic. Because the businesses that were to form the company's Americas Corporate Solutions division were the most mature, it was decided to launch the initiative, newly named START (Strategic Action Resource Team), there.

The kickoff meeting, held in April 2001, included strategy presentations by stakeholders, leaders, and sales support team members from each business unit. From there, beginning in 2001 and continuing through 2002, Grimmer worked with Barge and other colleagues to launch a START-sponsored sales training program (tracking each phase of a sales cycle). In each training session, marketing and business team members worked with client-facing relationship managers and business leaders to share experiences and refine the START program. Today, START training is ongoing.

In parallel with this training, Jones Lang LaSalle began to build its technological infrastructure to support the exchange and organization of knowledge, including sales-related pursuits. This systems work is ongoing as well.

About the time the START program commenced, Grimmer developed a chart to track the related growth in integrated marketing and sales activities among regions. The chart revealed positive trends from the beginning; it also revealed the need for more formal globalization of the business development efforts. "I saw strong engagement of our Americas' business partners with their counterparts in EMEA and Asia Pacific," Grimmer recalled. She continued:

> With Peter's support we started sharing our START training with other parts of the globe, identifying START resources in each region along the way. We trained a resource to move over to Asia Pacific in 2003, and identified EMEA resources in 2004. Also in 2004, we began global START meetings.
>
> We also established a monthly conference call to allow START members to report on client feedback and to help them update each other on new developments. These calls also enabled us to get their feedback on how the START program itself was working in their regions. As appropriate, we brought in guests from other regions, to share additional intelligence. The team's motto of *always better* kept us focused on continual improvement both for our staff and, ultimately, for the solutions and product that we were delivering to our prospects and clients.

By 2004 other Jones Lang LaSalle business units wanted access to START resources. An early adopter was the company's Capital Markets business unit. (Today, START is part of onboarding for sales professionals in other divisions.)

In 2004 and 2005, Grimmer and her START colleagues hosted "boot camps" as a way to help START team members gain better awareness of the business dynamics in each geographic region and become better business partners for global sales.

Along the way, they created shared tools and standardized templates to improve the group's efficiency, effectiveness, and decision making. They also utilized the company's marketing communications messages to differentiate the firm, and they incorporated proof points that validated the company's ability to deliver valued solutions.

By 2008 the START program comprised about 20 people worldwide and could point to extremely positive results. In one year alone, for example, the proposal win rates of the Corporate Solutions unit soared from 30 percent to well over 50 percent. In some areas, the company achieved 70 percent win rates. Grimmer herself brings deep knowledge to the notion of integrated marketing, sales, and client service, having worked on more than 100 proposals.

As might be predicted from the START program's support of strong revenue growth results, the marketplace began to notice. For example, the *Harvard Business Review* included Jones Lang LaSalle in its May 2007 article featuring companies that had busted internal silos to improve their customer focus.[4]

Today, members of the sales support teams pool their knowledge of clients' emerging needs and challenges. START team members work with colleagues to conduct voice-of-the-customer exercises after each client sales presentation, and then share their findings. They compare perspectives on how their solutions stack up against those offered by competitors. At each iteration of the program, they further formalize their marketing-to-sales processes and tools. The START group itself has become a hub of knowledge about the company's corporate clients. One could argue that the team's contribution now influences the firm's subject matter knowledge, management of information, and ultimately, the uniquely valuable solutions it develops for clients.

With its emphasis on skills growth, collaboration, shared accountability, and co-leadership, START also has served as a professional growth engine.

Indeed, START made it possible for many people to take on new leadership positions within Jones Lang LaSalle. Grimmer herself became the leader of Americas Corporate Solutions marketing in 2007.

Integrating Marketing and Business Development in Order to Expand Client Relationships

Although not its primary focus, the START program did include some thinking around expansion and growth opportunities. But as of late 2007, the Corporate Solutions unit's marketing functions had not been directly tied in to coordinating early-phase growth and renewal opportunities with the existing account base.

In 2007 Jones Lang LaSalle executives tapped Atlanta-based Paul Uber to direct the company's strategic initiative to expand the depth of its client relationships across Corporate Solutions. Grimmer and her colleague Sarah Stanley, then the manager of new business proposals for Americas Corporate Solutions, began to look at what was being done to build business with current clients.

In the area of account growth opportunities, they found evidence of functional disconnects between marketing and business development. For example, as soon as the company won new Corporate Solutions client assignments (even through START collaborations), the sales support team stepped away, even though a well-defined client loyalty program managed client events, gifts programs, and other neatly framed initiatives. In addition, the business development team was not involved in winning more services (that is, a broader palette of services than those for which the client currently engaged Jones Lang LaSalle), until a corporate client submitted a request for proposal. Also, the company's client relationship managers (CRMs), who had been responsible for new business development within their assigned accounts, needed additional support to maximize appropriate future opportunities. The CRMs were well known for excellence in managing their clients' real estate needs smoothly, but this commitment on occasion left them with less time to focus proactively on the client's emerging needs.

Building Power Tools to Drive a Company's Growth

After a few brainstorming calls among Uber, Grimmer, and Stanley, Uber and Stanley met for a daylong meeting in December 2007 to further outline how the company could better equip its Americas Corporate Solutions CRMs with new power tools to help them drive account growth. Uber, himself a national account executive, was in a position to guide the development of the firm's formal programmatic response and enable Stanley's transition to lead the newly named Account Growth Program. The program was positioned as a new resource for account directors and sales teams. Stanley's role was to teach new techniques, communicate, and facilitate the group's thinking.

By the end of December 2007, timed to dovetail with the Jones Lang LaSalle annual planning cycle, the program's parameters were set. There were few budget implications—most notably, some funds for technology support. In January 2008, Grimmer announced the new initiative to the Americas marketing team internally and then to the Americas Corporate Solutions account directors.

The Account Growth Program has three main goals:

1. *Build a stronger sales mindset toward account growth.* In late summer 2008, Uber hosted a two-day, deep-immersion sales training process for account directors and executives—those senior managers to whom all CRMs report in the Americas. Stanley became involved in teaching the "Account Growth Toolkit," a session that highlights for account directors and CRMs the main sales tools available to them.

2. *Become more proactive about account renewal and growth opportunities.* Traditionally, CRMs have focused on serving the client, and when renewals crop up, responding. Stanley, who joined Uber's biweekly Corporate Solutions account relationship conference calls, began to get a sense of the CRMs with whom she could work, and she began using the Account Growth Program's new Power Sales Tools to help them better anticipate growth opportunities. In particular, she recognized that the CRMs could benefit from a newly developed account success template. Stanley explained:

   At the end of each year, most of our clients like to get a report summarizing how we performed against their objectives. CRMs for many of our small to medium-size accounts don't have the resources to get these reports done, both for tracking their success as well as for communicating easily. And so, when renewal opportunities arose, they were challenged to deliver the best stories about the value that had been delivered.

Stanley and her colleagues on the account management team worked to resolve this situation quickly. Launched in April 2008, the new account success template was designed to be employed for accounts of any size or complexity and to be easily managed by on-account resources.

By April 2008, Stanley also had distributed a newly developed checklist tool, so that the CRMs could begin immediately to collect project success information. Not only valuable as a productivity tool, this new checklist was designed to help CRMs showcase the firm's value-added services, quickly and in a customized manner, when clients issued a new request for proposal.

3. *Increase the availability of timely account service information.* Because Corporate Solutions CRMs needed critical general and technical information on and evidence of the firm's value to clients in other regions and lines of business, Grimmer and Stanley developed three tools for their use:

- "Get Smart," a new electronic communication sent at the end of every month. Beginning in September 2007, this new communiqué was distributed to all the CRMs and anyone else who had a sales-related position in Corporate Solutions. It features content-only issues and facts that are of critical importance to clients — for example, if the firm wins a new client assignment in Dubai — or makes available updated statistics on the firm's project management capabilities.

- An analysis proving the value of integrated service delivery. CRM and team interviews will identify how bundled Corporate Solutions services help clients reduce cycle time, mitigate risk, or increase innovation.

- An account growth toolkit, a document-sharing technology that will be available on the firm's intranet and will feature a quick glance at the services Jones Lang LaSalle provides to Corporate Solutions clients, by geography. It will feature a quick recap of client issues and interest areas, key statistics for each Corporate Solutions account, and key contacts who can be of assistance. This matrix will be tested regionally and then offered globally.

Uber pointed out: "Our clients already realize significant value from Jones Lang LaSalle's ability to integrate across service lines and geographic regions. We recognized that driving that same high level of integration between our marketing, business development and service delivery teams would create additional value for our clients." He continued: "This program will allow our account teams to better anticipate our clients' emerging needs and serve them more responsively and productively."

The Power of a Company's Support of Its Professionals' Growth

Rather than framing its START and Account Growth programs as routine professional development requirements, Jones Lang LaSalle instead described them as being of strategic importance to the company. Shepherded by prominent senior leaders of the firm, the programs were deliberately conceived as enhancing the integration of marketing and business development functions—toward a global scope—while growing the competencies of the firm's employees. They fostered well-recognized shared accountabilities, formal collaboration arrangements, and shared leadership.

Lessons Learned and Early Results

As with any new or evolved enterprise function, structural change precedes an organization's cultural transformation. People need time to accommodate new resources, however welcome or effective those new resources are. Both Grimmer and Stanley were decidedly proactive; they had to introduce their new functions and support capabilities to their colleagues. Internal word-of-mouth and positive reviews made a difference in the success of these programs.

At the appropriate time, Uber, Grimmer, and Stanley plan to share their Americas Corporate Solutions integration experience, and the lessons they've learned, with their global counterparts. Their intent is to continue demonstrating a positive impact, revise the Account Growth Program as needed, and then introduce it to global colleagues.

Chapter 11

Cases: The Support Imperative

This chapter on the Support Imperative chronicles two firms — a management and engineering consultancy, and a temporary and contract staffing company — that successfully integrated administrative functions with marketing and business development functions. These stories underscore the potent market-focused results that can accrue when professional firms formally manage the connections among their "support" functions.

■ ■ ■

Integrating Marketing and Human Resources to Turn a Company of Experts into an Expert Company

R.W. Beck is a management and engineering consultancy. Its marketing and HR functions teamed up on the firm's first-ever initiatives on performance improvement and organization development to formalize how professionals could better collaborate and share accountabilities. The endeavor resulted in improved teamwork to market, sell, and deliver client services.

• • •

The way most professional firms work together looks like a patchwork quilt. The people in Paris operate one way; those in Singapore operate quite differently. Add to that the inclinations of most PSFs and B2Bs to grow through mergers and acquisitions, and the way people work together resembles an even crazier quilt.

On top of those variables, how does it feel to be a professional — an actuary, IT consultant, or what-have-you — trying to work effectively with colleagues to grow the enterprise's competitive edge? This professional's performance is judged on achieving hard results such as "revenues generated," or more subjective results such as "contribution to the firm's thought leadership."

But trying to team up successfully with some internal colleagues can be a dreadful experience. At least most professional firms make it explicit that *practitioners* must work together, and they regularly evaluate their success in doing so. But what about sharing accountability with "support" functions? What about asking them to formally collaborate with each other? Now there's an opportunity to get everyone in the enterprise rowing in the same direction.

I chose R.W. Beck as a case study because its management executives embarked on an integration endeavor for its support functions to help the firm make gains in marketing and business development. Their decisions represented some new steps for the firm, and incorporated both structural and cultural elements.

First, the firm purposefully reoriented its human resources function to include an emphasis on organization development and change management. Second, it created a formal partnership between marketing and human resources. Third, it developed a new performance management system to frame how all the firm's professionals could better collaborate and share accountabilities as they worked together. The net result of this new construct is improved teamwork to market, sell, and deliver R.W. Beck's client services.

R.W. Beck is a technical and business consulting firm that serves public and private infrastructure organizations and financiers worldwide. It promises "Insight with Impact" by translating industry knowledge into practical solutions specific to clients' needs. Founded in 1942 on the West Coast of the United States, the firm has more than 500 employees, who generate revenue of $106 million from 22 offices throughout the United States (and one in Singapore). R.W. Beck has grown rapidly through a number of important acquisitions strategically intended to deepen the firm's capability to offer both technical expertise and strategic business and financial acumen.

It is no accident that the firm has so succinctly articulated its value proposition, which is featured prominently on its Web site's home page: "Advancing the Business of Infrastructure." This phrase also telegraphs the firm's corporate decisions to build and maintain an infrastructure of its own, to advance its marketplace goals.

This story begins in 2005, when, during one of the firm's strategic planning sessions, R.W. Beck executives recognized that their organization was essentially a geographically based company of experts. The company operated through a series of individual business units comprised of specialists whose contribution to the betterment of the whole nevertheless originated from their own entrepreneurial silos. These leaders were determined to drive the firm's evolution into a national expert company that presented itself to the market as one entity, with one reputation and one vision of serving in the marketplace. According to Russ Stepp, the firm's CEO, "R.W. Beck has nearly 70 years of history. We wanted to make sure the firm will have at least 70 more. We had to address the firm's own sustainability."

But the enterprise lacked a cohesive business infrastructure. Every office operated as its own fiefdom, with multiple cultures. Even though the firm had recently adopted a new compensation system, there were widely varying approaches to rating people's performance. Employees in Orlando were rated differently than those in Nashville, and both groups were rated differently than employees in Seattle. Goal setting and accountabilities were all over the map. Consistent feedback mechanisms did not exist. Succession planning and leadership development were spotty.

And everyone thought that his or her way was the right way.

R.W. Beck's management executives feared that this way of working together could, in the near term, influence the firm's effectiveness in going to market. Even more, they knew it could affect the enterprise's survival. "We want to continually stay on top of marketplace dynamics and client needs. We want to maintain our foresight about what our clients are facing and the challenges they need to address," Stepp explained. "And so our goal was to make the organization and its employees even more resilient than they already were. We decided we needed to make significant changes."

This story hinges on three major initiatives: a performance review process that requires every professional to set explicit goals and accountabilities, a standardized calibration framework to help executives determine consistently how their professionals are performing, and a revamped leadership development program that is linked with both.

These three initiatives are powerful examples of how PSF or B2B executive managers, even in a partnership environment, can direct their professionals' day-to-day working relationships. R.W. Beck's management executives were not afraid to ask—even require—their people to act like a one-firm firm. Although these programs were designed to focus broadly on all aspects of the way R.W. Beck's people work together, they are also excellent examples of a major theme of this book: making marketing and sales a part of *everyone's* job.

Evolving from a Company of Experts to an Expert Company

The first formal steps toward change were taken in December 2007. The head of human resources, Susan Newton, interviewed more than 100 people in the firm's offices. All were asked for their opinions on the firm's current performance review process and ratings guidelines. They were encouraged to talk about what worked or did not work. And they were asked for suggestions about what they thought would advance the firm's goals. (Eventually, their remarks were incorporated into the new programs, making it easier to introduce the programs and to garner endorsement from the entire employee population.)

Taking these touch points as a development guide, R.W. Beck's executive and human resources managers set about creating the structural aspects of the new performance review program. It required everyone to set explicit goals and accountabilities. All aspects of the reviews had to be consistent across geographies and position levels. It was also important that each review address areas that R.W. Beck particularly wants to foster, including client focus (being a true partner, vested in each client's success); job knowledge and skills (combining technical and business acumen, a real differentiator for the firm); and personal attributes (being forthright and showing great integrity, judgment, and initiative). All were areas that promoted the firm's vision and mission and helped it stay true to the brand attributes that define its reputation in the marketplace. All were areas that enabled the firm to be a unified expert company.

It was important to develop the same type of structural guide for the company's new calibration process. The idea was to standardize, across the company, a well-recognized rating system that could objectively determine differences in performance levels and foster consistency when supervisors and managers conducted performance reviews. Newton recalled:

> When R.W. Beck rolled out this program, we were very clear that we would use calibration to ensure that performance ratings would be as consistent as possible across the organization, while supporting the identification of top performers and enabling leadership to differentiate when it came to rewards. The resulting discussion at the calibration session was

incredibly powerful and eye opening, resulting in a much more equitable and fair process.

As part of its internal program preparation, the R.W. Beck Leadership Team gathered for a discussion to help shape the new rating system. The team decided to embrace some new performance management "best practices." For example, the company had used a five-point scale in the past, with two ratings to highlight a performance that "exceeded" the norm for a particular performance level. The team realized there was no way to truly differentiate between the two descriptions; either a professional exceeded the norm or he didn't. It then agreed on a simpler four-point scale, with very clear guidelines and definitions of what each description meant, how they were different, and what a potential distribution might look like. The review and commitment-setting process allowed everyone to reflect on individual performance results. Stakeholder feedback and the calibration process provided supervisors and managers with information that would allow them to have meaningful performance discussions with their employees. The team considered these changes critical to helping the firm attain its goal to become an expert company.

Newton next worked with Stepp and other executive managers to map out the step-by-step deployment of the performance review process and calibration guidelines throughout the company. In doing so, they asked themselves: When in the company's business cycle would the process begin? What step should we take first, second, and so on? Who would initiate each performance review phase? Where would the performance review process go from there? How would it be managed across geographies? What technology system would support it?

The Only Person Who Likes Change Is a Wet Baby

Arguably, creating the framework and deployment map for a professional firm's internal performance review and rating program is the easy part. Executive managers knew R.W. Beck's people would likely react as would any other large group of people who have been comfortable with the way things had been done in the past. Declared Newton,

> The only person who likes change is a wet baby! In order to effectively introduce our new system, we knew we would need to inform people about the new program, and explain what would be expected.

Even more important, we needed to compellingly communicate with our employees about the real power behind these changes. We needed to illuminate them about this whole performance management system, and really integrate it into the culture of the company. We needed a new internal partnership to outline how it will help evolve R.W. Beck into an expert company.

And so began another first for R.W. Beck: a new formal partnership between the firm's marketing function, led by the vice president of strategic marketing, Jessica Reiter, and the firm's HR function. From the outset, the company positioned HR and marketing as partners on this very significant initiative. By demonstrating the shared collaboration and integrated accountabilities of these functions, they hoped to lead by example.

As head of strategic marketing, Reiter was responsible for corporate communications and was also R.W. Beck's brand champion. She considered it her job to ensure that the firm's brand infiltrated every strategic decision, every function, and every initiative. Management executives viewed marketing's partnership with human resources as a uniquely valuable opportunity to help every person in the firm coalesce around a new model of working together in a way that powerfully demonstrated the firm's brand promise.

For their first step, they created a communications plan with a firm-wide launch strategy. In January 2008, they developed and distributed memos, e-mails, and FAQs about the upcoming changes. In February 2008, Newton and CEO Russ Stepp traveled to the firm's major offices to deliver in-person presentations about the new management process. They walked people through the new process and introduced them to the new forms; they also fielded questions. For the benefit of the firm's smaller offices, Reiter arranged for a professionally recorded video of this presentation at a studio. The video recording was posted on the firm's intranet, along with copies of all related documents. Reiter said, "We wanted everyone to feel involved and comfortable asking questions. Our people were—and are—a part of our evolving management processes. We have a culture of inclusion and collaboration, and employees have always been interested and engaged. So it was easy to be open, forthcoming and very direct."

Beyond the initial communications launch, marketing and human resources geared up to introduce numerous tactical follow-up initiatives to support the continued integration of the firm's performance management process. Among them were a mentoring program, an online training course, new recruiting activities, and a new-employee onboarding orientation. From a strategic perspective, Reiter was including scenario planning in the firm's future strategic planning initiatives, with a close connection to people and performance in the marketplace.

Marketing and Human Resources: Becoming More Together Than Either Could Be Alone

Because some R.W. Beck professionals had been with the company for more than 25 years, everyone proceeded with enormous sensitivity to the culture. Stepp and the R.W. Beck Leadership Team expected this challenge, however, and took it in stride. As for the enormity of the tasks and the firm's aggressive timetable for developing and launching the new performance management program, they were grateful for the enthusiasm that was evident between Reiter and Newton.

But the biggest lesson learned for marketers and human resources teammates was the epiphany they experienced from their internal collaboration. Stepp explained, "Our marketing and human resource professionals became more than any of us thought possible; each is becoming an expert in what the other one is doing. The stronger this administrative partnership becomes, the closer we get to achieving our 'Expert Company' goal."

Using this powerful springboard, R.W. Beck's leaders are seeking even more integration of the firm's marketing and HR functions. Now that they have launched the cultural foundation for increased collaboration and shared accountabilities among the firm's technical professionals, they have begun to create additional structural frameworks to guide the ongoing pursuit of effectiveness in marketing and business development.

Specifically, an upcoming focus will be R.W. Beck's leadership program, Leadership Beck. The program will aim to build the firm's future leaders. Of the program's four modules, the third focuses on strategy, marketing, and sales. Led by Reiter, it outlines the firm's plans to grow its market opportunities, its brand promise, and the way it wants people to work together to market and sell.

Moving from Cost to Contribution: Integrating Marketing and Finance

Randstad is one of the world's largest temporary and contract staffing organizations. It forged innovative formal shared accountabilities and created a new culture of global collaboration between its marketing and finance departments, resulting in vast improvements in the productivity of the company's marketing expenditures.

• • •

The Randstad story begins by considering the intersection of three important issues.

The first is productivity. For any business, no matter the industry, revenues, or market share, productivity is the pathway to success. Executives spend their professional lives determined to achieve it, and employees strive to deliver it. At times, though, the journey toward optimal productivity can seem maddeningly elusive, like a destination that continuously moves just out of reach.

The second issue is helping clients deploy people productively. Very few global enterprises specialize in supplying temporary and contract staffing to companies worldwide.

The third issue is how a company effectively delivers its client value proposition to *itself*. Observers of the professional service arena will certainly recognize the cliché about the "cobbler's children"—that is, management consulting firms that don't manage themselves very well, or public relations and advertising firms that underinvest in their own marketing plans. It's a cliché many would love to leave behind.

To illustrate the Support Imperative, I searched for professional service businesses that have taken formal steps to integrate their marketing and business development functions with their other administrative operations. It was a challenge.

The Randstad Group (traded under the Euronext Amsterdam exchange symbol RAND.AS), which has its headquarters in Diemen, the Netherlands, is one of the largest temporary and contract staffing organizations in the world. Randstad's approximately 17,500 employees operate from nearly 3,000 branches in 20 countries throughout Europe, North America, and Asia. At the end of its 2007 fiscal year, the Randstad Group reported revenues of more than $10 billion (€9.2 billion), which represented a 12 percent increase in revenues over the previous year. Incredibly, this HR services giant enables the employment of an average of 369,200 people every day.

With a corporate vision to be among the world leaders in linking the supply and demand for workers, the company offers a wide range of services that cover almost every aspect of HR services, from staffing, which includes finding temporary personnel (flex workers and interim professionals) and permanent employees for clients, to the provision of a whole range of specialist services, such as HR consultancy and the management of HR processes.

Founded in 1960, for many years Randstad pursued growth organically. In early 2008, Randstad completed its acquisition of a major competitor, Vedior. With this acquisition, Randstad is now the second largest HR services company in the world.

"Show Me the Money!"

The Randstad Group's chief marketing officer Frans Cornelis joined the company in 2003, reporting to the company's CEO Ben Noteboom. With a deep corporate background from previous work with AT&T, Sara Lee, and the United Kingdom's chemicals and plastics giant ICI, and with educational credentials that include an MBA from INSEAD, Cornelis is no stranger to overcoming challenges.

Almost as soon as he began his job, Cornelis noticed a potential internal organizational challenge: Randstad's marketing and finance functions were not as effectively integrated as they could be. The company's chief financial officer, always interested in marketing's initiatives and helpful to the marketing team, was expending too much effort to lead a more thorough collaboration. Cornelis knew these functions could work better together.

But he quickly discovered some significant cultural background: several of Randstad's executive managers considered their expenditures on marketing to be costs, not investments. Marketing was operating too much in its own functional fiefdom—disconnected and marginalized. And finance, with its own priorities, was not as much of a functional ally as it should have been.

Cornelis knew that if the marketing teams didn't worry about the company's profits, they could not help the company progress. He wanted the company's marketers to be known internally as the most fanatical people about budgets. He began to tell his new team, "Finance can only improve the company's results by controlling its costs. They have the money. I can't help but talk to them! We in Marketing can help the company improve its already strong results, too—by developing new value."

From that moment, Cornelis set out to have marketing become more formally integrated with finance and to integrate in a way that matched the company's own value proposition to the marketplace: enabling productivity.

Finance and Marketing: True Colleagues

Cornelis's first step was to improve dramatically the use of the company's financial and other common systems to track marketing's costs and effectiveness. In 2004 he and his marketing team members sought finance's help to set up budget systems in which marketing's costs could be spotted in terms of direct productivity. He focused on the company's outside spending on media communications, PR, and advertising agencies, and on its graphic and marketing design costs. He labeled this initiative the "creative cost-to-effectiveness ratio."

To kick off this first step, he researched other companies' well-established marketing spending benchmarks and began laying the groundwork to move Randstad's marketing spending in line accordingly. To conduct his research, Cornelis and his marketing colleagues tapped their own networks of marketing leaders of other companies with whom they could compare expenditures. Their analysis produced startling revelations. In many units, Randstad's expenditures for its creative marketing initiatives stood at more than 20 percent of its entire marketing budget. Cornelis explained:

> We found certain Randstad departments were spending upwards of 250 percent of standard expenditures for the creative aspects of a marketing program. For example, unneeded duplication of design costs; conducting off-site logo brainstorming sessions; commissioning expensive consultants to produce costly flip charts; and, in one case, even sending an entire crew to Latin America to film a commercial.

Cornelis decided that Randstad would adopt the benchmark of a global consumer packaged goods company, whose expenditures for creative marketing initiatives ranged from 6 to 9 percent of its marketing budget. From there, beginning in 2004 Cornelis and Randstad's finance leaders initiated a series of programmatic steps to bring the company's marketing creative expenditures more in line with this benchmark. Unneeded cost duplication was weeded out by placing brand design under the direction of an international brand team and pooling the results. Also, the purchasing of big-ticket items for branch branding and branch furniture was centralized globally. By early 2008, Cornelis had reduced marketing's creative expenditures to 11–13 percent of its entire marketing budget for almost all units.

Even though marketing and finance had worked together well to reduce these creative expenditures, Cornelis knew that marketing had yet to fulfill its mission of adding value to Randstad. And so he discussed an idea with his new friends in finance. Instead of cutting budgets, the firm should plow savings back into buying more media or in more extensive local marketing. One very important opportunity was the rising importance of Web search engines and ad word marketing, which the firm could now adopt using the budgetary savings realized.

By the end of 2004, Cornelis was ready to embark on a second significant marketing-finance integration initiative. Once again, productivity was the name of the game. He began building a marketing operations management platform whose goal was to unify Randstad's brand around the world. At that time, Randstad's marketing team comprised 270 marketers worldwide, who until 2003 had been operating without an overarching global brand strategy. These marketing professionals were used to making narrowly focused brand decisions related to their own region or line of business.

From 2003 to mid-2005, Cornelis and his marketing team members refurbished Randstad's brand. In 2005 the company celebrated the global rollout of its new "Good to Know You" campaign. As team members led this rollout, they developed a centralized buying program to manifest the brand, down to the most tactical level. For example, they pooled contracts around the world for all brand-related expenditures, even down to office furniture and artwork.

The 2008 Vedior merger nearly doubled the size of Randstad's marketing team to 500, and added some 30 new countries to the firm's scope. Even still, the company's marketing operations management platform provided centralized guidance for marketing professionals so that they could make more globally appropriate and cost-effective branch implementation decisions.

Without having put the new centralized buying program and marketing operations management platforms in place, the task of absorbing and training all these new marketing people would have been very difficult. Instead, they became quickly productive. Cornelis commented on the magnitude of these linked marketing-finance initiatives:

> The centralized buying program cost savings were in the order of 20 to 25 percent on all furniture and branch branding materials. We used the same

system to launch to the 2005 worldwide celebration of our "Good to Know You" campaign. It would have been impossible to organize without it, at least not for anywhere near the same cost, as it involved ten simultaneous, worldwide, identical events linked by satellite. This was managed by our own people. A bill for undertaking this initiative with outside organizers would have run into the tens of millions.

Beginning in 2005, marketing collaborated with the finance department again to co-develop yet another integration initiative, this time related to local measurement and the achievement of productivity. Cornelis wanted to be able to say, "Look, you got your money back." He and his finance colleagues conceived of several new measurement processes:

- *Requiring investments in local marketing actions to link back to the company's gross margins in the same region.* Cornelis asked his finance colleagues to develop systems and measurements on how much money Randstad could expect to make on its investments in certain specific brand awareness tactics, including radio and e-mail. Using the company's official reporting systems, Randstad's financial professionals were able to report by 2007 that, within three months and in real cash terms, 80 percent of the company's local marketing projects made back its original additional local marketing investment, measured by increased gross margin above the average national growth rate.

- *Tracking brand awareness.* Cornelis began tracking awareness of Randstad's brand in 2004, prior to the company's introduction in 2005 of its "Good to Know You" brand campaign. Every spring and fall, he tracks awareness of the brand in all areas where Randstad is active, including the top 10 global markets for its services. Awareness has increased dramatically. The company set a target to maintain its brand awareness among competing companies so that it was within the world's top three, and to increase awareness each year by more than the competition. In order to help his colleagues visualize the company's progress, Cornelis developed a brand awareness chart (figure 11.1) that compares top-of-mind awareness of the brand in question against the size of the target group in that market. The measure depicts absolute "fan club" size numbers that can be added up between markets of various sizes. Cornelis remarked, "It is the most honest way we can think of to measure this." When presenting the chart for external consumption, the company masks the actual track-

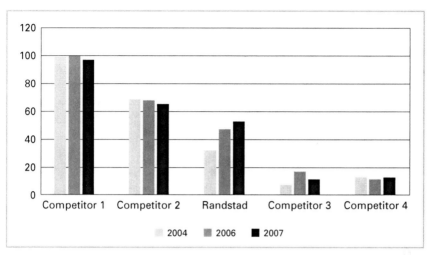

Figure 11.1 Randstad's Rise of Awareness in Top 10 Global Markets
Source: TNS Global. Reprinted by permission.

ing percentages. The main point remains the same, of course; Randstad can factually measure its marketplace progress.

- *Using comparisons to help Randstad analyze its marketing return on investment.* Cornelis reviewed the marketing expenditures of two of its competitors, Adecco and Manpower, both of which were twice as large. By simply obtaining Adecco's publicly disclosed financials, Cornelis was able to show that Randstad, while spending roughly the same absolute amount of marketing money as Adecco, was more profitable, was growing faster organically, and was making substantially larger gains in brand awareness over several years in a row since 2005. Manpower lagged far behind in these measures compared with both Adecco and Randstad over the same period. In fact, Randstad moved up from number four to clear number three in the global league table (the list of the largest global HR services firms by revenue) over that period.

Marketing and Finance: Moving Beyond Cost Effectiveness to Significant Functional Integration

Like Randstad, many professional service businesses have taken steps to optimize their expenditures on marketing. It's like plucking low-hanging fruit; it's always a good idea to become more cost-effective. But the real reason Randstad is a case in this book is because the company went beyond the obvious tactical steps to produce better marketing results more cost effectively. Randstad's executive managers took additional critical steps to ensure that finance and marketing functions shared formal accountability for producing results. They required real operational integration by directing marketing and finance to co-develop related performance measurement goals. Cornelis explained:

> At Randstad, our general managers have extremely well defined responsibilities. Each of them has a detailed description of duties and areas of control. As CMO, I am charged with making progress on achieving Randstad's marketing goals. In 2005, we went to the CFO and asked him and his people to help us set up what eventually became more than five major and some 15 derived specific measurement targets. He said, "Do you really mean it that you want to be measured on achieving these more than 20 marketing measurement goals?" We replied, "Yes, if you help us."

And so, since 2005 Randstad's CMO and CFO have formally shared responsibilities and control for improving marketing results as cost effectively as possible. For example, finance is required to track marketing expenditures using co-developed measurement tools. Marketing and finance compensation and rewards are also linked. C-level leaders get compensated once for achieving big targets. After that, they hand off the implementation and achievement of programmatic goals to other members of their teams, who also share formal collaboration arrangements, accountabilities, compensation, and rewards for achieving marketing results as cost effectively as possible.

Randstad's formal integration of marketing and finance is manifested during its annual goal-setting cycle. Once the company's plans are announced internally, instructions are sent out to the controllers of the operating companies. These instructions include marketing metrics, and, without fail, these leaders come to Cornelis's department and ask to jointly develop the plan to realize their targets. They know they will be monitored and measured, but also compensated and rewarded for their own contributions to Randstad's growing market share. In fact, there is an annual prize for the operating company that posts the largest increase in market share.

Integration Challenges That Had to Be Overcome

As with every substantive organizational shift, Cornelis and his colleagues encountered speed bumps as they led Randstad to make both its tactical and strategic changes in marketing-finance integration.

For example, after setting up the company's new marketing-finance systems, they found that their next challenge was to improve the quality of the data posted. Sometimes, it took months, and in some cases more than two years, to iron out the wrinkles and to avoid "garbage in, garbage out" types of errors. Both marketers and controllers had to be educated on the importance of measuring costs and cost categories properly.

Also, it was still sometimes difficult to control the temptation to cut the marketing budget at the first sign of concern. In one case, a full two years was required to gradually recover from a four-month spending block in one particular country.

Last but not least, marketing and finance colleagues discovered that much more international cooperation inevitably required new forms of communication and knowledge-sharing. In particular, they realized everyone had to have a good mastery of English because it was the common business language. They also learned the importance of everyone helping to build and synchronize each other's understanding and skill sets in order to deliver on the company's new requirements. Locally, for example, marketers needed to share their knowledge with their finance colleagues, who were less trained in these subjects.

The learning exchange—and productivity gains—continue to this day. Cornelis concluded:

> The key lesson is that it is all a matter of organizing *and communicating* internally. To win outside, one must start on the inside. One would think that the marketers would be excellent communicators, but sadly this is not a skill that is learned a lot in marketing education. Typically, marketers tend to communicate within their own circles—with agencies, other marketers, seminar participants and the like.
>
> Yet marketers *must* become expert at communicating to general managers and CFOs! Our work has demonstrated that this kind of skill growth and cultural change—across departments—makes excellent sense if a company wants to grow its marketplace position. The marketing and finance integration efforts we've undertaken have produced a noticeable, and very positive, change in the company's results.

Glossary

Erasing Silos Begins with Shared Understanding

In preparing to write this book, I interviewed numerous senior-level professional service management executives, marketers, and business developers. At almost every interview, we found ourselves having to clarify terms in order to have a meaningful conversation. Clearly, this lack of a shared comprehension of terms illustrates one of the fundamental "disconnects" in professional service marketing and business development. I began asking these advisors if it might be appropriate to include a glossary in my book. The resounding answer was "Yes!"

■ ■ ■

administration/administrative   Functions that support a business enterprise in delivering its value proposition to the marketplace. Examples of well-recognized administrative functions are human resources, information technology, legal, facilities, and finance. Many administrative functions house other functions. For example, finance includes accounts payable and accounts receivable.

alignment   Juxtaposing activities between functions within a business enterprise so that interface between functions is smooth and effortless. Not to be confused with *integration*.

business development   One-to-one activities of finding or responding to targeted prospects, initiating and pursuing a conversation that leads to crafting and proposing customized solutions they will buy, and agreeing on price and assignment scope. *Business development* is the preferred term for selling in many professional service sectors, and it should not be confused with sales support or *marketing*.

campaign   Programmatic initiative around which to implement integrated marketing and business development processes. Often based on time- or event-driven issues, a campaign is also easily trackable because of defined targets, goals, and timetables. In the IT arena, a good example was Y2K.

centralized marketing   Marketing and business development functions that are best managed or coordinated "centrally," that is, by an individual or focused team, on behalf of the broader enterprise. Functions that are optimally centralized include firm-wide targeting and segmentation, public and media relations, Web site management, brand management, account and relationship management, and the client relationship database.

client service   The means by which a service offering is "delivered" by PSF or B2B practitioners to their clients. Aspects of service delivery include the quality and quantity of in-person or electronic interactions, behavioral or relationship style, speed, accuracy, convenience, and other client-determined measures of performance quality.

cross-selling   Selling a firm's additional services to its existing clients, i.e., clients moving from buying from a single service to buying two or more services from that firm's portfolio of service offerings.

data mining   Capturing, organizing, and analyzing valuable client data to the point that one can discern past and potential client and marketplace patterns. Data mining can be implemented using a contact or client relationship management database that houses a broad scope of client data related to a PSF's or B2B's interactions with or research about a prospect or client.

demand creation/demand generation   Product or service-oriented marketing activities designed to increase the number of qualified prospects for a firm's service offerings. Increasingly, this term is used by PSF and B2B marketers and business developers because it conveys an actionable, documentable, and measurable process. Demand creation seeks to elicit a client's unambiguous response to a PSF or B2B outreach—the "demand." The client then becomes known as a "lead."

disconnect(s)   See **silos**.

executive managers   PSF and B2B leaders who serve on executive committees or internal boards; managing partners or chief executives and their C-suite colleagues; practice or sector leaders; and geography or line-of-business heads. Managers include anyone who has decision-making responsibilities—or who shares in making growth decisions, even in a partial way—for the management and marketplace future of a PSF or B2B service organization.

expertise-oriented marketing and business development   Activities based on the individual's (or smaller group's) *intellectual capital* and direct client contact. Examples are thought leadership publishing, speaking engagements, firm-sponsored seminars and events, sponsorships, relationship building, proposals, and, of course, project delivery.

fee-earning practitioners   See also **revenue-generating practitioners**. The people whose expertise and experience, intellectual capital, and credentials are the basis of a professional firm's offerings to the marketplace. Fee-earning practitioners are a PSF's or B2B's "products" from whom clients seek value-added solutions.

formal initiatives   See **infrastructure**.

function/functions/functional   *Organizational* processes or tasks that result in desired outcomes. Often, functions have recognizably distinct operational boundaries, such as human resources, information technology, or marketing. Typically housed within functions, roles are a set of *individual* tasks that contribute to a desired outcome. Roles may be identified by a position title such as chief marketing officer. A role could be a subset of a function, say, a marketing coordinator whose job is to implement a variety of steps in a process, or a CMO whose role is advisor, not implementer.

informal initiatives   See **infrastructure**.

infrastructure   An enterprise's set of usually formal, recognized, and management-sanctioned business frameworks, tools, processes, protocols, or policies. Formal processes or tools (structures) may be organizationally acknowledged in position descriptions and reporting relationships; internal presentations; initiatives, plans, or programs; defined teams; and timetables and checkpoints. Formal initiatives are often supported by a firm's administrative or operational procedures such as compensation and rewards, technological systems, and the like. Infrastructure also comprises informal initiatives that may be culturally supported or understood as "the way we do things here." "Informal" should not be considered a negative or less-than-optimal approach. Informal also implies initiatives that are not documented in a firm's policies or procedures, or those that could be found by an outsider looking for evidence.

integration   Structural frameworks and cultural models that result in interdependent collaboration and sharing of accountabilities between discrete functions within a professional or business-to-business service firm. Through goal-setting and measurement tools, integrated functions formally acknowledge each other's interdependence and potential for co-contributions to a firm's success. Integration does not mean *alignment*; alignment implies that functions juxtapose each other, but are not formally required to work together interdependently.

intellectual capital   Sum of an expert's education and training, professional acumen, and experience. Intellectual capital serves as the basis of a PSF's or B2B's service offerings. Not to be confused with (but related to) *thought leadership*.

lead generation   See **demand creation/demand generation**.

longitudinal research   Research whose analysis typically compares the same information from time period to time period. Not to be confused with cross-sectional or latitudinal research (whose analysis and expected findings are not dependent on comparisons of data over periods of time).

management executives   See **executive managers**.

marketing   Activities to define the market, build market share, and generate demand.

Market definition activities include client and market research, market share and trends analysis and forecasting, consumer buying or risk behavior analysis, targeting and segmentation, pricing strategy, and competitive intelligence.

Market share building and demand generation activities include differentiation, positioning, and branding; internal marketing (including shaping and harnessing a firm's cultural norms for the purpose of enhancing its uniqueness and brand equity); analytics activities, including data mining, ROI measurement, and client satisfaction and loyalty assessments; promotions and marketing communications (including events, speaking engagements, seminars, trade shows, advertising, public and media relations, articles and white papers, brochures or other collateral, and any kind of Internet-related, social, or digital media channel management); and service portfolio development and management (also known as innovation).

marketing communications (also known as marcom)   A communications activity in which a strategic message is delivered through a variety of print, in-person, or digital channels with the intent to shape the perceptions of a potential PSF or B2B client and generate demand. Marcom activities include advertising, branding, direct marketing, graphic design, marketing, packaging, promotion, publicity, sponsorship, public relations, sales, sales promotion, and online marketing.

market/marketplace   Universe of current and potential PSF or B2B service buyers or purchase decision makers and influencers.

matrixed organizational structures   Multiple interdependent business units organized by geography, service line, industry focus, or other units deemed appropriate for a professional firm by its executive managers. May or may not have separate profit and loss structures.

nonrevenue-generating professionals   Staff members in nonrevenue-generating and/or administrative functions, most often found in larger PSFs or B2Bs, who help support their firm in delivering its value proposition to its marketplace. These in-house functions typically include marketing and business development, and other administrative areas such as finance, human resources, professional development, legal, and the like.

offshoring   Practice of transferring the implementation of in-house but core business functions to a nondomestic geographic location, often for cost-saving or optimized resource allocation reasons.

onboarding   Practice of acclimating a new employee or team member into an enterprise. Encompasses the traditional notion of "employee orientation," but is understood to be a broader, more systematic, and more accelerated process of assimilating people into a business group.

outsourcing   Practice of transferring the implementation of noncore business functions to an outside provider, often for cost-saving or optimized resource allocation reasons.

pipeline   Stepwise process through which PSFs and B2Bs identify, pursue, and win engagements with potential clients. Often depicted as a flowchart, pipelines portray the movement of an inquiry to a qualified lead to a request for proposal to a proposal presentation to a sale, retained client, or cross-selling initiative.

pricing   Activity related to determining how much of a professional fee to charge for a service or productized service. Price is related to how much the client values the service.

professional and business-to-business service firms   Private or public business enterprises whose main source of revenues derive from the intellectual capital, credentials, licensure, experience, and expertise of their people (their "products"). Recognized professional service sectors include accounting, advertising, architecture, construction and construction management, a range of engineering specialties, executive search, a legion of consultancies (including economics, marketing and public relations, management, IT, human resources, research, and strategy and operations), law, and others.

rainmaker/rainmaking   A professional who sells his or her services, and the practice of selling professional services.

revenue-generating practitioners   See **fee-earning practitioners**.

role   See **function**.

segment/segmentation/segmenting   Subgroup of people or organizations that share one or more characteristics that might cause them to have similar product or service needs. A segment is distinct from other segments, and its members exhibit common attributes or behaviors. Segments also meet general criteria such as by industry or public versus private sector. Segmentation is the process of identifying and selecting segments that best match a PSF's or B2B's service offerings. It employs a variety of factual information, including demographic, geographic, attitudinal, or behavioral data.

selling   See **business development**.

service delivery   See **client service**.

service offering   Packaged set of intellectual capital. Examples are architectural design, an accounting audit, legal counsel, and market research.

silos   Lack of or barrier to organizational cooperation, communication, and shared accountability between business units, functions, and colleagues. The term is based on the farming structure that is typically built tall and narrow to house and protect grain. Silos can occur within any organizational construct. In matrixed professional service enterprises (where functions are managed or revenues are tracked by practice groups or lines of business, geographies, industries, or the functional purview of clients), silos may result in lower go-to-market effectiveness, productivity, and results.

structure   See **infrastructure**.

targeting   Process of selecting the clients a firm wishes to service. The decisions involved in targeting strategy include which segments to focus on and how many services — and which — to offer to each segment.

thought leadership   Output and manifestation of a person's intellectual capital. In a PSF or B2B environment, thought leadership is typically packaged for marketing purposes into research analysis and reports, articles, books, white papers, speeches, and seminars. Thought leadership is not intellectual capital; it connotes forward-thinking, cutting-edge, and innovative intellectual capital.

value proposition   Benefits (tangible and intangible) a client receives for its engagement of a PSF or B2B, especially in relation to what the client could have received from a different service provider.

Integration Imperative Templates

This appendix provides templates for each of the three structural imperatives outlined in the book: Process Imperative, Skills Imperative, and Support Imperative. These templates provide representative detail of how the Integration Imperative's frameworks and cultural paradigms could be applied in a professional or business-to-business service firm. The templates address scenarios that are pertinent to revenue-generating practitioners, marketing and business development professionals, and/or administrative personnel.

■ ■ ■

The Process Imperative

		The Process Imperative				
The 11 Organizational Competencies of _Marketplace Masters_		**D** **Define** and identify the most strategically important clients	**A** **Acquire** the most strategically important clients	**R** **Retain** the most strategically important clients	**B** **Build** the firm's revenues with the most strategically important clients	**I** **Increase** the perceived value of the firm to all audiences
Looking out	Studying a firm's clients using qualitative and quantitative research	Segmenting the market Targeting the "right" clients and prioritizing which clients to pursue, respond to, or avoid Pricing				Growing the firm's overall brand value, thought leadership equity, and innovation Building broad awareness of the firm and its favorable reputation
	Researching the market using economic forecasts and trend analyses					
	Researching competitors by gathering competitive intelligence					
Digging deeper	Embracing competitive differentiation (positioning and brand) strategies		Establishing a firm's value, protection from copycats, attractiveness, and credibility, with a narrow and sustainable focus Successfully winning engagements with those "right" prospects and clients	Fostering increasingly significant firm-client relationships Successfully keeping current engagements with targeted clients	Increasing each current client's use of the firm's entire service portfolio (cross-selling) Expanding the firm's penetration into that client's "share of wallet"	
	Mining client data					
	Aligning marketing strategies with culture					
	Using account planning and relationship management programs					
	Using measurements to increase strategic focus and competitive advantage (the three Client Metrics)					
Embedding innovation	Building an R&D process					
	Using technology to build new services					
	Using incentives and rewards to stimulate innovation					

Table B.1 The Process Imperative

The Skills Imperative

Skills growth stage	For expertise-oriented M/BD, "collaborate and mentor"	For centralized M/BD, "cooperate"	Your perceived status	Your M/BD approach	Your M/BD level
Owner/ Management executives	• Be an industry influencer/shaper • Be a thought leader/rainmaker • Develop new service offerings or service delivery approaches	• Provide input and advice to senior M/BD pros on the creation and dissemination of firm-wide differentiation, positioning, and branding strategies • Provide support to M/BD when needed (i.e., getting colleagues to cooperate). Includes championing compensation and rewards to support firm-wide M/BD strategies	Recognized guru	Highly proactive	Tiers 1 and 2 and up
Principal/ senior manager	• Pursue industry leadership • Lead practice area • Drive revenue/profit	• Serve as internal champion of M/BD initiatives	Recognized cross-industry expert	Proactive	Tiers 2–3, higher end
Senior consultant	• Develop a trusted relationship with clients • Engender strong confidence and credibility with outside publics • Build a good M/BD portfolio	• Serve on internal committees to develop and shape centralized M/BD strategies and their implementation. Act as eyes and ears, etc.	Recognized industry expert	Proactive/ opportunistic	Tiers 2–3
Consultant	• Gather some staffing influence • Build credibility with clients • Be able to carve out specific project roles • Start amassing M/BD expertise	• Help gather practice, region, or line-of-business M/BD input into the creation or update of centralized M/BD strategies and tactics	Some externally recognized expertise	Opportunistic/ proactive	Tiers 3–4, higher end
Research associate	• Accept being staffed on projects • Serve as part of team when asked	• Help gather local M/BD input into the creation or update of centralized M/BD strategies and tactics	Minimal externally recognized expertise	Reactive	Tiers 3–4

Table B.2 The Skills Imperative for Revenue-Generating Practitioners

Note: Tiers 1 and 2 and up = the most highly regarded, most selective marketing and business development (M/BD) opportunities; the most widely distributed. Tiers 2–3, higher end = well-regarded but midlevel M/BD opportunities; smaller or regional distribution. Tiers 2–3 = well-regarded but midlevel M/BD opportunities; smaller or regional distribution. Tiers 3–4, higher end = respectable lower-level M/BD opportunities; small or local distribution. Tiers 3–4 = entry-level M/BD opportunities; very small or local distribution.

Skills growth stage	For expertise-oriented M/BD, "lead, collaborate, and mentor"	For centralized M/BD, "implement and cooperate"	Your perceived status	Your M/BD approach	Your M/BD level
CMOs-CBDOs/ Owners/ Executive manager	• Lead and ensure the continuous improvement of the firm's entire expertise-oriented M/BD program. • Ensure the best integration possible for expertise-oriented and centralized M/BD.[a]	• Lead and ensure the continuous improvement of the firm's entire centralized M/BD program.[b]	• Acknowledged guru status and voice of influence among cross-industry M/BD peers.[c] • Acknowledged guru status among the majority of the firm's internal practitioner clients (and beyond).[d]	Highly proactive	Tiers 1 and 2
Vice president, marketing/ Business development	• Lead projects for expertise-oriented M/BD.[e]	• Lead the development and ensure the implementation of some critical enterprise-wide centralized M/BD strategies and tactics.[f]	• Highly recognized expertise among industry-specific M/BD peers, and some recognition in cross-professional industry circles.[g] • Acknowledged leadership among a growing percentage of the firm's internal practitioner clients.[h]	Proactive	Tiers 2–3, higher-end
Marketing/ Business development director	• Manage projects for expertise-oriented M/BD.[i]	• Lead projects to create or update centralized M/BD strategies and tactics.[j]	• Recognized expertise among industry-specific M/BD peers.[k] • Strong exposure to the firm's internal practitioner clients.[l]	Proactive/ opportunistic	Tiers 2–3
Marketing/ Business development manager	• Take increasingly specific responsibility for expertise-oriented M/BD.[m]	• Take increasingly specific responsibility for the creation or update of centralized M/BD strategies and tactics.[n]	• Some recognized expertise among M/BD peers.[o] • Some exposure to the firm's internal practitioner clients.[p]	Opportunistic/ proactive	Tiers 3–4, higher end
Marketing coordinator	• Serve as part of expertise-oriented M/BD team when asked.[q]	• Help provide local implementation for the firm's centralized M/BD tactics.[r]	• Minimal externally recognized expertise among M/BD peers.[s] • Minimal exposure to the firm's internal practitioner clients.[t]	Reactive	Tiers 3–4

Table B.3 The Skills Imperative for Marketing and Business Development Professionals

Note: Tiers 1 and 2 and up = the most highly regarded, most selective marketing and business development (M/BD) opportunities; the most widely distributed. Tiers 2–3, higher end = well-regarded but midlevel M/BD opportunities; smaller or regional distribution. Tiers 2–3 = well-regarded but midlevel M/BD opportunities; smaller or regional distribution. Tiers 3–4, higher end = respectable lower-level M/BD opportunities; small or local distribution. Tiers 3–4 = entry-level M/BD opportunities; very small or local distribution.

a Examples: recommending and overseeing the practitioners' broadest and most integrated pursuit of thought leadership and selling strategies and ensuring that all thought leadership activities and selling strategies integrate with the firm's broadest market, client, and competitor research findings. More examples: providing significant input into every critical expertise-oriented M/BD decision; initiating new expertise-oriented M/BD strategies where none had existed before; building on deep trusted relationships and continuously growing new relationships with a broad cross section of the firm's key clients and prospects; leading the optimization and evolution of the firm's service portfolio, including developing new service offerings or service delivery approaches.

b Examples: recommending and overseeing the optimal integration of all centralized M/BD strategies and tactics; providing input into every critical centralized M/BD decision; initiating centralized programs where they will improve the firm's marketplace effectiveness; serving as internal champion of integrating the firm's expertise-oriented and centralized M/BD initiatives.

c Examples: serving on or chairing the national board of the firm's industry associations or professional marketing societies; being widely sought after for original content or contributions to books and high-end bylined thought leadership articles; being in high demand as a prestigious speaker and commentator on professional service marketing strategies or tactics; and being in a position to shape the future direction of the professional service M/BD field.

d Examples: serving on the firm's executive committee or board; being elected as a partner or equity shareholder; being sought after to lead critical enterprise-wide M/BD projects; being one of the firm's key influencers on decisions for new M/BD strategies; and driving enterprise-wide market share, revenue, and client value growth strategies.

e Examples: recommending and overseeing the creation of a thought leadership program that links practitioner research to a series of leveraged vehicles (such as book, e-book, newsletter series, bylined articles, speeches, Web 2.0 podcasts and online self-assessment quizzes, intranet communications, and incorporation into new service offerings and sales proposals); leading firm-wide cross-selling programs; recommending and overseeing a linked networking and recruiting program for practitioner relationship management, candidate referrals, and new-hire mentoring; advising on new enterprise-wide M/BD incentive and rewards programs; and fostering deep, trusted relationships with the firm's key clients.

f Examples: recommending and overseeing the creation or upgrade of the firm's new client loyalty measurement program; leading the re-creation of the firm's differentiation strategy; recommending and overseeing the firm's new centralized relationship management program; and serving as internal champion of centralized M/BD initiatives.

g Examples: leading a national committee of the firm's industry associations or professional marketing societies and publishing bylined thought leadership articles or making speeches on industry-specific professional service marketing strategies or tactics.

h Examples: leading M/BD projects; initiating new M/BD strategies for the firm; and conceiving of and leading new programs to improve the practitioner's M/BD effectiveness.

i Examples: helping create and manage media relations strategies; shaping the firm's thought leadership initiatives; co-developing publishing programs; co-creating practice area or geographic sales strategies; co-developing practitioner research agendas; managing some aspects of the firm's innovation initiatives; and establishing or maintaining a trusted relationship with the firm's key clients.

j Examples: project management for a new or critical upgrade of the firm's Web site; managing market/prospect/competitor research for numerous proposals; leading the vendor selection for the firm's new brand strategy project; and serving on the firm's growth strategy committees.

k Examples: leading a committee of the local chapter or serving on a regional or national committee of the firm's industry associations, professional marketing societies, or networking groups.

l Examples: managing M/BD projects; making suggestions and decisions on the firm's M/BD strategies; and making acknowledged contributions to improving the firm's M/BD effectiveness.

m Examples: drafting and serving as the media contact for press releases; conducting research and editing for practitioner articles; helping prepare practitioners for sales presentations; leading some aspects of the content for practitioner research, proposals, or presentations; and serving as project manager for sponsored events.

n Examples: assisting with a strategic upgrade of the firm's client relationship database; conducting market/prospect/competitor research for proposals; and assisting with the rollout of a new logo and positioning tagline.

o Examples: serving on a committee of the local chapter of the firm's industry associations, professional marketing societies, or networking groups.

p Examples: scheduling local M/BD-oriented meetings and taking responsibility for some meeting content.

q Examples: proofreading press releases, practitioner articles, or sales proposals; helping develop documents or exhibits for proposals or presentations; and assisting with sponsored events.

r Examples: updating client relationship databases or media relations lists; compiling proposal materials; and monitoring the firm's adherence to brand image standards.

s Examples: joining and attending local chapter meetings of the firm's industry associations and professional marketing societies or networking groups.

t Examples: taking notes and distributing them from M/BD-oriented meetings.

The Skills Imperative Mapped Against the Process Imperative

Skills growth stages of the Skills Imperative		The Process Imperative				
Practitioners	**Marketing and business development professionals**	**D** Define and identify the most strategically important clients	**A** Acquire the most strategically important clients	**R** Retain the most strategically important clients	**B** Build the firm's revenues with the most strategically important clients	**I** Increase the perceived value of the firm to all audiences
Owner	CMOs–CBDOs/ owners/executive managers	X	X	X	X	X
Principal	Vice presidents, marketing/ business development	X	X	X	X	X
Senior consultant	Marketing/ business development directors	X	X	X		X
Consultant	Marketing/ business development managers	X	X			X
Research associate	Marketing coordinators	X				X

Table B.4   Applying the Skills Imperative to the Process Imperative

The Support Imperative

Mapping the Support Imperative Against the Process Imperative

Tables B.5 through B.9 provide a short list of suggestions for professional firms' administrative functions to integrate into the Process Imperative's stepwise marketing and business development functions. From these suggestions, each enterprise can develop its own integration approaches.

Table B.5 features the Support Imperative mapped against the "Define" step; table B.6 features the Support Imperative mapped against the "Acquire" step; and so on.

		D **Define and identify the most strategically important clients**
Segmenting the market Targeting the "right" clients and prioritizing which clients to pursue, respond to, or avoid Pricing	HR	LEAD: Analyze professionals' productivity by service line to determine relationship, if any, to pricing and revenues or other financial patterns. CO-LEAD with M/BD: Train practitioners to conduct qualitative research and competitive intelligence. ASSIST: Define and prioritize strategically important clients to acquire.
	Finance	LEAD: Analyze profit margin trends by segments and targets. LEAD: Forecast pricing scenarios and revenue trends by segments and targets. CO-LEAD with M/BD: Train practitioners on optimal communication with clients/targets about pricing and reporting back to finance and M/BD about price perception shifts. ASSIST: Define and prioritize strategically important clients to acquire.
	IT	LEAD: Develop tracking capabilities to determine competitor access of firm Web materials. CO-LEAD with M/BD: Determine search engine optimization (SEO) tactics to track search and access patterns by segments and targets. ASSIST: Define and prioritize strategically important clients to acquire.
	Legal	LEAD or CO-LEAD: Define and prioritize strategically important clients to acquire.
	M/BD	LEAD: Conduct qualitative and quantitative studies on firm's clients and potential clients. LEAD: Define and prioritize strategically important clients to acquire. LEAD: Prioritize future segments and targets. CO-LEAD with IT: Determine SEO tactics to track search and access patterns by segments and targets. CO-LEAD with HR: Train practitioners on optimal communication with clients/targets about pricing and reporting back to finance and M/BD about price perception shifts. CO-LEAD with HR: Train practitioners to conduct qualitative research and competitive intelligence. CO-LEAD with Finance: Forecasting and trend analysis.

Table B.5 Applying the Support Imperative to the "Define" Step of the Process Imperative

		A Acquire the most strategically important clients
Establishing a firm's value, protection from copycats, attractiveness, and credibility, with a narrow and sustainable focus Successfully winning engagements with those "right" prospects and clients	HR	LEAD: Develop strategies and undertake tactics to recruit, hire, measure the performance of, compensate, and reward the account planners, seller-doer practitioners, and operational professionals to acquire strategically important clients. LEAD: Develop and implement change and performance management strategies and tactics to guide the firm's desired culture regarding acquiring clients. CO-LEAD with M/BD: Train seller-doer practitioners and other M/BD professionals to follow the firm's client acquisition processes.
	Finance	CO-LEAD with IT and M/BD: Analyze data-mined purchasing patterns for current and past clients, by segments and targets.
	IT	CO-LEAD with Finance and M/BD: Analyze data-mined purchasing patterns for current and past clients, by segments and targets.
	Legal	LEAD: Ensure the firm avoids conflicts of interest in its client acquisition strategies and tactics, or defends against perceptions of same.
	M/BD	LEAD: Develop client acquisition strategies and tactics for direct and indirect marketing and business development for the firm, practices, service lines, industries, geographies, and individual practitioners. LEAD: Measure effectiveness of client acquisition strategies and tactics and incorporate findings into future client acquisition/retention plans. LEAD: Manage client satisfaction and client loyalty measurement programs and incorporate findings into future client retention/growth plans. CO-LEAD with Finance and IT: Analyze data-mined purchasing patterns for current and past clients, by segments and targets. CO-LEAD with HR: Train seller-doer practitioners and other M/BD professionals to follow the firm's client acquisition processes. ASSIST: Work with HR to ensure that the above client acquisition strategies and tactics align with the firm's desired culture.

Table B.6 Applying the Support Imperative to the "Acquire" Step of the Process Imperative

		R Retain the most strategically important clients
Fostering increasingly significant firm-client relationships Successfully keeping current engagements with targeted clients	HR	LEAD: Develop strategies and undertake tactics to recruit, hire, measure the performance of, compensate, and reward the account managers/relationship managers, seller-doer practitioners, and operational professionals to retain strategically important clients. LEAD: Develop and implement change and performance management strategies and tactics to guide the firm's desired culture regarding retaining clients. CO-LEAD with M/BD: Train seller-doer practitioners and other M/BD professionals to follow the firm's client retention processes.
	Finance	CO-LEAD with IT and M/BD: Analyze data-mined purchasing patterns for current and past clients, by segments and targets. ASSIST: Define and prioritize strategically important clients to retain.
	IT	CO-LEAD with Finance and M/BD: Analyze data-mined purchasing patterns for current and past clients, by segments and targets. ASSIST: Define and prioritize strategically important clients to retain.
	Legal	LEAD: Ensure the firm avoids conflicts of interest in its client retention strategies and tactics, or defends against perceptions of same. ASSIST: Define and prioritize strategically important clients to retain.
	M/BD	LEAD: Develop, monitor, and revise client satisfaction and client loyalty measurement programs, and incorporate findings into future client retention and growth plans. LEAD: Define and prioritize strategically important clients to retain. Develop client retention strategies and tactics for direct and indirect marketing and business development for the firm, practices, service lines, industries, geographies, and individual practitioners. LEAD: Measure effectiveness of M/BD strategies and tactics and incorporate findings into future client retention/growth plans. CO-LEAD with IT and Finance: Analyze data-mined purchasing patterns for current and past clients, by segments and targets. CO-LEAD with HR: Train seller-doer practitioners and other M/BD professionals to follow the firm's client retention processes. ASSIST: Work with HR to ensure that the client retention strategies and tactics align with the firm's desired culture.

Table B.7 Applying the Support Imperative to the "Retain" Step of the Process Imperative

B		
Build the firm's revenues with the most strategically important clients		
Increasing each current client's use of the firm's entire service portfolio (cross-selling) Expanding the firm's penetration into that client's "share of wallet"	HR	LEAD: Develop strategies and undertake tactics to recruit, hire, measure the performance of, compensate, and reward the account planners/relationship managers, seller-doer practitioners, and operational professionals to build the firm's business with strategically important clients. CO-LEAD with executive managers: Develop and implement change and performance management strategies and tactics to guide the firm's desired culture for building its book of business. CO-LEAD with M/BD: Train seller-doer practitioners and other M/BD professionals to follow the firm's client growth processes.
	Finance	LEAD: Develop and monitor funds, compensation, and reward programs that support the firm's pursuit of innovation. CO-LEAD with IT: Analyze data-mined purchasing patterns for current and past clients, by segments and targets. CO-LEAD with M/BD: Manage the firm's service portfolio, including analytics and forecasting on revenues for new services. ASSIST: Define and prioritize strategically important clients with which to build the firm's business.
	IT	LEAD: Develop and monitor the effectiveness of technologies or systems that support or increase the firm's service revenues or profits. CO-LEAD with Finance: Analyze data-mined purchasing patterns for current and past clients, by segments and targets. ASSIST: Define and prioritize strategically important clients with which to build the firm's business.
	Legal	LEAD: Ensure the firm avoids conflicts of interest in its client revenue growth strategies and tactics, or defends against perceptions of same. LEAD: Monitor the business arena for legal impediments to potential new services. ASSIST: Define and prioritize strategically important clients with which to build the firm's business.
	M/BD	LEAD: Develop client revenue growth strategies and tactics for direct and indirect marketing and business development for the firm, practices, service lines, industries, geographies, and individual practitioners. LEAD: Measure effectiveness of M/BD strategies and tactics and incorporate findings into future client revenue growth plans. LEAD: Assess client satisfaction and client loyalty measurement programs and incorporate findings into future client revenue growth plans. LEAD: Define and prioritize strategically important clients with which to build the firm's business. LEAD: Develop and manage service portfolio and innovation programs. CO-LEAD with HR: Train seller-doer practitioners and other M/BD professionals to follow the firm's client revenue growth processes. ASSIST: Work with HR to ensure that the client revenue growth strategies and tactics align with the firm's desired culture.

Table B.8 Applying the Support Imperative to the "Build" Step of the Process Imperative

		I Increase the favorable perception of the firm with all audiences (includes employees, suppliers, referral sources, influencers)
Growing the firm's overall brand value, thought leadership equity, and innovation Building broad awareness of the firm and its favorable reputation	HR	LEAD or CO-LEAD: Develop and implement initiatives to recruit and hire people (regardless of function or role) who have skills to contribute to the favorable perception of the firm with all its audiences and who can help grow the firm's overall brand value. LEAD or CO-LEAD with Finance: Create, monitor, and revise rewards and incentives programs that support increasing the favorable perception of the firm with all its audiences. ASSIST: Demonstrate the firm's desired brand value, thought leadership equity, and innovation in professional interactions.
	Finance	LEAD: Create, monitor, and revise appropriately branded financial documents (e.g., paychecks, invoices, and supplier contracts). LEAD or CO-LEAD with HR: Create, monitor, and revise rewards and incentives programs that generally support increasing the favorable perception of the firm with all its audiences and specifically support growing the firm's overall brand value, thought leadership equity, and innovation. ASSIST: Demonstrate the firm's desired brand value, thought leadership equity, and innovation in professional interactions.
	IT	LEAD: Create and maintain technology-oriented M/BD programs that support increasing the favorable perception of the firm (i.e., Web sites, podcasts, intranets, extranets, client databases, and software applications) and support the creation or deployment of technology-enabled innovation. ASSIST: Demonstrate the firm's desired brand value, thought leadership equity, and innovation in professional interactions.
	Legal	LEAD or CO-LEAD: Create and monitor the firm's legal interests regarding brand value, thought leadership equity, and innovation. ASSIST: Demonstrate the firm's desired brand value, thought leadership equity, and innovation in professional interactions.
	M/BD	LEAD: Create, monitor, and revise the firm's programs that support increasing the favorable perception of the firm with all its audiences. LEAD: Develop, monitor, and revise the firm's differentiation, positioning, and branding strategies and tactics. Develop, monitor, and revise the firm's thought leadership programs. Develop, monitor, and revise the firm's service portfolio, R&D, or innovation management program. ASSIST: Demonstrate the firm's desired brand value, thought leadership equity, and innovation in professional interactions.

Table B.9 Applying the Support Imperative to the "Increase" Step of the Process Imperative

Endnotes

Introduction

1. Paul Dunay, comment on "Sales Is from Mars and Marketing Is from Venus—A CEO's Perspective," Buzz Marketing for Technology, March 2, 2008, http://buzzmarketingfortech.blogspot.com/2008/03/sales-is-from -mars-and-marketing-is.html.
2. Jon Miller, comment on "Sales Is from Mars, Marketing Is from Venus— Podcast," Marketing and Strategy Innovation Blog, March 4, 2008, http://blog.futurelab.net/2008/03/sales_is_from_mars_marketing_i.html.
3. Gale Crosley, CPA, "The Marketing Director and Business Developer Challenge: Help Them Become a Power Couple!" reprinted with permission from Moore Stephens North America, *Networker* (Spring 2007), www.crosleycompany.com/cpa-accounting-practice-articles-marketing -director-bd-challenge.asp.
4. Barbara Sullivan and Graham Ericksen, "Bridging the Marketing–Sales Chasm," *strategy + business*, Leading Ideas Online, December 18, 2007, www.strategy-business.com/li/leadingideas/li00056?pg=all.
5. Cindy Commander, Meagan Wilson, and Jane Stevenson, "The Evolved CMO," research report sponsored by Forrester Research and Heidrick & Struggles, 2008.
6. Mike Schultz, comment on "Marketing and Selling Make Nice," Services Insider blog, January 22, 2008, www.whillsgroup.com/pages/30606 _marketing_and_selling_make_nice.cfm.
7. Julie Schwartz, "Critical Skills for Services Success: The Services Market- ing Competency Report Card," research report, Information Technology Services Marketing Association (ITSMA), March 2007, www.itsma.com/ research/abstracts/OLB070306.htm.
8. Suzanne Lowe, "Doing Things Differently—Orchestrating Improvements in Professional Services Marketing Processes," The Marketplace Master, October 2007, www.expertisemarketing.com/newsletter/2007/issue42 -oct2007.html.
9. Suzanne Lowe, "Doing Things Differently—An Example from Smith- Group," The Marketplace Master, April 2007, www.marketplacemasters .com/newsletter/2007/issue36-apr2007.html.
10. David Maister, *Strategy and the Fat Smoker: Doing What's Obvious But Not Easy* (Boston: Spangle Press, 2008), 11.
11. David Maister, e-mail message to Suzanne Lowe, April 8, 2009.

Chapter 1

1. Robert Buday, "Integrating Marketing and Business Development in Professional Services Firms: Findings from a 2007 Bloom Group Survey," research report, Bloom Group LLC, December 2007, 9.
2. Ibid., 19.

3. Suzanne Lowe and Larry Bodine, "Increasing Marketing Effectiveness at Professional Firms," research report, Expertise Marketing LLC and Larry Bodine Marketing Inc., February 2006, 30.
4. Ibid., 54.
5. Ibid., 69.
6. Ibid., 66.
7. Buday, "Integrating Marketing," 13.
8. Ibid., 12.
9. Ibid., 14.
10. Suzanne C. Lowe, *Marketplace Masters: How Professional Service Firms Compete to Win* (New York: Praeger, 2004), 9–12.
11. Ibid., 16–19.
12. Buday, "Integrating Marketing," 19.
13. Commander, Wilson, and Stevenson, "The Evolved CMO," 4.
14. Larry Bodine, "Offshoring Marketing: How Law Firm CMOs Can Prioritize Their Efforts," Need-to-Know News, LawMarketing Portal, August 3, 2006, www.lawmarketing.com/pages/articles.asp?Action=Article&Article ID=542. Reprinted with the permission of *Law Firm Inc.* magazine, copyright 2006, ALM Properties, Inc.
15. Suzanne Lowe, "Are PSF Marketing and Business Development Functions *Stuck in a Rut?*" research report, Expertise Marketing LLC, March 2008.
16. Diane Schmalensee and Dawn Lesh, "Making Marketing Indispensable in Service Firms," research report, Schmalensee Partners, September 2008, 2–3.
17. Gregor Harter, Edward Landry, and Andrew Tipping, "The New Complete Marketer," *strategy + business*, issue 48, reprint no. 07308 (Autumn 2007), www.strategy-business.com/media/file/sb48_07308.pdf.
18. Massachusetts Institute of Technology, Course 15: Business to Business Marketing, http://student.mit.edu/catalog/m15c.html#15.833.
19. Kellogg Graduate School of Management, Course Catalog and Schedules: Services Marketing and Management, www20.kellogg.northwestern.edu/dpco/offdtl.asp?coursecatalogid=881.
20. Columbia Business School, Courses at Columbia Business School, Services Marketing, www4.gsb.columbia.edu/courses/detail/102423/Services+marketing.
21. Chicago Graduate School of Business, Kilts Center for Marketing, Curriculum, 37303, Marketing of Services, and 37201, Developing New Products and Services, http://research.chicagogsb.edu/marketing/curriculum.aspx.
22. Harvard Business School Executive Education, Leading Professional Service Firms, www.exed.hbs.edu/programs/lpsf/.
23. Miller Heiman, Industry Expertise, www.millerheiman.com/our_expertise/industry_expertise/index.html.
24. Society for Marketing Professional Services, Current Domains of Practice, www.smps.org/AM/PrinterTemplate.cfm?Section=Domains_of_practice2, and Overview of the CPSM Program, www.smps.org/AM/Template.cfm?Section=Certification.
25. Legal Marketing Association, LMA Education Overview, www.legalmarketing.org/education/intro.

26. The Chartered Institute of Marketing, Professional Development, Qualifications Available, www.cim.co.uk/ProfessionalDevelopment/Qualifications/QualificationsAvailable.aspx.
27. PSMG: Professional Services Marketing Group, Professional Services Marketing Qualification, www.psmg.co.uk/page.cfm?id=870.
28. Netherlands Institute of Marketing, NIMA Top Brands, www.nima.nl/englishsummary.

Chapter 2

1. Lowe and Bodine, "Increasing Marketing Effectiveness," analysis cell F1230.
2. Lowe, *Marketplace Masters*, 7–8.
3. Ellen McGirt, "The Most Dangerous Job in Business," *Fast Company*, June 2007, www.fastcompany.com/magazine/116/next-most-dangerous-job-in-business.html.
4. Ibid.
5. Lowe, *Marketplace Masters*, 62.
6. Gary Hamel, with Bill Breen, "Making Innovation Everyone's Job," *The Future of Management*, Harvard Business Online, November 26, 2007, http://discussionleader.hbsp.com/hamel/2007/11/making_innovation_everyones_jo.html.
7. Maister, *Strategy and the Fat Smoker*, 4.
8. Buday, "Integrating Marketing," 5–7.
9. American Bar Association, "History of the American Bar Association," www.abanet.org/about/history.html.
10. Legal Marketing Association, "LMA Fast Facts," www.legalmarketing.org/about-lma/intro/fast-facts.
11. Legal Sales and Service Organization, "About LSSO," www.legalsales.org/welcome/about.cfm.
12. American Institute of Certified Public Accountants, AICPA Media Center—AICPA History and Background, www.aicpa.org/MediaCenter/History_Background.htm.
13. Association for Accounting Marketing, "History of AAM," www.accountingmarketing.org/history.asp.
14. American Institute of Architects, "About the American Institute of Architects," www.aia.org/about/index.htm.
15. Society for Marketing Professional Services, "About the Society for Marketing Professional Services," www.smps.org/AM/PrinterTemplate.cfm?Section=About_SMPS.
16. Association of Management Consulting Firms, "Fact Sheet," www.amcf.org/memFacts.asp.
17. Association of Executive Search Consultants, "Frequently Asked Questions," www.aesc.org/article/faqs/?PHPSESSID=1d296bf492f2274fd2fc0b7b3371b186.
18. PM Forum, "What Is the Professional Marketing Forum?" www.pmforum.co.uk/about/index.aspx.
19. Professional Services Marketing Group, "PSMG Conference Overview," www.psmgconference.co.uk/.
20. Lisa Bowman, e-mail message cc'ed to the author, January 24, 2008.

21. Betsi Roach, e-mail message to Kyle Sheldon-Chandler, January 2008.
22. Ashley Mercurio, e-mail message to Kyle Sheldon-Chandler, January 23, 2008.
23. David Munn, e-mail message to Kyle Sheldon-Chandler, January 23, 2008.
24. Amy Kotz, "Desperately Seeking CMOs: Lots of High-paid Vacancies. But Does M Stand for Masochist?" *American Lawyer*, December 1, 2007, www.law.com/jsp/PubArticle.jsp?id=1196417065551.
25. Janet McColl-Kennedy, Jill Sweeney, and Geoff Soutar, "Marketing Still a Dirty Word to Many Professional Service Firms," *UQ News Online*, February 17, 2006, www.uq.edu.au/news/index.html?article=9008.
26. McGirt, "Most Dangerous Job in Business."
27. Greg Welch, "Chief Marketing Officer Tenure Improves According to Annual Spencer Stuart Study," June 1, 2007, www.spencerstuart.com/about/media/45/.
28. Granville Loar, "2006 Accounting Marketing/Sales Responsibility and Compensation Survey," research report, Association for Accounting Marketing, May 2007, 1.
29. Laura Schreier, "Like Ad Campaigns, Tenure Is Short for Legal Marketers," *Hartford Business.com*, November 11, 2007, www.hartfordbusiness.com/news3781.html.
30. Milo Sindell and Thuy Sindell, *Sink or Swim! New Job. New Boss. 12 Weeks to Get It Right* (Cincinnati: Adams Media Corporation, 2006), 7.
31. Thomas J. DeLong, John J. Gabarro, and Robert J. Lees, *When Professionals Have to Lead: A New Model for High Performance* (Boston: Harvard Business School Press, 2007).
32. Thomas DeLong, comment in "New Challenges in Leading Professional Services," Working Knowledge, Harvard Business School, posted January 22, 2008, http://hbswk.hbs.edu/item/5773.html.
33. Ibid.
34. Ibid.
35. David Maister and Patrick McKenna, *First Among Equals: How to Manage a Group of Professionals* (New York: Free Press, 2002).

Chapter 3

1. Suzanne Lowe, "Doing Things Differently—A Conversation with Yoh's Jim Lanzalotto," The Marketplace Master, July 2007, www.expertise marketing.com/newsletter/2007/issue39-jul2007.html.
2. Suzanne Lowe, "Doing Things Differently—Reinventing the Marketing and Sales Function at Professional Service Firms," The Marketplace Master, September 2007, www.expertisemarketing.com/newsletter/2007/issue41-sep2007.html.
3. Suzanne Lowe, "Doing Things Differently—An Example from Thornton Tomasetti," The Marketplace Master, June 2007, www.expertisemarketing.com/newsletter/2007/issue38-jun2007.html.
4. Bob Liodice, "Unraveling the Contradictions: Making Marketing Masterful in an Era of Change," research report, Association of National Advertisers (ANA) and Booz Allen Hamilton, October 11, 2004, abstract, www.boozallen.com/news/659394?lpid=981228.

Chapter 4

1. Philip Kotler and Gary Armstrong, *Principles of Marketing*, 12th ed. (Upper Saddle River, NJ: Pearson Education, 2007).

Chapter 5

1. Fred Reichheld, *The Ultimate Question* (Boston: Harvard Business School Publishing, 2006).
2. Ford Harding, "Cross Markets Aren't So Different," The Marketplace Master, August 2008, www.expertisemarketing.com/newsletter/2008/issue52 -aug2008.html.

Chapter 6

1. My thanks go to my former employer Tom Kuczmarski, founder of management consultancy Kuczmarski & Associates, where I first encountered a version of this growth matrix for the firm's professionals.
2. Lowe and Bodine, "Increasing Marketing Effectiveness," 9.

Chapter 7

1. David Maister, comment in "Meet the MasterMinds: David Maister on *Strategy and the Fat Smoker*," Management Consulting News, January 2008, www.managementconsultingnews.com/interviews/maister _interview_2.php.
2. Suzanne Lowe, "How Well Do PSF Marketing and BD Work with Others?" research report, Expertise Marketing LLC, April 2008, 2.
3. Ibid.

Chapter 8

1. Suzanne Lowe, "PSF Marketing and BD Integration: Does It Benefit Clients?" research report, Expertise Marketing LLC, May 2008.
2. Ibid., 2.
3. Ibid., 3.
4. Ibid., 2–5.

Chapter 9

1. "The Incredible Shrunken Headhunters," *BusinessWeek*, March 2002, www.businessweek.com/careers/content/mar2002/ca2002038_7665.htm.
2. *The Best Lawyers in America*, 2008, www.hollandhart.com/newsitem.cfm ?ID=987.
3. www.hollandhart.com/newsitem.cfm?ID=940.
4. www.hollandhart.com/articles/MLF50.pdf.

Chapter 10

1. "What Is Lean?" www.lean.org/WhatsLean/Principles.cfm (1 of 3).
2. "The Second Annual *Marketing the Law Firm* 50: The Top Law Firms in Marketing and Communications," *Marketing the Law Firm*, Law Journal

Newsletters, www.lawjournalnewsletters.com/issues/ljn_marketing/20_7A/news/147710-1.html.

3. Robert S. Kaplan and David P. Norton, *The Balanced Scorecard: Translating Strategy into Action* (Boston: Harvard Business School Press, 1996).

4. Ranjay Gulati, "Silo Busting: How to Execute on the Promise of Customer Focus," *Harvard Business Review* (May 2007), 2, http://harvardbusinessonline.hbsp.harvard.edu/b01/en/common/item_detail.jhtml;jsessionid=NOXX04WL53JRGAKRGWDR5VQBKE0YIISW?referral=4320&id=R0705F&_requestid=280635.

Index